development aide are
separate but the

red.

The Refugee System

in tense focuse on the global north
humanitarian aide. knoledge production
is controled by the HCNR

what is the global south?

the global North is more weathy
  ⅃ the Grand Comprimise
          we give you money you
              keep the refugees.

Nick maginske
        ⅃ discresion on who can
              enter
women who experanced sexual assault
weren't allowed in for fear of connection
to issue

the vertual frontecie

47% arent apart of the signed treaty

How many people are in camps? →

For Mazen and Nedal – RA
For Marian and Gabriela – DSF

The Refugee System:
A Sociological Approach

Rawan Arar
David Scott FitzGerald

polity

First published in 2023 by Polity Press

Polity Press
65 Bridge Street
Cambridge CB2 1UR, UK

Polity Press
111 River Street
Hoboken, NJ 07030, USA

ISBN-13: 978-1-5095-4278-9
ISBN-13: 978-1-5095-4279-6(pb)

A catalogue record for this book is available from the British Library.

Library of Congress Control Number: 2022932997

Typeset in 10.5 on 12pt Sabon
by Fakenham Prepress Solutions, Fakenham, Norfolk NR21 8NL
Printed and bound in Great Britain by TJ Books Ltd, Padstow, Cornwall

The publisher has used its best endeavours to ensure that the URLs for external websites referred to in this book are correct and active at the time of going to press. However, the publisher has no responsibility for the websites and can make no guarantee that a site will remain live or that the content is or will remain appropriate.

Every effort has been made to trace all copyright holders, but if any have been overlooked the publisher will be pleased to include any necessary credits in any subsequent reprint or edition.

For further information on Polity, visit our website:
politybooks.com

Contents

Tables and Figures

Tables

Figures

Abbreviations

3RP	Regional Refugee and Resilience Plan
ASEAN	Association of Southeast Asian Nations
CIREFCA	International Conference on Central American Refugees
DIDR	development-induced displacement and resettlement
DP	displaced person
ECOWAS	Economic Community of West African States
EU	European Union
GCC	Gulf Cooperation Council
GCR	Global Compact on Refugees
IDP	internally displaced person
IGCR	Intergovernmental Committee on Refugees
ILO	International Labour Organization
INS	Immigration and Naturalization Service
IOM	International Organization for Migration
IRC	International Rescue Committee
IRO	International Refugee Organization
ISIS	Islamic State of Iraq and Syria
NGO	nongovernmental organization
OAU	Organization of African Unity
PICMME	Provisional Intergovernmental Committee for the Movement of Migrants from Europe
POW	prisoner of war
PRC	People's Republic of China
ROC	Republic of China
ROVR	Resettlement Opportunity for Vietnamese Returnees

UNCCP	United Nations Conciliation Commission for Palestine
UNHCR	United Nations High Commissioner for Refugees (UN Refugee Agency)
UNKRA	United Nations Korean Reconstruction Agency
UNRRA	United Nations Relief and Rehabilitation Administration
UNRWA	United Nations Relief and Works Agency for Palestine Refugees in the Near East

1

A Systems Approach to Displacement

When violence threatens, some people flee. Others remain. How do families decide to leave, where to relocate, and whether to keep moving? What conditions and government policies shape their limited options? Departing from refugee studies based on isolated siloes of knowledge about just one setting, our sociological approach explains the entire refugee system. Changes in one part of the system reverberate elsewhere. Earlier migrations shape later movements. Blocked paths of mobility in one place redirect migration along other paths. Government policies today are shaped by historical legacies, behaviors of other states, and the actions of displaced people. All these processes are forged by deep inequalities of power.

The Salvadoran refugee system is a case in point. El Salvador's economy has long been dependent on the United States, but it did not have a strong tradition of migration to the United States until the onset of its civil war in 1979. The Salvadoran population in the United States increased from 94,000 to 465,000 between 1980 and 1990, during a civil conflict that included a Cold War dimension of a proxy fight between the United States and communist adversaries such as Nicaragua, Cuba, and the Soviet Union. Only 2.6 percent of Salvadoran applicants during this period were granted asylum in the United States, which favored asylum for people from countries led by communist governments rather than rightwing US allies like El Salvador. Many Salvadorans lived in the United States without papers or under a tenuous temporary status. Few voluntarily returned after the war ended in 1992.[1]

Some Salvadoran youth formed new gangs for protection from established gangs. Deportations of gang members by US authorities inadvertently spread groups such as Mara Salvatrucha and 18th Street back to El Salvador, where they prospered in a social fabric weakened by civil war. Criminal violence, forced gang recruitment, extortion, and bloody reprisals by police became new reasons for Salvadorans to flee abroad. With little chance of obtaining visas to travel legally to the United States, most attempted to cross Mexico as irregular migrants. Mexican government crackdowns at the behest of Washington drove Salvadorans to travel through remote areas that left them more vulnerable to violence from gangs, including offshoots of the same organizations that had been transplanted earlier from the United States to El Salvador. Salvadorans who reached the United States to ask for asylum usually had to make their case based on the threat of violence from nonstate actors, such as gangs, if they were returned to El Salvador. Along with other Central Americans, they sometimes traveled north in caravans to achieve safety in numbers. Spectacular images of hundreds of people walking down the highway fed into restrictionist narratives in the United States of a migrant "invasion," which generated further US pressure on the governments of Mexico and Central American countries to stop the caravans.[2]

The Salvadoran experience demonstrates several lessons drawn out by a systems approach to displacement. Intervention by a powerful state in the core of the world system (the United States) in the system's periphery (El Salvador) generates the movement of people in the opposite direction. Forced displacement subsequently channels migration for work and family reunification, as well as coerced movement back to El Salvador in the form of deportations. New push factors then generate migration, as people flee from criminal violence and economic precarity. The core state uses a transit state (Mexico) to try to block further movement. A systems perspective shows this interactivity among states, sequences of migration, and feedback loops in which past outputs of displacement processes become inputs into new iterations.

By contrast, accounts of refugee movements in the news usually tell simple stories about isolated events that cause people to flee their homes for safety wherever they can find it. "Few refugee news stories make the connection between 'there' and 'here'," finds researcher Terence Wright. "Sympathetic coverage of those in far-off lands affected by disaster and war appears in stark contrast to the media treatment of those seeking asylum in the West."[3] Photographs of Syrian refugees taken in tented settlements in Lebanon suggest that such dire conditions make them worthy subjects of humanitarian aid, while asylum-seekers in Europe, from the Moria camp on the Greek island of Lesbos to the "Jungle" in the French port of Calais, are characterized as disorderly, defiant, and dangerous. These diverging interpretations of camp settings privilege the perspective of rich host countries, while neglecting the drivers of displacement. An analysis of World Refugee Day coverage in US newspapers found that "the media are overwhelmingly more likely to address refugees as locally situated, often totally divorced from the circumstances and context which led to the refugees' arrival in the United States."[4] The intervening period between flight from the country of origin and arrival in a country of resettlement is also forgotten, even though most resettled refugees were displaced for years in transit countries. People born into a stateless refugee status may have never even seen their country of origin.

International organizations try to avoid the political embroilments of assigning blame for conflicts that produce refugees by glossing over the reasons for displacement. For example, an account published by the UN Refugee Agency (UNHCR) in 2019 explains how the "Iraqi refugee crisis" unfolded:

> The Iraqi refugee crisis is the result of decades of conflict and violence in the region. In 2014, an escalation of violence surged when the Islamic State (ISIS) launched attacks in northern Iraq. As a result of the conflict, millions of families were forced to flee their homes and half of the country's infrastructure was destroyed.[5]

The report does not mention state actors involved in displacing Iraqis, such as the Iraqi government or the US-led invasion in 2003, which resulted in the displacement of millions of Iraqis and the emergence of ISIS. Critiques of the United States may jeopardize an important relationship with the top financial supporter of UNHCR operations. Naming the Iraqi state might jeopardize the UNHCR's access to internally displaced people in Iraq. By contrast, holding ISIS rhetorically accountable does not threaten relationships with donors and states of origin.

Similarly, when the Bali Process, an international forum led by Australia and Indonesia to combat human trafficking and smuggling, analyzed the 2015 Andaman Sea emergency in which members of the Muslim Rohingya minority fled ethnic cleansing in Myanmar, its report avoided even using the name Rohingya. The report only noted "the events of May 2015, specifically the movements of mixed populations." In this account, "mixed populations" simply appeared, and the focus of states in the Bali Process was how to manage them.[6] These accounts deliberately ignore why refugees fled in the first place.

The systems approach to displacement breaks not only with popular representations of refugees, but also with scholarly and advocate narratives insisting that "refugees are not migrants."[7] The boundary between refugees and migrants is rooted in legally consequential distinctions, not always sociological realities, as discussed in the following chapter. By avoiding the tendency to separate migration, refugee, and conflict studies, we can examine the interplay among different kinds of immobility, movement, and their governance.[8] By refugees, we mean a subset of migrants who have crossed an international border in large part to escape the threat of violence or persecution, or people who have crossed a border and are afraid to return home because of such a threat. At the same time, our analysis incorporates individuals who fall outside official refugee labels and are on the fringes of studies of forced migration. An approach toward the decision-making of people facing violence and persecution, which we call the new economics of displacement, illuminates linkages between systems of economic and refugee migrations. Moving beyond a narrowly circumscribed definition of refugees makes it possible to draw on highly elaborated theories of international migration that show how movements are shaped by links among places of origin, transit, and host societies within a global system of control.

The refugee system

This book draws on pathbreaking work on systems approaches to migration to explain the refugee system. We build on foundational studies of rural–urban migration systems by geographer Akin Mabogunje, regional migration systems by demographers Mary Kritz, Hania Zlotnik, and Douglas Massey and colleagues, and theoretical elaboration by demographer James Fawcett and development studies scholar Oliver Bakewell.[9] Our approach is closest to that of *Escape from Violence*, published in 1989 during the waning days of the Cold

War, by political scientist Aristide Zolberg and colleagues. We assess developments in the more than three decades since its publication, historical evidence of the construction of the refugee regime that went unrecognized in their seminal text, and greater attention to forced immobility and internally displaced persons (IDPs). Their macro approach is integrated with greater theorization of how policies from above interact with refugee decision-making at all stages of immobility, movement, and settlement.[10] We refine and deploy the systems approach with illustrative examples of its elements drawn from a global universe of cases.

The refugee system is an interactive set of processes within, among, and transcending states that produce immobility and movement related to violence and persecution. Ideological, military, economic, and political power shape the system. Its processes include feedback mechanisms linking elements across time and place. Our fundamental orientation toward understanding the system is derived from key thinkers in historical sociology, but eclectic tools from across the social sciences, history, and law illuminate particular contexts.[11]

A systems approach does not require writing a history of the world to understand a given situation. For example, in a pointed essay reviewing Betts and Collier's argument that Syrian refugee migration to Europe in 2015 was determined by the policies of European countries, especially the stance of German chancellor Angela Merkel, historian Benjamin Thomas White showed how refugee movements were shaped by conditions across different kinds of states. Without using the word "system," he deployed a systems approach to demonstrate how, in addition to the policies of Greece, Hungary, and Germany, movement into Europe was also shaped by circumstances outside Europe. These included shifting patterns of external intervention in Syria's civil war; a welcome that was wearing thin in the primary host countries of Jordan, Lebanon, and Turkey; and refugees' fading expectations of local integration in neighboring countries or return to Syria.[12] One could extend the analysis to show how mass refugee movements into Europe then fed back into policy-making, namely the EU–Turkey deal, in which the EU, led by Merkel, paid Turkey to contain Syrian refugees. The EU later turned a blind eye to the Turkish government's pushbacks of Syrian refugees and its incursion into northern Syria to set up a so-called safe haven with Russian support. Syrians in different parts of Syria, as well as other Middle Eastern countries and throughout the Global North, decided to stay in place or move as they interacted with shifting policies around the globe.

A systems approach shows how *refugeedom* – the relationship between refugees, state, and society – interacts with *refugeehood* – the experience of becoming and being a refugee.[13] In 2015 the world witnessed the death of two-year-old Alan Kurdi, a Syrian refugee boy of Kurdish origin, who drowned in the sea between Turkey and Greece during his family's failed attempt to reach Europe to ask for asylum. Images of Alan's small, lifeless body on the Turkish shore were shared millions of times, but the family's experience is rarely discussed in its entirety. The story of the Kurdi family's tragedy reveals the importance of integrating the study of state policies with the theorization of refugee decision-making.

Alan's parents, Abdullah and Rehanna, met in late 2010 in an olive orchard in Kobani, a Syrian town near the border with Turkey. They married in Damascus and were living there when the war began in March 2011. The family became internally displaced the following year and fled back to Kobani. As the violence in Syria escalated, resources, food, and medicine became increasingly difficult to find. Abdullah decided to cross the border into Turkey to work and send money back home. ISIS soon gained control of Kobani, prompting Rehanna and her two sons, Ghalib and Alan, to join Abdullah in Turkey. Life in Istanbul was challenging. The boys were out of school. Their parents feared the children had no real future. Abdullah reached out to his sister Tima, who had emigrated to Canada decades earlier. As a Canadian citizen, Tima could help sponsor refugees to resettle there. She had already begun the process for another sibling, however, and did not have the financial resources to sponsor Abdullah's family of four. As she tried to raise the money, the family faced an additional obstacle. The Canadian government required the family's Syrian passports, which the Kurdis could not obtain. With Canadian resettlement out of reach and the family's situation worsening in Turkey, Abdullah made the tough decision that the family would travel by boat to Europe to seek asylum. The Greek island of Kos was only five kilometers away. The Kurdis had already braved dangerous terrain in Syria. Abdullah believed they could make the journey. Several of his cousins had recently received asylum in Germany and Sweden.

With passports and visas, the Kurdis would not have needed to put themselves in jeopardy. They could have traveled on one of the many ferries across the strait. But as Syrians, for whom visas to European countries were practically impossible to obtain because European governments wanted to keep out likely asylum-seekers, the Kurdis would have to travel clandestinely. Abdullah asked Tima for $5,000 to pay the smugglers. She sent him the money and later recounted his texts as he deliberated which day to try to reach Greece: "The waves were too high. I would not do it," he said on August 21, 2015. "Water so calm today. But the smugglers had a rubber dinghy. I won't take a rubber dinghy," Abdullah texted his sister on August 27.[14] Tima's worst fears came true on September 2. Alan, his older brother Ghalib, and his mother Rehanna drowned at sea. Abdullah was the sole survivor.

Alan Kurdi's story seized the attention of audiences around the world, fueled humanitarian campaigns, and became the subject of numerous academic studies. The response, however, has largely neglected the Kurdi family's broader experience of displacement and insecurity, which began years before that sorrowful day in 2015. System-wide constraints and opportunities shaped how the Kurdis navigated displacement inside Syria, family separation across the Syrian-Turkish border, refugeehood in Turkey, the flickering promise of resettlement in Canada, and the hope of asylum in Europe. Members of the Kurdi family made the best decisions they could about their future, despite many unknowns. State policies throughout their journey and in countries half a world away influenced their decision-making. Alan Kurdi's death, and the hundreds of thousands of people who would traverse the seas for a chance to live in Europe, would in turn shape policies in Europe and beyond.

Against siloed approaches

The systems approach to displacement differs markedly from siloed knowledge production about refugees. Table 1.1 shows six characteristics of siloed approaches. The first three characteristics include the tendency to be ahistorical (most policy studies), the failure to explain – or purposefully neglect – the causes of displacement beyond generic gestures to "root causes" (UNHCR *Global Trends* reports), and the use of an exclusively legal definition of refugees to define the scope conditions of research and governance (most legal and policy studies). These first three trends are linked to a dual imperative in

Table 1.1: Siloed vs. systems approaches to forced displacement

Siloed approaches	*Systems approach*
Ahistorical (most legal and policy studies)	Historical institutionalist attention to complex causal sequences, path dependency, and feedback loops
No specific explanation of displacement (UNHCR *Global Trends* reports)	Starting point is the politics of exit, and the new economics of displacement framework to understand decision-making by households and individuals
Exclusively legal definition (most legal and policy studies)	Sociological definition of people fleeing the threat of violence or persecution
Studies begin with refugees who have already crossed an international border (FitzGerald & Arar 2018)	Attention to factors creating immobility as well as mobility, and IDPs as well as refugees
Focus on three "durable solutions" in a single country (humanitarian organizations)	Attention to cross-border ties
Single isolated stage of displacement divorced from other stages (most social science studies)	Intersection of conflict/refugee/migration studies shows feedback linking policies and actions at each stage

which knowledge producers, in addition to publishing reports and datasets, are responsible for providing potentially lifesaving services or conferring protected statuses to displaced people. Policymakers, lawyers, humanitarian professionals, and members of international organizations use "categories of practice" as opposed to "categories of analysis."[15] Categories of practice allow states and international organizations to define, assess, count, and move refugees. A siloed approach serves its purpose in an asylum hearing, for example, but it does not reveal the underlying dynamics of refugeedom.

The other three characteristics of siloed approaches include ignoring those who do not move, sometimes because they have been killed;[16] a focus on so-called "durable solutions" of return, local settlement, and resettlement that take place in a single country (humanitarian organizations);[17] and the study of a single isolated stage of displacement, such as asylum-seeking or resettlement, that is divorced from other stages (most social science studies). These siloed tendencies in the academy build on the work of policymakers, lawyers, and humanitarian professionals. In doing so, academic studies often adopt the same scope conditions of analysis and ultimately employ categories of legal and humanitarian practice even though they are not providing services or protection to displaced people. Drawing on UNHCR's annual *Global Trends* reports, for instance, scholars are likely to give attention to refugees and IDPs, but neglect those who are besieged, interned, or otherwise unable to move toward safety.[18] Scholars who turn to policy reports about refugee resettlement will rarely learn about refugees' lives before arriving in the country of resettlement, even when refugees have already been displaced for decades in third, fourth, or fifth countries.

The limitations of siloed approaches become especially clear when we consider how displaced people see the world through interactive connections among places of origin, transit, and destination. Their histories do not begin the day the war started. The experience of displacement does not begin the moment a person crosses an international border. Neither does refugeehood end the day legal status is secured. Refugees often have family members dispersed over long distances and across borders. Their obligations and opportunities are not confined to one particular state.

Power

Refugee experiences and policies are shaped by different forms of power – the capacity to make social actors do something against their wishes. We draw on sociologist Michael Mann's typology of four sources of social power – economic, military, ideological, and political – to show how each type of power and their interactions shape systems of forced immobility and displacement.[19] Rather than a legal approach asking what states *should* do in matters of displacement according to interpretations of international and domestic law, we first establish *why* states and people act the way they do, which requires analyzing how power works, before offering our own suggestions in the conclusion about how that power might be used more humanely.

Explanations of patterns of international migration begin with economic power. Many influential accounts draw on Immanuel Wallerstein's concept of world systems.[20] Rather than compare discrete nation-state units, world systems theory conceives of a single global system of capital accumulation emerging in the sixteenth century and morphing in various ways since then, as core countries in the system, beginning with Western Europe, penetrated the periphery to extract economic surplus. World systems theory, and related theories of dependency, have been extremely generative in the study of international migration. Labor migration tends to follow paths laid down by interventions such as settler colonialism, state-sponsored recruitment of temporary labor, and postcolonial migrations to former metropoles. European colonial recruitment of Indian and Chinese indentured servants in the nineteenth century, often as a replacement for African slaves in Caribbean colonies, follows this model, as does US recruitment of *braceros* from Mexico in the two world wars and Western European post-World War II recruitments of "guest workers" from countries around the Mediterranean.[21]

Refugees often follow paths created much earlier through the core's economic and military domination of the periphery. For example, 140,000 Cubans sought asylum in the former colonial metropole of Spain between 1961 and 1977.[22] Imperialist as well as colonial ties structure refugee flows.[23] One million Cubans migrated to the United States, which occupied Cuba from 1898 to 1902 and dominated much of the economy until the 1959 revolution. Haitians fleeing government oppression and economic collapse beginning in the 1970s headed for the United States, which had occupied Haiti from 1915 to 1934 and long dominated its economy, and to Quebec, which, along with Haiti, is a centuries-old Francophone legacy of French settler colonialism in the Americas.[24] Refugees often follow earlier labor migration routes between semi-peripheral and core countries. During the war in the former Yugoslavia in the 1990s, many Croatian and Bosnian refugees went to Germany along pathways laid by German recruitment of Yugoslav "guest workers" in the 1960s.[25]

The systems approach explains feedback loops between labor and refugee migrations. The causes of a flow can change in response to developments in both origins and destinations. Labor migrations often channel subsequent refugee flows, which in turn can generate family reunification, as among many Bosnians living in Sweden in the 1990s.[26] A movement that began as voluntary may become involuntary in subsequent stages, such as when West African labor migrants in Libya became persecuted during the Libyan civil war in 2014 and many fled to Europe.[27] War can reshape pre-existing labor migration streams, by making continued migration more difficult and bottling up labor migrants abroad who are afraid to repatriate for fear of suffering violence or conscription. This dynamic can then change the economic sectors in which labor migrants work in host countries, from temporary to more permanent niches. Such dynamics have emerged in a wide range of countries, including Ethiopia, Haiti, Israel/Palestine, Mexico, Mozambique, Sri Lanka, Sudan, Tanzania, and Turkey.[28]

Military power also shapes refugee flows in ways that complement the economic understandings of world systems theory. The exercise of military power generates refugee flows as wars, ethnic cleansing, and persecution push refugees out. External powers often apply a carrot-and-stick approach to shape those conflicts to their advantage. The slow dissolution of the Ottoman Empire produced the largest waves of refugees in the late nineteenth and early twentieth centuries as an expanding Russian empire and interventions by Britain and France accelerated nation-state formation and ethnic cleansing.[29] The Cold War involved military interventions around the world. External military interventions then drove greater outflows and the perpetuation of armed conflicts.

Refugee destinations are not arbitrary. Military interventions can structure movement *after* a conflict as well. For example, military interventions by the core in the periphery shape postcolonial flows. Postcolonial settler repatriation, such as the movement of European settlers in Algeria to France after Algerian independence in 1962, often falls out of siloed refugee studies, in part because repatriating colonists are not legally protected by the Refugee Convention as they continue to enjoy the protection of their state of nationality. However, their movement was less than voluntary in many cases. A systems approach is attuned to these movements, which are quintessential expressions of world systems theories' emphasis on core interventions in the periphery and feedback loops of migrations in the opposite direction.

Refugee arrivals are often the consequence of other forms of military interventions abroad. The flow of Indochinese refugees to the United States was a direct result of the US war in Indochina. Although rarely recognized legally as refugees, Salvadorans, Guatemalans, and

Nicaraguans first came to the United States in large numbers during the 1980s as a consequence of civil wars in their countries in which foreign powers, including the United States, played a major role.[30] The United States has historically had special programs for resettling collaborators in countries where it has militarily intervened, from Laos in the 1970s to Afghanistan from the 2000s to 2020s.[31] Similarly, when France withdrew from Algeria in the 1960s, it accommodated the migration to France of 88,000 Harkis – indigenous North Africans who had fought with France against national liberation forces.[32]

Military power not only produces new refugees and destinations, but also manages them, providing relief, control, deterrence, and forced repatriation. Military intervention, or its threat, has been used to contain potential refugees, such as the NATO intervention in Libya in 2011, or efforts to prevent refugees from reaching their destinations by blocking maritime and land routes.[33] During and immediately following World War II, the Displaced Persons Branch of the Supreme Headquarters Allied Expeditionary Force exercised jurisdiction over displaced persons (DPs) in Europe and used the basic design and techniques of military camps to control these populations. British and US soldiers carried out forced repatriation to the Soviet Union, their ally, of liberated Soviet prisoners of war (POWs).[34] The fact that displaced person camps in Europe were under Allied military control shaped solutions to the mass displacements. After the war, the United States in particular wanted to withdraw its responsibility for the camps, which prompted the Truman administration to push for more resettlement slots in the United States and other Allied countries and to recognize the state of Israel in 1948 as a destination for displaced Jews.[35] Three decades later, the US military transported and housed more than 100,000 refugees from Vietnam to the United States. The CIA airlifted 2,500 allied Hmong military officials and their families from Laos to Thailand, and then on to the United States.[36] Military power can thus generate and pre-empt flows, shape their destinations, control and protect displaced people, or return them to harm's way.

Ideological power is a critical component of the refugee system. The generation of refugee flows has often been driven by nationalism, the ideology that a homogeneous national people deserves its own nation-state. Responses to refugees are equally ideological. The belief that there is something wrong with a state persecuting groups of its subjects is a historically elaborated notion that is not universally held to this day. Humanitarianism and human rights are the central contemporary ideologies used to describe, understand, and advocate for people caught in armed conflict and refugees. These ideas have been inscribed into law. Notions of who constitutes a "social group" deserving of legal protection have changed over time because of deeper shifts in ideologies, for example, about gender and sexuality. The ideology of state sovereignty, which includes the principle that states should have the exclusive authority to control who is admitted and allowed to stay in their territories, collides with the ideologies of humanitarianism and human rights in ways that limit the scope and implementation of the refugee regime.

Refugee movement and experience are shaped by political power as well. While Mann defines political power more narrowly as the "centralized and territorial regulation of social life" through the state, we adopt a more capacious definition that includes international organizations, such as the UNHCR, the UN Relief and Works Agency for Palestine Refugees in the Near East (UNRWA), and the International Organization for Migration (IOM), as well as nongovernmental organizations (NGOs) such as Human Rights Watch and the International Rescue Committee (IRC), given the importance of parallel or surrogate states in refugee management, as elaborated in Chapter 6. Since the 1960s, most of the people categorized by the UNHCR as refugees have remained outside the most powerful countries of the West or Global North. Relationships between governments of the Global North and South strongly shape refugee policies. Incentivized by money, aid in kind, trade concessions, the promise of liberalized visas, and other rewards, countries in the Global South contain most refugees in part to prevent them from traveling to the Global North to seek asylum. Countries in the Global South are active participants in these negotiations, as they link the issue of refugee control and relief provision to their other foreign policy interests. States in the Global North and South are not always able to get everything they want in these negotiations given their complex interdependence.[37]

We draw on the observation of sociologist Stephen Castles, that "forced migration is not the result of unconnected emergencies but rather an integral part of North–South relationships."[38] Our amendment is to avoid reducing the cause of all forced migration to the interventions of powerful states. Relationships among states

Figure 1.1: A billboard at the entrance to the UNHCR's Za'atari refugee camp in Jordan, which hosted 80,000 Syrians in 2016, thanks wealthy donor states for their aid. Photo by Rawan Arar.

within the Global South also shape forced migration. Myron Weiner examines combinations of entry and exit policies, such as where one country promotes exit and another restricts entrance, both countries promote flows, both promote restriction, or the country of origin restricts exit while the other promotes entrance. These policies are highly interactive. "Often the entry rules set by one country are shaped by the exit rules set by another," he notes.[39] Policies controlling mobility and integration in one country affect policies in others through specific mechanisms of diffusion and iterative cycles of adjustment to migration patterns that have been changed by the policies of other countries.[40]

Potential refugees develop their aspirations and make decisions about movement within the constraints and possibilities of configurations of economic, military, political, and ideological power. In the classical formulation of Kritz and Zlotnik, an international migration system is defined as "a network of countries linked by migration interactions whose dynamics are largely shaped by the functioning of a variety of networks linking migration actors at different levels of aggregation."[41] The systems approach helps explain why people move to particular places and how they make those choices. Rather than a simple cause and effect model of refugee decision-making based on push factors in the place of origin and pull factors in the destination that channel refugees in one direction, the systems approach emphasizes interactions of power and ties that shape human flows.[42]

Beyond "solutions"

Much refugee research is defined by the policy categories of "durable solutions" – voluntary return, local integration, and resettlement, an approach characterized by a methodological nationalism rooted in the assumption that the nation-state is the natural unit of analysis and container for people's lives.[43] By contrast, the systems approach examines the interdependence of "all stages of the refugee displacement cycle."[44]

For example, despite the fact that fewer than 1 percent of the world's refugees are resettled, far more are affected by resettlement policies. The carrot of resettlement is dangled in ways that discipline refugees in countries of mass hosting. Many refugees aspire to return to their countries of origin or to settle locally, but for those who wish to resettle, the dream affects their lives in the first host country. For example, when hundreds of thousands of Chinese from the People's Republic of China (PRC) fled to Hong Kong in the 1950s, the World Council of Churches noted: "Even though the majority of Hong Kong refugees may never get to some other place, it is psychologically very important that a few are able to emigrate. The hope of resettlement abroad helps to reduce the despair and unrest at being hopelessly blocked in Hong Kong."[45] In the 1970s, Vietnamese who had reached Malaysia, whose government sometimes pushed boats filled with Vietnamese refugees back out to sea, did not publicly protest the grim conditions in Malaysian camps for fear that it would jeopardize their chances of resettlement in a Western state.[46]

Ties among countries structure refugee experiences, and the process of refugee movement and settlement further reshapes those ties through diasporic engagement. The United States granted sanctuary to Vietnamese refugees in the aftermath of the US defeat in Indochina in the 1970s. The second generation of Vietnamese Americans decades later became conduits for commerce and other ties between Vietnam and the United States after the re-establishment of diplomatic relations in 1995.[47]

In another feedback loop, the style of raising funds in the Global North to finance mass hosting in the Global South makes resettlement in the Global North more politically difficult. In 1959, the UNHCR sponsored World Refugee Year to raise funds, including for Chinese from the PRC who had fled to Hong Kong. Historian Laura Madokoro notes that international campaigns that emphasized the material deprivation of Chinese refugees in Hong Kong paradoxically made them seem alien and unsuited for permanent resettlement as new citizens and economic actors in English-speaking settler societies.[48] Contemporary fundraising campaigns pose similar risks. Objects of pity may inspire donations; they do not look like ideal neighbors.

Just as earlier migrations shape later refugee movements, so too do earlier refugee reception policies shape later receptions. Lebanon hosted an estimated 1.5 million Syrian refugees after the Syrian conflict began in 2011. Syrian refugees constituted more than a fifth of the population living in Lebanon, making it among the leading refugee host countries in the world on a per capita basis.[49] Yet the Lebanese government refused to establish formal refugee camps for Syrian refugees, in part to avoid repeating the experience of Palestinian refugees in Lebanon. Palestinian refugees arrived in 1948, but, except for a small minority of Christians allowed to become Lebanese citizens as part of a project of religious demographic engineering, the Muslim majority remained stateless and were required to live in camps. After the Palestine Liberation Organization was expelled from Jordan and established its major base in Lebanon in the 1970s, becoming a kind of state within a state, Lebanon became a major target of Israeli bombing. Palestinian refugees were caught up in the ethnic and religious conflicts within Lebanon, in which foreign powers from the United States to Syria and Iran intervened, culminating in the 1975–90 civil war, Israeli invasions in 1978 and 1982, and other conflicts. As a consequence, Lebanese political leaders have been reticent to permit geographic concentrations of recognized refugees that might become permanent.[50] Refugee policies are not just shaped by the past in a given country. They diffuse across countries and time, as governments copy each other, and international organizations, NGOs, think-tanks, and academics spread knowledge of practices.

Breaking away from an analytic overreliance on policy categories allows for a critique of the "sedentarist bias" of the international refugee regime. All three permanent solutions are predicated on a goal of ending movement.[51] Analyzing possibilities beyond the durable solutions framework of three static endpoints, to accommodate refugees' ongoing mobility and ties among hosts as well as countries of origin, suggests a wider array of policy solutions. "Migration and mobility may not only enhance existing solutions: they offer a means of connecting them," notes Katy Long.[52] Experts have urged freedom of secondary movement and a choice of residence for refugees at least since jurist Jacques Rubinstein's call in 1936.[53] Assessing the viability of such proposals requires widening the field of analysis to include myriad actors, interests, and types of power.

Limits of the systems approach

Concepts that are too broad lose analytical leverage. The international migration systems framework elaborated by Kritz and others includes the political, demographic, and economic context; migration flows between at least two countries or group of countries; and historical, cultural, colonial, and technological links among those countries. Akin Mabogunje's scheme is even more capacious, as it includes numerous subsystems and adjustment mechanisms. Anthony Richmond's typology of "reactive migration" includes twenty-five basic types.[54] At worst, the systems perspective would be a "kitchen-sink" approach, which, in trying to explain everything, explains nothing. Readers enamored of parsimony will be dissatisfied. But it should not be surprising that many factors shape a phenomenon as complex as the relationship between violence and mobility. The challenge remains to elaborate for the study of refugeedom what other work has been done to explain the international labor migration system.[55]

We distinguish our approach from some uses of systems theory in the study of international migration, in that we do not see a system as a quasi-organic entity or machine that inherently seeks equilibrium.[56] Attention to processes that transcend nation-state borders, analysis that moves beyond the three "durable solutions" framework, and a focus on power are elements shared with a "transnational" approach to displacement.[57] However, the systems approach focuses not just on the links of displaced people across borders; it pays equal attention to the interactions of states and other actors. Rather than a "people-centered perspective," we examine the interplay among individuals and much larger institutions and historical forces.

Our approach is to focus on the links across countries rather than the purely internal dynamics in each case. Of course, processes within a country's borders are also critical in shaping every stage of displacement, and these internal and external processes interact. Once policies are established at the national level, their implementation is still subject to all kinds of micro-institutional and personal dynamics. A vast body of case studies establishes the importance of these domestic processes.[58] We neither dismiss their importance nor attempt to adjudicate how consequential they are vis-à-vis the system level. Such a judgment would be highly contextual and could only be accomplished with much narrower scope conditions than those of this book. Our goal, rather, is to reveal dynamics that would remain obscured in siloed studies of a given country, group, or stage of displacement. The utility of any theoretical perspective is whether it shows something important that other perspectives miss.

The road ahead

The following chapters lay out the benefits of a sociological approach to understanding decision-making of people threatened by violence; policies in countries of origin, hosting, and transit; and the linkages among them. Chapter 2 summarizes debates among different approaches toward defining refugees. Constructivists argue that refugees are not a reality outside the act of naming them and the consequences of acquiring that label. Realists object, and assert that refugees have distinctive characteristics. Sociological realists define refugees as a subtype of migrant who has been displaced across an international border by the threat of violence. Within the realist camp, there are disputes about how far to push the boundaries of who should be legally recognized as a refugee. A focus on subjective self-identities brackets all the questions of realist definitions to center on how individuals define themselves to make sense of their experience. We then show how a systems approach reveals a matrix of movement and coercion, ranging from those who cannot move because they have been killed, to those who come and go freely as voluntary migrants. A visual representation of the "(im)mobility chessboard" (see Figure 2.4) brings together experiences that are usually discussed in siloed bodies of literature about armed conflict, ethnic cleansing, refugee studies, and international migration studies. We highlight the connections among categories and how the same individuals can move among them.

Chapter 3 describes the development of the legal regime around refugees from overlapping policies aimed at managing different forms of mobility. Rather than taking a narrow approach that focuses on the origins of refugee law in the interwar period or the 1951 Refugee Convention, we take a systemic view that illuminates how different strands of law and norms came together to influence the contemporary refugee regime. Refugee law is rooted in the realist notion that certain classes of individuals deserve exceptional protections related to punishment, slavery, extradition, and migration control. Over time, the regime has become secularized, formalized in multilateral agreements, and applies increasingly universalistic criteria to the refugee definition. The construction of the refugee regime and its use have been shaped by power relations among states more than the objective characteristics of displaced individuals. The chapter also provides a narrative historical scaffolding for many of the examples in the subsequent analytical chapters, which refer to cases that may not be uniformly familiar. Readers interested in learning more about particular episodes and historiographic debates will find detailed sources in the endnotes.

Chapter 4 examines how people who face violence and persecution calculate the costs of migration and weigh the risks of staying. We consider the degree and character of violence that refugees face, which can be generalized or targeted against an individual or ethnic group in the case of genocide and ethnic cleansing. Economic factors also play a role in decision-making, especially when the escalation of war leads to currency devaluation, the breakdown of work and business, and the scarcity of basic goods. After refugees leave their home country, they face the question of whether to attempt to migrate further. The prospect of return looms at every stage of migration. We introduce a model for refugee household decision-making called the "new economics of displacement," which takes into consideration how families manage multiple risks and goals. Through a longitudinal case study of the Asfour family from Syria, we show how members of one family attempted to manage the risks of the armed conflict from its outbreak in 2011 through the next decade.

Chapters 5–8 are organized by analytical categories of the type of displacement at moments of exit, hosting, and cross-border engagement. Rather than a chronologically organized case study of a country, region, or group of refugees, we examine what motivates states and other actors to try to manage different types of displacement. We show how military, economic, political, and ideological power operates in systems of immobility and mobility. The strategies and practices of these actors are influenced by historical sequences and links to other parts of the system. A dialectical process then reshapes the system itself.

Chapter 5 details how the ability of people to flee violence and persecution is shaped by exit policies of states and nonstate combatants. Many states have historically restricted the exit of their citizens and subjects. Others tolerate or even deliberately try to expel targeted groups. These policies are developed interactively with policies of potential host states. Particular types of conflict are more likely to produce refugees, including nation-state building from multiethnic empires and civil wars with foreign interventions.

In Chapter 6, we demonstrate that the global system of refugee management is dependent upon states that are not signatory to the 1951 Refugee Convention and states in the Global South more broadly. States in the Global South not only host most of the world's refugees, they also facilitate highly controlled refugee movement to the Global North through resettlement, and restrict the onward movement of asylum-seekers through containment measures pushed by powerful Northern states. We identify variation across Southern host states by breaking away from the refugee/migrant binary, in which only UN-recognized refugees are counted, and invite readers to consider the many Global Souths.

Chapter 7 examines host country interests from the perspective of powerful countries such as the United States, Germany, Britain, Australia, and Canada. Attempts to control and select refugees for admission reflect their foreign policy interests interacting with economic and demographic goals and ideologies of ethnocentrism, humanitarianism, and nationalism. A systems approach highlights how even some lobbying groups that appear to be "domestic" in fact have interests shaped by earlier migrations and transnational experiences and goals. One of the ways that powerful states try to limit refugee flows is by pushing control out from their borders into the territories of countries of origin and weaker states in the Global South.

Refugees often maintain and forge new ties to their places of origin, from long-distance engagements to repatriation. Chapter 8 identifies the remittances, visits, communications, and political organizing that constitute these ties. We then turn to the conditions that favor or inhibit cross-border connections. Conditions in countries of origin, as well as host country politics, international organizations, and migration patterns, affect homeland engagements.

The Conclusion recaps the main arguments about the merits of a systems approach revealed in the empirical chapters. We then establish the similarities and differences between policies in powerful and weaker host states. Finally, we make a set of recommendations to policymakers, journalists, and researchers working on displacement issues.

2

Who Is a Refugee?

Governments go to extraordinary lengths to control migration. Nearly 31,000 kilometers of walls divide states around the world. Of all pairs of adjacent countries, more than a fifth have fortified borders. European navies off the coast of Africa intercept small boats heading for Europe. Federal US agents interrogate and search the bags of US-bound passengers at airports in Abu Dhabi, Toronto, and Dublin.[1] Australia pays the remote island republic of Nauru to hold asylum-seekers who try to reach Australia by sea without a visa. Most controls are bureaucratic. Filipino and Mexican siblings of US citizens wait more than two decades to obtain their family reunification visas *after* meeting all qualifications.

In a world of restrictive immigration policies, legally recognized refugees acquire rights that are denied to other migrants and *may* be granted preferential admission. Around the world between 2010 and 2019, national governments granted some form of protection to 5 million people applying for asylum out of 16.2 million applications received at their borders or inside the granting countries. Twenty-nine countries had active overseas refugee resettlement programs for refugees selected from abroad. The United States, Canada, and Australia have dominated resettlement schemes since the late 1970s, with 3.4 million resettled in the United States alone between 1975 and 2019. Yet in 2019, before the Covid-19 pandemic, all countries together across the globe resettled only 107,800 refugees, just 0.5 percent of the world's refugee population under the UNHCR's mandate.[2]

The world's recognized refugee population reached 26.4 million in 2020, of whom 20.7 million fell under the mandate of the UNHCR.

The UNHCR has been directed by the UN's General Assembly to provide international protection and humanitarian assistance to most groups of refugees since its formation in 1950. In 2020, the UNHCR estimated that 86 percent of the world's refugees lived in poor and middle-income countries. The top host countries – Turkey, Pakistan, Uganda, Germany, and Sudan – hosted four out of ten UNHCR mandate refugees. UNRWA registered 5.7 million Palestine refugees under its mandate in Jordan, the Gaza Strip, West Bank, Syria, and Lebanon. The UNHCR categorized an additional 48 million people in 2020 as IDPs, people who were forcibly displaced but did not cross an international border.

Given the high stakes of the refugee designation, policymakers, advocates, academics, pundits, and forced migrants themselves disagree about who is a refugee. The term confusingly blends the analytical categories of social science, categories of everyday speech in which a refugee is someone who moves under any condition of hardship, and more specific categories of legal practice.[3] Immigration restrictionists are especially keen to root out people whom they call "bogus refugees" and to define them against some "genuine" standard. The construction of the categories also matters analytically because it shapes explanations of why refugees move, their experiences, and policymaking around displacement.

Constructivists

Constructivists and realists debate who is a refugee from an analytical perspective.[4] For constructivists, refugees are not a reality outside the act of naming them as such and the resultant consequences. Refugee categorization says more about the categorizing institutions than the characteristics of categorized people.[5] As Cynthia Hardy puts it, "a refugee only exists insofar as he or she is named and recognized by others."[6] Some constructivists argue that the effort to determine who is a refugee, and who is not, is doomed to failure. "Determination procedures, no matter how sophisticated, cannot uncover the truth," Hardy argues.[7] Ethnographic accounts show how judges, asylum officers, and lawyers make legal classifications that reflect unwritten expectations of how a victim should act, rather than making the correct choice according to the black letter of humanitarian protection law.[8] A challenge for refugee status determination is that, while the extent to which migration is compelled by violence lies on a continuum, individual cases must be shoehorned into a limited number of categories. Partly as a result, categories of protection have proliferated that fall short of asylum in terms of their duration and rights. Limited humanitarian protections include the "B-status" in Scandinavia in the 1960s, Complementary Protection in the UK since 2003, and Temporary Protected Status in the United States since 1990.[9] Political scientist Giulia Scalettaris concludes that "definitions of categories of people (such as 'refugees,' 'migrants,' 'IDPs,' etc.) arising from the refugee and humanitarian regime are not necessarily meaningful in the academic field from an analytical point of view."[10] It would be misleading to use an individual's legal designation to explain her social conditions beyond those that are produced by the categorization itself.

Constructivists point out that many basic claims about refugees are misleading because of differences across time over how refugees are defined. According to the UNHCR, "We are now witnessing the highest levels of displacement on record."[11] This assessment is reproduced by humanitarian organizations, journalists, and scholars. Charity agencies seek donations to cope with a disaster whose size has "overwhelmed the international community."[12] Supporters of refugee resettlement programs ask for more slots "amidst the worst refugee crisis in history."[13] Mass media generate eye-catching claims about unprecedented flows that sell more copy and generate more clicks.[14] Prominent scholars make similar claims.[15] Many pundits and politicians argue that borders must be more tightly controlled to prevent a huge wave of refugees from "swamping" their countries. Stakeholders across the political spectrum agree that refugee flows are at an all-time high, even as they disagree on their causes and effects. Yet the shared premise of an unprecedented emergency is simply the effect of changes in definitions and counting protocols.

The UNHCR database portrays the growth in the number of displaced people, rising from fewer than 2 million in 1951 to 82.4 million in 2020. These data include recognized refugees who fled across a border, asylum-seekers at a border or inside another country asking for recognition as refugees, and IDPs. Reliance on the UNHCR database alone distorts our understanding of the magnitude and causes of displacement. It underestimates past refugee migration because it leaves out flows related to imperial demise and relies on figures whose production is influenced by changing counting rules and legal classifications. The 1951 start date in the database leaves out both world wars and much of the transition from empires to nation-states, including 14 million people displaced by the 1947 partition of India. An estimated 175 million people were displaced by World War II alone, mostly in Asia; these displacements represented 7.6 percent of the world's population, compared to 1 percent of the world's population displaced in 2020.[16]

Increased attention to IDPs, rather than increased numbers of IDPs in the real world, also shapes claims of an unprecedented displacement crisis. More than 4.2 million IDPs emerged in the UNHCR database overnight in 1993. Systematic record-keeping did not register the earlier internal displacement of millions of people. Just to give two examples, the Assyrian empire in ancient Mesopotamia forcibly transferred an estimated 4.5 million people over 300 years, mostly in the seventh and eighth centuries BCE.[17] More than 30 million people were estimated to have been displaced during the Taiping Wars in China between 1850 and 1864, the size of the entire population of Britain at the time.[18] Finally, the international legal definition of refugees did not systematically include non-Europeans until 1967. Partly as a result, huge populations of refugees displaced before 1967 are not counted in the UNHCR database. Constructivists highlight the historically contingent ways that refugees and other forced migrants have been defined.[19]

Realist perspectives

Realists, on the other hand, consider refugeedom to express a reality in the world regardless of whether refugees are named as such. Refugees are a particular social category rooted in their unique experience. "With a different past and with motivations at variance with those affecting voluntary migrants, the refugee moves from his homeland to the country of his settlement against his will," states E. F. Kunz. The refugee "is a distinct social type."[20]

As Chapter 3 explains in detail, most, but not all, states agree on the legal definition of a refugee. According to the 1951 Refugee Convention, a refugee is someone who,

> owing to a well-founded fear of being persecuted for reasons of race, religion, nationality, membership of a particular social group or

political opinion, is outside the country of his nationality and is unable or, owing to such fear, is unwilling to avail himself of the protection of that country; or who, not having a nationality and being outside the country of his former habitual residence as a result of such events, is unable or, owing to such fear, is unwilling to return to it.[21]

Some regional international instruments give a more expansive definition. Many national laws incorporate the UN definition, others are narrower, while still others follow a more capacious standard.[22]

The legal concept of "recognizing" refugees is based on the premise that refugees are an ontologically given category out there in the real world waiting to be seen for who they *are*. As the UNHCR explains in its refugee status determination handbook:

> A person is a refugee within the meaning of the 1951 Convention as soon as he fulfils the criteria contained in the definition. This would necessarily occur prior to the time at which his refugee status is formally determined. Recognition of his refugee status does not therefore make him a refugee but declares him to be one. He does not become a refugee because of recognition, but is recognized because he is a refugee.[23]

By insisting that being a refugee precedes, and is independent of, the act of classification, realists stand on firmer rhetorical ground to demand refugee protection.

Expansive realists

The realist camp is further divided into expansive and classical realists. The former wish to bring more types of forced migration under the refugee umbrella, while the latter try to hold the line according to classical interpretations of the legal standard of the 1951 Convention and its 1967 Protocol (discussed in Chapter 3).

For many expansive realists, IDPs should be included within the refugee category and given international protection. The only difference between an IDP and a refugee is that an IDP never crossed an international border. It is likely that most refugees were IDPs first, at least for a short period, as few refugees are able to leave their country without traveling some distance through it. People trying to flee their country but who die before doing so perish as IDPs rather than refugees simply because they did not make it out. Expansion of legal displacement categories to include IDPs introduces the issue of whether foreign governments and international organizations have the authority to intervene and violate the sovereignty of the state where displacement is taking place. As explained in Chapter 3, there has been movement in that direction since the 1990s.

During the Syrian conflict that began in 2011, thousands of IDPs camped in the deserts of southern Syria within view of the Jordanian border. After initially allowing Syrians to pass freely, the Jordanian military in 2015 prevented them from moving across a narrow strip of territory between the states commonly referred to as "no man's land." Displaced Syrians who were clearly within Syria were unquestionably IDPs, but how should the people in no man's land be classified? Some humanitarian agencies took an expansive realist stance by insisting that these forcibly displaced people were already in Jordan, and, therefore, were refugees who should be able to secure greater international protection. The government of Jordan insisted that the estimated 70,000 people in no man's land were not refugees, but IDPs. Ultimately, the Jordanian government worked with select aid agencies to support this group, but with vastly more limited resources than was offered to those fortunate enough to have crossed into Jordan proper.

As with refugees, there are numerous episodes of mass internal displacement that predate the term "IDP." The Japanese invasion of China between 1937 and 1945 displaced an estimated 95 million Chinese people within their country.[24] It was only China's vast size and the fact that parts of the country remained unoccupied by Japan that these people were IDPs rather than de facto refugees. It is difficult to establish who is an IDP, as opposed to a refugee, when international borders change quickly, such as during the dissolution of states or military campaigns. During and after World War II, "displaced person" was often used as an umbrella term to describe people forced to flee from their homes by fighting and persecution, regardless of whether they were inside or outside their country of nationality.[25]

Some expansive realists further argue that the refugee definition should be augmented to include people forced to move for reasons beyond violence and persecution. "It is imperative that the definition of a 'refugee' be widened to include all those in peril from natural and unnatural disaster," argued Anthony Richmond in 1993,[26] a

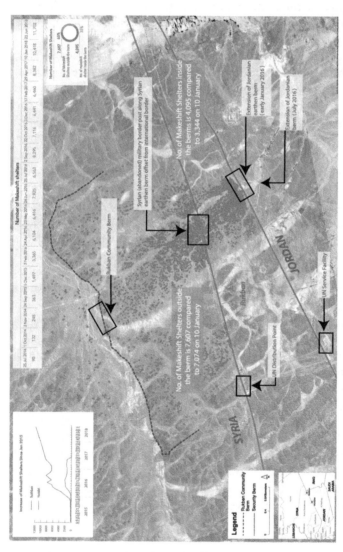

Figure 2.1: A satellite photo of the border between Jordan and Syria in June 2018. The UN estimated that 11,702 makeshift shelters (identified with a dot on the map) housed around 70,000 people inside Syria and a "no man's land" between Syria and Jordan. Map by United Nations Office for the Coordination of Humanitarian Affairs. The boundaries and names shown and the designations used on this map do not imply official endorsement or acceptance by the United Nations.

Figure 2.2: A Chinese family flees Shanghai during the Japanese invasion in September 1937. The Second Sino-Japanese War (1937–45) displaced an estimated 95 million people in China, far more than all displacements in Europe at the time. Photo by AP.

position that has gained adherents in light of extreme climate change and its potential to contribute to population displacement.[27] Indeed, protection for those unable to return home because of "natural calamity" was written into US refugee law beginning in 1953.[28] The State Department's report on implementation stated that the "term 'refugee' as used in the Act is broad enough, for example, to include the victims of the floods in Holland, Italy, or Japan [and] the earthquakes in Greece."[29] After an earthquake devastated the Azores, the US Congress passed a law granting additional visas to Portuguese, "who, because of natural calamity in the Azores Islands subsequent to September 1, 1957, are out of their usual place of abode in such islands and unable to return thereto, and who are in urgent need of assistance for the essentials of life."[30] The 1965 immigration act included a preference for "persons uprooted by catastrophic natural calamity."[31]

Many other groups of people are forced to migrate, including slaves, indentured servants, and trafficked persons. Forced migration also includes development-induced displacement and resettlement (DIDR), such as the forced relocation of communities to build large dams or other modernization projects. The DIDR phenomenon fits much more easily within a sociological definition of forced migration than in a legal refugee category.

Classical realists

"Classical realists" defend the 1951 Convention refugee definition, which applies only to people outside their country who, if they are returned to their home, face persecution on one of five specific grounds – their race, religion, nationality, political opinion, or membership in a particular social group. These authors warn that expansive definitions could compromise the legitimacy of policies for classically defined refugees "if the public no longer believes that those who claim the status truly are specially jeopardized."[32] For classical realists, the 1951 definition is tied to a recognition of the limitations to intervention from abroad that is embedded in the Westphalian system of state sovereignty. They fear that if they were to yield to the proposals of the expansive realists, individuals fleeing violence and persecution would be less able to secure special protections. Classical realists may believe that people forced to move because of climate change or disaster should receive some kind of support, but they object to a broadening of the refugee definition because it may have negative practical consequences for refugees currently protected under the 1951 Convention.

Several small island states are facing imminent mass displacement as a result of climate change. Yet despite their populations' protection needs, at the 2018 negotiations for the Global Compact on Refugees these states did not advocate expanding the 1951 Convention definition to include climate refugees.[33] Instead, they supported expanding temporary work permits and humanitarian visas for climate-induced *migrants*. The 2018 Global Compact for Safe, Orderly and Regular Migration became the first international migration agreement to recognize climate-induced displacement. These policy positions reflect an interest in including climate-induced displacement under the aegis of *forced migration*, while hewing to the political and legal constraints that reserve the *refugee* label for instances of people faced with the threat of violence and persecution.

Sociological realists

Sociological realists are more agnostic about whether the legal refugee definition should be expanded or restricted, but they accept the ontological reality that some people move in large part because of violence or persecution. For purposes of sociological and historical analysis, we follow Zolberg et al. in defining refugees as those who have crossed an international border because of violence, including the threat of violence behind persecution, or those who are afraid to return to their country because of its threat.[34]

The timing of the violence that partly constitutes the refugee category varies. "Anticipatory refugee movements" are undertaken by someone who "leaves his home country before the deterioration of the military or political situation prevents his orderly departure."[35] In these situations, it is only with hindsight that the objective threat of violence can be fully established. Understanding decision-making in anticipatory movements requires an analysis of the subjective assessments of those who stay and those who flee. Other refugees lack the protection of their state of origin as a result of past violence, which, in the case of protracted refugee situations, took place many years or even generations earlier. Stateless people often inherit their status.[36] Thus, the source of violence that generates the refugee condition can be in the intergenerational past, recent experience, the present, imminent, or in the hypothetical future if one were to return home.

Bracketing the serious concerns about legal definitions that divide the classical and expansive realists, sociological realists emphasize that particular individuals and groups may be de facto (sociological) refugees even if they are not assigned the legal label. They may even be known primarily under other labels. Sociological refugees can be students, defectors, freedom fighters, and settlers. For Zolberg et al., "unrecognized refugees" include groups such as Jews expelled from Iberia in the late fifteenth and early sixteenth centuries who were refugees *avant la lettre*, or contemporary asylum-seekers who fled persecution but whose claim is rejected.[37]

One of the quintessential labor migrations to the United States, from Mexico, bears elements of refugeehood. As with many movements, migrating to work and migrating to flee violence were sometimes intricately bound together. Yaqui people in the northwestern Mexican state of Sonora who resisted Mexico's federal government were exterminated or faced deportation to the remote southeastern territory of

Yucatán. Thousands fled to the US territory of Arizona in the early twentieth century, following paths of earlier groups who had gone to work in agriculture and mining. Yaqui people were not recognized in the United States as refugees, but as migrant workers.[38] During the Mexican Revolution (1910–20), the United States became a sanctuary for Mexican rebels and soldiers, their families, and civilians seeking safety. The US Army established a temporary camp for 8,000 Mexican refugees near Eagle Pass, Texas, and for 5,000 refugees at Fort Bliss outside El Paso. "Experience on this border has demonstrated that the most practicable way of handling a situation such as described is to give refugees temporary asylum in the border towns," an immigration service supervisor reported back to Washington. When conditions improved in Mexico, the refugees would be required to repatriate.[39] War in Mexico between an anticlerical government and Catholic rebels broke out twice in the 1920s and 1930s, sending thousands of Catholics north and the entire Church leadership into exile in San Antonio, Texas.[40] Today we would call all these groups and individuals "unrecognized refugees" whose movement was channeled by earlier labor migrations.

Figure 2.3: Refugees during the Mexican Revolution head toward Marfa, Texas, after the Battle of Ojinaga in January 1914. Photo by Bain News Service/Library of Congress.

The question of which groups should sociologically qualify as unrecognized refugees is not always straightforward. Frank Caestecker argues that historians of refugeedom should not be hamstrung by using legal categories alone, but he questions whether historians can be refugee "eligibility officers for the human past."[41] The undesirable alternative for analysts is to exclusively examine cases in which a politically charged process has legally defined certain groups or individuals as refugees, while ignoring the other cases.

Historical questions around the categorizations of unrecognized refugees matter for at least two reasons. First, they highlight the changing connections among countries of origin and potential destinations. The question of who was a refugee did not become a major legal question at the turn of the twentieth century because of relatively open European access to the United States, which functioned as an escape valve for unrecognized European refugees.[42] By contrast, in the 1930s, when even longstanding countries of immigration became much more selective, the question of whether there was a special obligation for states to admit people categorized as refugees became critical. Most governments decided they did not have such an obligation. The escape valve for Jews fleeing fascism closed. Once the postwar international refugee regime was put into place, the question of categorization became even more important, as legal prohibition of *refoulement* became widespread.

Second, the question of unrecognized refugees in the historical record calls into question the common assertion that today's refugees are fundamentally different. Claims that "the distinction between forced migration and economic migration is becoming blurred as a result" of increasing global inequality, for example, look shakier when it becomes evident that forced and economic migration have often been intertwined.[43] Legal scholar Bhupinder S. Chimni has sharply criticized "the myth of difference" – the idea that there are great dissimilarities between refugees in Europe around World War II and the early Cold War, on the one hand, and post-Cold War refugees from the Third World on the other.[44]

The claim that there was a golden age of dissident refugees who were recognized because they plainly had fled targeted political persecution, unlike today's "mixed flows" of people, is a historical distortion.[45] French officials in 1933 considered many German Jews to be "self-proclaimed refugees" seeking economic advantage in France.[46] In 1949, following the division of Germany by the occupying Allies, West Germany's cabinet estimated that only 7 percent of escapees from East Germany were facing targeted persecution, but, politically, the West could not send them back because of West Germany's claims to represent all of Germany.[47] However, West Germany did not always welcome Germans from the East with open arms. The 1950 Federal Emergency Admission Act required refugees to show they faced "imminent danger to life and limb, to personal liberty, or other compelling grounds" for attempting to exit the East. Over the next two years, more than 60 percent of refugee status applicants were rejected for not meeting this standard. The 173,000 applicants declared "illegals" were not deported and were finally given legal status in 1952. A 1956 CIA report concluded: "Information obtained through the refugee screening process indicates that the mass movements from East Germany to West Germany have taken place primarily because of economic or personal reasons and that such motives as opposition to the Soviet system as such or belief in Western democracy have played a relatively minor role."[48] A 1953 study of 300 Polish, Hungarian, and Czech refugees found a majority defected because of economic rather than political push factors.[49] After the Hungarian Revolution in 1956, many in the West questioned whether escapees from Eastern Europe were refugees, given the economic rewards of moving from East to West, and the fact that many of those who moved were not targeted dissidents, but, rather, average subjects of repressive regimes.[50] Similarly, as Zolberg and colleagues argued in 1989 during the waning Cold War, "except for a clear minority of political exiles, it is difficult to establish whether Cubans are refugees or economic migrants."[51] The question of "mixed flows" is as old as the refugee regime itself.

Self-identities

Categorization as a refugee can confer legal advantages, but it often comes bundled with social stigma. In her 1943 essay titled "We Refugees," German Jewish refugee and theorist Hannah Arendt began by stating: "In the first place, we don't like to be called 'refugees.'"[52] Someone who is legally categorized as a refugee may avoid using that label, or only use it situationally, to avoid its association with weakness and victimhood. In other cases, the refugee label may be a point of pride. In her study of Syrian refugee identity, political scientist Wendy Pearlman interviewed a Palestinian refugee from Syria seeking asylum in Germany, who explained:

> I was born as a refugee. My father was born as a refugee. My grandfather was kicked out of Acre. So now, I am refugee for the third time. I don't have a problem with this word. I defend it. I am with this word. But I think the word "refugee" is sensitive because of how it has been used here in Germany. So, some people now prefer to use "newcomers." But for me, I don't like "newcomers." It doesn't mean anything. "Refugee" means to seek for refuge and find shelter. But "newcomers" means that you just came for no reason. "Refugee" is a legal [category] with legal benefits given to you by law. "Newcomer" takes [the politics out of it].[53]

This Palestinian man recognized a societal cost to the refugee label and noted that some people prefer to adopt the "newcomer" label to avoid judgment. For him, however, taking the politics out of the refugee label would also separate him from a generations-long struggle that had become a part of his identity.

Focusing on the self-understandings of individuals and communities highlights the fact that some legally recognized refugees do not consider themselves to be refugees or represent themselves in those terms, or at least only deploy the refugee category in particular situations. On the other hand, some people who are not legally recognized as refugees consider themselves to be refugees to their core.[54] People who understand themselves to be refugees or members of an ancestral refugee community have sometimes been particularly influential advocates for new refugees, as we outline in Chapter 7. The gap between state-given and self-assigned categories is highlighted in the account of the Asfour family in Chapter 4. As resettled refugee Wajih Asfour explained, the day he arrived in Canada, the Canadian government added one refugee to its population count. But for him, he had reached safety and stopped being a refugee.

Are refugees migrants?

A related debate that crosscuts all three realist perspectives disputes whether refugees are migrants. Sociologically, we consider refugees to be a subset of migrants. It is often difficult in practice to identify what distinguishes refugees from other migrants. Most sociological

definitions of refugees are oriented around a set of related dichotomies that define refugees in contrast with "migrants," or at least
in contrast with other types of migrants. The common thread in
many of these categorizations is that refugees have less agency. Their
movement is described as involuntary, forced, reactive, or lacking
in choice.[55] However, all migration takes place on a continuum of
coercion. At one pole, the only choice is death or submission to being
transported as a slave, prisoner, or expellee. In other constrained
contexts, there is a greater menu of options, but all choices are
risky and undesirable. At the other extreme, privileged people with
resources can migrate "out of the 'joy' of mobility, for adventure and
to see the world."[56] In between these extremes are people who must
leave to achieve expectations of a dignified life.

Another longstanding criterion used to distinguish refugees from
migrants is that refugees leave for political reasons, while migrants
have economic aspirations.[57] The US Congress on several occasions
in the nineteenth century drew a distinction between refugees and
other immigrants. In 1834, Congress granted thirty-six sections of
land in Illinois and Michigan to 235 Polish (settler) exiles. The exiles
had fled the Polish–Russian War for the expected safety of Austria,
only to be expelled to the United States.[58] Congressman Churchill
C. Cambreleng of New York supported their request. The reasons
for their migration was "totally different from those of any other
people," he told the House. "They are compelled, by the utmost
rigor and perfidy of the Russian government, to say farewell to their
sweet home."[59] The political/economic dichotomy is only useful in
some cases and obscures the multiplicity of motivations that drive
many movements. States can use economic tools to punish opponents
and despised minorities by cutting off their access to employment,
markets, education, and land. Economic crises often have political
causes. Economic crises generate political unrest. Wars raise the
risk of falling victim to generalized violence as well as the inability
to maintain one's livelihood in a collapsing economy.[60] A further
complication of the political/economic dichotomy is that individuals'
goals, and opportunities to achieve them, often change over the
course of time and multistage movements.[61]

Many stakeholders are leery of considering refugees as a subcat-
egory of migrants. For key actors in the UNHCR, many legal
scholars, and advocates, "refugees are not migrants,"[62] or being a
refugee is "only incidentally comparable to being a migrant."[63] This

position aims to maintain the privileged category of refugee for under-standable policy reasons. For legal scholar James Hathaway, the risk of not categorizing refugees as a distinct group is that "officials will fail to take account of the specificity of the duties that follow from refugee status if refugees come to be seen as no more than (forced) migrants." Defending a strictly legal definition, Hathaway observes that, "even if all that binds refugees is their common international legal status, that is more than enough. In the real world, legal status – and the rights that go with various forms of legal status – routinely identify and constitute fundamental social and political categories."[64]

On the other hand, some social scientists suggest there are normative as well as historical reasons to reject the sharp divide between migrants and refugees. "An artificial separation between 'refugee' and 'migrant' ostensibly removes the humanitarian imper-ative for states to admit the needy in all but a minority of cases, opening up opportunities to restrict migration," argues Katy Long. Another unintended consequence of the institutional separation of the international management of refugees from migrant workers in the early 1950s is that refugees became the objects of humanitarian assistance whose economic agency is snubbed.[65] Oliver Bakewell persuasively argues that when scholars rely too much on formal legal and policy categories, it "limits the extent to which research can offer a radical analysis of the situation of forced migrants," including people who move and settle outside of any formal programs or legal statuses. In his view: "Studies arising too closely from policy concerns can tend to skew the basis for research, constraining the questions asked, the areas of study, the methods used and the analysis. Such research often produces narrow, short-term answers to its (limited) questions, which then contribute to the development of inappropriate policies."[66]

To understand how power operates in the production of knowledge about refugees and to maintain a critical distance that is not beholden to states or other political actors, it is useful to separate categories of practice, such as the statutory definition of refugees, from categories of analysis, such as the sociological definition used in this text.[67] For example, an exclusive focus on whether a given person or group should be granted legal protection makes it difficult to analyze the interactions between different motivations for moving and changes in reasoning over time. The refugee versus migrant question is usually only assessed at the point of entry into a country where authorities are seeking to determine the worthiness of admission by reconstructing the rationale for exit. The tasks of the refugee status determination officer and the scholar do not always overlap.

The distinction between categories of legal practice and categories of sociological analysis become especially clear when considering asylum cases in which the person seeking protection must be recognized by the state as a member of a "particular social group," which is one of the five grounds for protection outlined in the 1951 Refugee Convention along with race, religion, nationality, and political opinion. Women who flee domestic violence are often in a precarious position. The Refugee Convention does not explicitly mention sex or gender as a protected ground. During treaty negotiations, a Yugoslavian proposal to include discrimination on the basis of sex in the refugee definition was rejected by the other delegations. Since the 1990s, however, the UNHCR and a number of states have issued guidelines for gender-related discrimination through an expansion of the "social group" category to include victims of severe domestic violence, female genital cutting, rape, and "honor" crimes. Refugee claims have been successfully made on the basis that states failed to protect their own citizens from such crimes at the hands of nonstate actors, though the scope of such cases remains legally and politically contested.[68]

Table 2.1 summarizes different theoretical approaches toward defining refugees and gives examples of how they might inform a position regarding an asylum-seeker who is not explicitly protected by the Convention definition of a refugee based on her gender alone, but who may qualify as a member of a particular social group as the victim of domestic violence in which her state of nationality refuses to intervene and provide protection.

Hathaway's "plea to go back to more of a 'dating' relationship" between refugee and migration studies, rather than a full union, is worth pondering.[69] Given the diversity of goals within refugee and migration studies, and the legal and political uses of the refugee category, the notion of dating might even be too much for some. The idea that refugees are only incidentally comparable to other migrants is sociologically false, but, like many myths, it can have social utility. We believe there is a greater likelihood that refugees will be denied their existing meager protections than that special protections for refugees will be extended to broad groups of other migrants. Immigration control historically preceded exceptions for refugees,

Table 2.1: Theoretical approaches toward defining refugees

Theoretical stance	Principle of categorization	Example
Constructivists	Refugees are not a reality outside the act of naming them and the resultant consequences. There is no inherent difference between refugees and migrants.	The decision whether to grant her asylum reflects the institutional histories and political interests of the adjudicator, not the applicant's distinct experience.
Realists	Refugees are a social category rooted in their unique experience, regardless of whether they are named as such.	
Classical realists	Refugees are only those facing persecution as legally defined in the 1951 Convention. Expansive definitions should be resisted because they may compromise the legitimacy of policies for classically defined refugees.	The asylum-seeker is a refugee if a successful legal argument can be made that she is a member of a "particular social group" whom her state of nationality persecutes or fails to protect. The asylum-seeker is not a refugee based on gender persecution alone.
Expansive realists	The 1951 Convention definition should be expanded to include many forms of forced migration including "climate refugees," internally displaced persons, and victims of domestic violence.	Because this woman fled her home to escape from a violent husband, she should be considered a refugee and protected by the receiving state.
Sociological realists	Agnostic about the legal definition, but accept the ontological reality that some people move in large part because of violence or persecution. Refugees are a subtype of migrant.	She is a refugee because she fled violence.
Self-identities	Brackets the legal definition to focus on how individuals define themselves to make sense of their experience.	If she identifies with the refugee label, then she is a refugee.

and there is little reason to see why getting rid of refugee exceptions would result in the end of immigration control. In the immediacy of applied policy, upholding the classical distinction is sensible.

Yet understanding the interaction between forced displacement and other types of migration is critical for explaining the origins and consequences of refugee policy and how people threatened by violence try to make a more secure life for themselves and their communities. Preferential policies for refugees only have a rationale in the context of an immigration system that filters who may enter a country and creates hierarchies of status after arrival. Selection, integration, and expulsion criteria for refugees overlap with the politics and policies regulating all kinds of migrations. Rather than attempting to separate the study of refugees from that of other migrants, we take a systems approach that shows how policies designed to manage one kind of mobility spill over into others.

The focus on displacement in refugee studies and a refugee definition constituted by movement across a border hides the experiences of those who are forced to stay in place by a conflict – in other words, those who face "involuntary immobility."[70] For legal scholar Andrew Shacknove:

> Whether a person travels ten miles across an international border or the same distance down the road into a neighboring province may be crucial for determining logistical and diplomatic action. Conceptually, however, refugeehood is unrelated to migration. It is exclusively a political relation between the citizen and the state, not a territorial relation between a countryman and his homeland. Refugeehood is one form of unprotected statelessness.[71]

One of the potential downsides of using a legal definition of refugees to define the scope of study is that experiences of immobility are less visible. Analyzing the experience of refugees alone samples on the dependent variable and assumes what should be explained – why some people move while others in similar predicaments stay put.

The systems approach reveals a matrix of possible experiences rather than focusing in isolation on a single type. We include people displaced by violence as well as illustrative examples of other forms of forced and voluntary migration. Within groups subject to persecution, people may find themselves in different categories at different times, or different members of the same group may experience different categories simultaneously. One reason is that persecuting governments wield many tools and strategies that can include mass killings, expulsions, enslavement, and internment in concentration camps. To capture a broad range of (im)mobility and coercion, Figure 2.4 depicts where different types of people fall along these two axes. The x axis shows the degree of movement away from home, beginning with domestic relocation and extending to international relocation and return. The y axis shows the degree of proximate coercion – the level of violence or its threat applied close in time – that propels movement or staying in one place. We conceptualize these axes as continua of coercion and movement rather than discrete stages to emphasize that they are part of a large potential universe of experiences. Movement among these dimensions is not always in a single direction. Like a chessboard, it is theoretically possible for an individual to move forward, backward, and sidewise. As on a chessboard, some actors have a greater capacity than others to move in different directions. For pawns in the weakest position, movement is impossible. Opportunities to move are enabled and constrained by interactions with other actors.

The most immobile people include nonmigrants who voluntarily stay at home, at bottom left of Figure 2.4. They represent the majority of the world's population. At top left, the most involuntary immobile people are those who have been killed at home and cannot move. Of the living, the most coerced are those who are currently besieged, targets of persecution hiding underground or attempting to "pass," but who could conceivably escape in the future. Moving within their country of origin under extreme levels of coercion are those killed while in transit, followed by prisoners, internees in concentration camps, and people subject to forced internal relocation. At top right, some of the most mobile people also suffer high degrees of coercion, such as refugees sent back to their country of origin and voluntary migrants who are forcibly deported.[72] The highest degree of mobility for individuals under low levels of coercion are authorized immigrants or voluntary returnees, at bottom right.

There are many possibilities among these four extreme poles. Refuseniks have requested permission to leave their country but the authorities refuse their request, forcing them to live under persecution. Among those who have moved within their country of origin, the most coerced are stuck in "safe havens," such as Syrians living in a border strip of northern Syria occupied by Turkish forces.

Degree of proximate coercion	Domestic		International		International return
High	killed at home	killed in transit	killed crossing border	transported slave	killed on return
	besieged, targets in hiding	prisoner, internee, internally relocated	expellees; detained asylum seeker, closed camp refugee	indentured servant	refouled refugee, deportee
	refusenik	IDPs in "safe havens"; spontaneous IDPs	open camp refugee, tolerated spontaneous settler	unauthorized migrant "guest worker"	pressured returnee
Low	voluntary nonmigrant	internal migrant	asylee, resettled refugee	authorized immigrant	voluntary returnee
		Domestic	International		International return

Degree of movement

Figure 2.4: The (im)mobility chessboard.

Less coerced are spontaneous IDPs who have fled localized conflict in search of a safer area. The least coerced have simply moved as voluntary internal migrants.

Among those who try to flee across a border, those facing the highest coercion are killed while exiting or entering, followed by those forcibly expelled. Some asylum-seekers are detained or forced to live in restricted areas, often for years, and are pushed toward the top of the graph because they are immobile unless they accept repatriation.[73] Many refugees are confined in closed, heavily securitized camps, such as Jordan's Cyber City. Less coerced are those living in open camps who can come and go, such as UNRWA refugee camps for Palestinians in Jordan, and those who have spontaneously settled and are tolerated by local authorities. Other refugees range up and down this scale depending on shifting policies or the whim of local officials. Resettled refugees have fled high levels of coercion in the past, but in the present, they voluntarily participate in resettlement programs. Asylees, refugees who were granted asylum after applying at a granting country's borders or from within its territory, generally enjoy few restrictions on their movement once that status is granted.

Among those who move to work, transported slaves are by far the most constrained. Slavery can also be a way for persecutors to extract labor from targets of persecution before working them to death. Slavery, expulsion, and genocide can be different facets or stages of persecution. At a much lower level of coercion, indentured servants are forced to work for the same employer for multiyear terms. Temporary migrant workers are able to travel internationally, but they usually labor under serious constraints, especially under the *kafala* system in Gulf Cooperation Council countries or the 1942–64 Bracero program in the United States. Among repatriates, the highest degree of coercion in return involves forcible deportation and refoulement, but there are lesser forms of coercion, such as when a combination of withdrawing carrots and the use of sticks pressures refugees to return.

Are refugees victims?

People seeking humanitarian protection must often distort their complicated experiences into simplified stories in which they are victims with little control over their lives.[74] Many refugees object to being treated as victims because it strips them of their fundamental humanity.[75] However, it is difficult to imagine a definition of refugees that does not involve some element of being a victim of violence or persecution. As Emma Haddad puts it, "the victim-like definition is necessary for the survival of the concept in theory and the survival of the individual in practice."[76] It is possible to define refugees as victims in this way without labeling them as *merely* victims. The conceptual problem is not so much the notion of victimization, but rather, any implication that refugees are *helpless* or *passive*, when in fact they often exercise their agency in resourceful ways despite the difficulties in which they find themselves.

Refugees are victims of violence or its threat. At the same time, a minority may themselves use violence. Legally, the 1951 Refugee Convention does not apply to those who have committed a "crime against peace, a war crime, or a crime against humanity" as defined by international law.[77] Sociologically, refugees include soldiers of defeated armies and released prisoners of war who face persecution if they are returned.[78] Indeed, as described in Chapter 3, the League of Nations first established its refugee institutions to deal with the repatriation of Russian prisoners of war in the 1920s. A reaction against the forced repatriation of Soviet prisoners of war after World War II was a critical factor in the creation of international refugee agencies and the consolidation of the principle of non-refoulement.

Communities of former refugees can produce new refugees. Refugee settlers and their descendants in North America fleeing religious and political persecution in Europe displaced Native Americans.[79] The children of Ottoman refugees displaced from the Balkans and the Caucasus were overrepresented in the genocide and displacement of Armenians from Anatolia during World War I.[80] Refugees from Europe joined Zionist forces to push Palestinians off their land in 1948, thus unleashing the *Nakba* (catastrophe) for Palestinians, while establishing the state of Israel.[81]

There is a long history of refugee groups who use force to try to achieve their political goals. Waldensian refugees fleeing religious persecution in Savoy for sanctuary in Switzerland in the late seventeenth century invaded Savoy three years later. They "may well be the first successful militarized refugee group," notes political scientist Phil Orchard.[82] The failed attempt by CIA-sponsored Cuban exiles to overthrow the Castro regime by landing at the Bay of Pigs in 1961 has been called a "refugee invasion."[83] During its 1971 conflict with Pakistan, the Indian government trained and provided weapons to Mukti Bahini refugees who helped establish an independent Bangladesh. Refugee camps have been home bases for militarized organizations in Cambodia, Central America, Africa, Afghanistan, and the Middle East. At the same time, most refugees are not involved in perpetuating violence. In the only attempt of which we are aware to quantify the phenomenon, Sarah Kenyon Lischer found that between 1987 and 1998, "95% of all refugee-related violence [took] place, on average, in fewer than fifteen states," and that the number of refugee *groups* involved in political violence declined by half to 30 percent in 1998. The number of individuals within those groups who deploy violence is infinitely smaller.[84]

Identifying refugees *simply* as victims, which is motivated by some contemporary humanitarian constructs of refugees, ignores the varieties of relationships between victimhood and victimizing that a historical lens reveals. Stating that refugees are not simply victims can be an affirmation of universal human dignity. It is also an analytical move that shows how refugeedom is implicated in a much broader set of historical processes such as settler colonialism and state-seeking nationalism.

The following chapter explains how ideologies of protection for refugees and others facing persecution have developed over many centuries and become instantiated in different bodies of law. Whether one takes a realist or a constructivist position toward the refugee category, the shifting *legal* definitions are highly consequential, and their origins are far more complex and surprising than a siloed approach that begins history with the 1951 Refugee Convention conveys.

3

Making a Legal Refugee Regime

Regimes are constituted by unwritten norms and written legal instruments. The latter include national laws, treaties that create binding legal obligations, such as the 1951 Refugee Convention, and treaties that create nonbinding moral commitments, such as the 1948 Universal Declaration of Human Rights. In standard accounts of the refugee regime, history begins in the twentieth century and Europe lies at the center of the story. For historian Philipp Ther, focusing on Europe is inevitable "because the history of refuge and refugees has European origins."[1] Philosopher Giorgio Agamben dates the "first appearance of refugees as a mass phenomenon" to the collapse of the Russian, Austro-Hungarian, and Ottoman empires at the end of World War I.[2] According to anthropologist Liisa Malkki, "it is in the Europe emerging from World War II that certain key techniques for managing mass displacements of people first became standardized and then globalized," and "the principal elements of international refugee law and related legal instruments grew largely out of the aftermath of the war in Europe."[3]

To be sure, the 1951 Refugee Convention that remains in force was drafted in response to European displacement around World War II. Focusing on the Convention is understandable from the perspective of legal practitioners who depend on it to advocate for refugees. The Convention includes several principles that are fundamental to the contemporary legal regime. Article 2 defines who is a refugee protected under the Convention. Article 3 provides that states should not discriminate against refugees because of their race, religion, or country of origin. Article 31 prevents states from penalizing refugees who used illegal means to enter if they came directly from a country where they were threatened. Article 33 prohibits refoulement, which is the forcible return of refugees to a country where they will be persecuted. These elements form the core of the contemporary refugee regime. None of them appeared *ex nihilo* in 1951.

Siloed perspectives on refugee law that focus primarily on the 1951 Refugee Convention ignore fundamental legal developments outside Europe and before the twentieth century. A systems approach provides an alternative perspective by examining how religious beliefs, ideologies, and laws in different domains interact to produce the contemporary legal regime. The treatment of refugees arises from distinct bodies of law and softer norms that regulate emigration, immigration, slave trafficking, extradition, asylum, refugee relief and protection, and refugee resettlement. We examine the many origins and manifestations of refugee-related laws – laws that may not use the term "refugee" but which have influenced the development of contemporary protections. Policies and decisions about who is worthy of protection reflect inequalities of power.

Paying attention to interactions of different bodies of law around the world shows there have been three major developments in legal refugee regimes. The first trend is the secularization of the authority that grants asylum and the grounds for granting it. A second development since World War II is the use of increasingly universalistic criteria for defining refugees, rather than ad hoc designations of particular groups. The third development is the growth of formal, multilateral agreements around refugees. These multilateral agreements have narrow historical precedents, going back at least as far as the 1555 Treaty of Augsburg's provision granting a qualified right of some persecuted European religious minorities to exit their countries. Multilateral agreements began to create a formal international refugee regime in 1889 in South America with rules about extradition and diplomatic and territorial asylum.

Secularization of religious roots

The belief that people fleeing violence should be granted protection has deep religious roots across cultural contexts. "Asylum" derives from the classical Greek concept of *asylon hieron*, the inviolable sanctuary of the temple.[4] The Temple of Osiris in Ancient Egypt, the

Kaaba in Arabia, biblical "cities of refuge," Puʻuhonua o Hōnaunau in Hawaiʻi, and many other sacred places have also served as sanctuaries for different types of people in flight. In China, the Confucian principle to "embrace gently the guests from afar" was invoked by the Qing empire to welcome Torghut Mongolians fleeing Russian persecution in 1771.[5]

The scriptures of Judaism, Christianity, and Islam include key episodes of forced migration. In Judaism, forced relocation in the Babylonian Captivity and the Exodus from Egypt are fundamental to understandings of diaspora and resilience in the face of persecution. In Islamic tradition, the *hijra*, in which the prophet Muhammad and his followers fled from Mecca to Medina to escape an assassination plot, is so central that it marks the start of the Islamic calendar. The Arabic term for refugee/emigrant, *muhajir*, recalls this flight. The Quran is replete with exhortations to protect "those that fled their homes or were expelled from them, and those that suffered persecution," which have become the basis for asylum in Islamic law.[6] After the Catholic monarchs in Iberia expelled Jews and Muslims beginning in 1492, in what was "the first case of an entire country purged of unwanted minorities," most of the Muslims fled to North Africa.[7] Jews fled to various parts of Europe and the Mediterranean, where the Ottoman sultan regularly gave them sanctuary.[8] Asylum in the Ottoman Empire was the flipside of expulsion from Europe.

The Christian story of the flight of the Holy Family to Egypt to escape King Herod's persecution, and the parable of the Good Samaritan who helped an injured traveler in distress despite their ethnic differences, have been routinely invoked by Christian leaders. These lessons influenced the development of long-distance humanitarianism and movements to provide sanctuary to refugees.[9] Many of the first converts to Islam fled persecution in Arabia for the safety of Abyssinia, where the Christian emperor protected his guests from extradition.[10] The medieval Catholic Church granted asylum in churches, but states appropriated the authority to grant asylum in France (1515), Spain (1570), and England (1625).[11]

The word "*réfugié*" emerged in French in the late sixteenth century to refer to Calvinist religious dissenters from the Low Countries who found sanctuary in France. King Louis XIV revoked religious tolerance for the Huguenots in 1685 and violated the provisions in the 1648 Peace of Westphalia that allowed individuals who faced religious persecution to leave the country.[12] "Refugee" entered the

Figure 3.1: A detail from *The Saint Bartholomew's Day Massacre* (*Le Massacre de la Saint-Barthélemy*, *c.* 1572–84), by François Dubois (*c.* 1529–84), represents killings of Huguenots in Paris on August 24, 1572. Huguenots were the first group to be called "refugees" in French and English. Oil painting on wood, 94 × 154 cm. Lausanne, Musée cantonal des Beaux-Arts, Don de la Municipalité de Lausanne, 1862, inv. 729 © Musée cantonal des Beaux-Arts de Lausanne.

English language to describe Huguenots who illegally fled France for safety in Britain.[13] Huguenots received relief from government and civil society, including private sponsorship by subscribers who pledged to directly pay particular refugees – a forgotten precursor to contemporary private resettlement schemes in countries like Canada.[14] The Edict of Potsdam in 1685 welcomed Huguenots to Brandenburg and granted them a degree of autonomy, land, tax holidays, and exemptions from tariffs on the goods they brought with them. In what may have been the world's first state-sponsored refugee resettlement program, Friedrich Wilhelm I sent an agent to Geneva in 1687 to arrange free transportation to Germany for Huguenot refugees.[15]

During the "long nineteenth century" from the French Revolution to World War I, the refugee protection regime in Europe and the

Mediterranean shifted from sanctuary for people fleeing religious persecution to secular political exiles. In Latin America and the United States, asylum was selectively granted to people fleeing political crimes and persecution. In 1917, the United States created a preference for people fleeing religious persecution, followed by the selective inclusion of both kinds of persecuted people after World War II.[16]

Non-refoulement in slavery and extradition law

The norm of non-refoulement precedes international refugee law. Non-refoulement was selectively inscribed into policies around fugitive slaves beginning in the seventeenth century in the Americas and international antislave trading during the nineteenth century. Non-refoulement in extradition law gathered strength during the long nineteenth century and culminated in its first multilateral expression in South America in 1889. Examining this history illuminates how norms and practices develop, how they diffuse across jurisdictions, and how state officials use their discretion to decide who will be safe from forced return.

Asylum has an early history in regulations of escaped slaves that has been forgotten in most accounts of the refugee regime. As early as 1664, Catholic Spain's Caribbean colonies offered protection for escaped slaves, from other European colonies, who sought to convert to Catholicism. These protections were strongest for those fleeing Protestant English and Dutch enslavers, especially after a 1750 Spanish decree. By giving safe haven to escaped slaves, the Spanish Caribbean colonies could bleed competitor colonies of their labor forces. Yet these protections were not always upheld. By the late eighteenth century, Spanish authorities returned fugitives as they feared that enslaved people escaping from Haiti would spread revolution and those fleeing Britain's colonies would spread abolitionism.[17]

Great Britain was the dominant slave-trading power in the Atlantic for more than a century, transporting 2.5 million African slaves in the eighteenth century alone. It banned the slave trade in its empire in 1807 and slavery itself in 1833. Over the nineteenth century, Great Britain negotiated treaties with Spain, Portugal, the Netherlands, France, Brazil, and the United States to outlaw the international slave trade. The British Navy enforced the ban by intercepting ships carrying enslaved people. While there was no provision in British law or the treaties to return the estimated 150,000–200,000 intercepted slaves to their homes, British authorities sometimes offered a form of refuge. Britain sent most liberated slaves to its colony of Sierra Leone. Resettlement to the colony did not mean that intercepted slaves lived free of state coercion. By the 1840s, the Liberated African Department in Sierra Leone increasingly allowed military conscription of freed slaves or sent them to the West Indies as indentured servants.[18] From 1833 to the 1860s, Britain's colony of Upper Canada admitted 40,000–50,000 escaped American slaves and protected them from extradition as long as they had not committed major crimes.[19] The distinction between the worthy proto-refugee and the excluded criminal has continued throughout the history of refugee reception.

Britain gave its naval officers wide latitude to decide when to refoule intercepted slaves. An 1876 policy ordered officers "to be guided by considerations of humanity" when deciding whether to return slaves or provide a de facto form of diplomatic asylum and transport them to a colonized sanctuary in Aden, Mombasa, or the Seychelles. Still, geopolitics remained a consideration. The 1876 policy specified that when British ships were in another state's territorial waters, the commander should "avoid conduct which may appear to be in breach of international comity and good faith." In practice, intercepted slaves were sometimes sent to Zanzibar, where slavery remained legal, in the interest of diplomacy. The policies of other sea powers varied. By 1876, Germany, Italy, and the United States did not surrender slaves encountered at sea back to their enslavers; Portugal and the Netherlands would surrender them routinely; and France and Russia gave discretion to officers on the scene.[20] The law and implementation varied, but an incipient principle of not returning people into the arms of their enslavers was becoming established among the Western powers. The application of the principle of non-refoulement was motivated by both moral and diplomatic considerations.

The refusal to extradite persons charged with political offenses abroad constituted another early form of asylum. Unlike other criminal offenses, political crimes are motivated by commitment to a cause. The founding scholars of international legal thought in seventeenth- and eighteenth-century Europe – Hugo Grotius, Samuel von Pufendorf, and Emmerich de Vattel – debated the principles for states to grant asylum to individuals wanted by other states.[21] An informal

US policy against extradition for political crimes dating to 1791 was formalized in an 1843 treaty with France. A distinction in immigration law between those who had only committed political offenses and criminal offenders was written into the 1875 Immigration Act, which allowed the admission of the former.[22] The exception carried over into subsequent laws for certain classes of political offenders. The Immigration Act of 1903 excluded from admissibility "persons who have been convicted of a felony or other crime or misdemeanor involving moral turpitude; polygamists, anarchists, or persons who believe in or advocate the overthrow by force or violence of the Government of the United States or of all government or of all forms of law, or the assassination of public officials." Yet the 1903 law exempted "persons convicted of an offense purely political, not involving moral turpitude."[23] In effect, this was a preference for some political refugees without using that term.

Provisions preventing extradition for political crimes were written into Belgian law in 1833 and copied throughout Europe. The refusal to extradite foreigners for political crimes committed abroad sometimes protected high-profile revolutionaries. For example, Sun Yat-sen fled to London after his failed rebellion against the Qing dynasty in 1895. Chinese agents kidnapped and held him in the Chinese legation in London for several weeks as they tried to arrange his extradition. After British authorities refused to cooperate, the Chinese agents finally released Sun from the legation.[24] He went on to become the first President of the Republic of China (1911–12).

The first multilateral agreement refusing extradition for foreigners being sought for political crimes in their home countries was introduced in the 1889 Treaty on International Penal Law signed in Montevideo by Argentina, Bolivia, Paraguay, Peru, and Uruguay.[25] The jurists who negotiated the treaty explicitly drew on ancient Greek traditions of asylum as well as national laws and bilateral extradition treaties of European states. Thirty-three years before any multilateral European treaties existed to manage refugees, Latin America took the lead in creating a regional asylum regime.[26]

Diplomatic and territorial asylum

States limit their responsibility toward potential asylum-seekers by controlling *where* a person can request protection. States have jurisdiction over exceptional spaces outside their borders, like embassies and consulates abroad. Diplomatic asylum is a status granted to asylum-seekers in such spaces by diplomats, or by military commanders of their camps, warships, and aircraft on foreign soil. Diplomatic asylum is rare and usually reserved for elites to meet the granting government's foreign policy goals. When providing sanctuary is an accepted norm among states, governments of the asylee's country of nationality are less likely to see another state's grant of diplomatic asylum as a hostile act.[27] In these ways, diplomatic asylum can facilitate interstate relationships. On the other hand, granting asylum to the national of a hostile state can further inflame tensions.

Most European states ended grants of diplomatic asylum by the twentieth century. The United States has granted it sparingly since the nineteenth century.[28] By contrast, Latin American states have a sustained tradition of offering dissidents and deposed leaders diplomatic asylum. Multilateral treaties, beginning with Article 17 in the 1889 Congress of Montevideo, institutionalized diplomatic asylum in South America. Sixteen countries in the Conference of American States signed a 1928 treaty laying out diplomatic asylum obligations. Inter-American treaties in 1933, 1939, and 1954 entrenched the region's strong norm.[29] Deposed leaders have depended on diplomatic asylum to survive falls from political grace. Mutual asylum agreements are an insurance policy for elites in the region.

Territorial asylum applies to people who reach a granting state's territory to seek protection. The Huguenots in Britain, the Netherlands, and German-speaking Protestant states were the first people called refugees to receive formal legal protection, but these protections were granted through ad hoc designations, not a general asylum law.[30] The first state to create a general asylum provision was France. Its 1793 Constitution granted asylum to strangers banished from their countries "for the cause of liberty." While the constitution was not implemented, it set the groundwork for nineteenth-century grants of asylum to political exiles.[31] At the same time, tens of thousands of French royalists fled the French Revolution, primarily to England. Some officials feared that revolutionaries sent to overthrow the British government lurked among deposed royalist refugees. In response, Parliament passed the first major British law to give the government wide powers to control the entrance of outsiders, making distinctions between worthy refugees and nefarious foreign agents. The 1798 Aliens Act recognized asylum for French exiles fleeing "oppression and tyranny" as opposed to those who would enter Britain for "hostile purposes."[32] In historian Caroline Shaw's account, Britain's rise as a world power then gave it the self-assurance to loosen its laws and allow any foreigner to enter Britain between 1826 and 1905.[33]

National policies did not operate in isolation. During the long nineteenth century, the United States received the vast majority of transatlantic migration. When the United States kept its doors open, so too did states in Europe. Most East European Jews who arrived in Britain in the 1880s were in transit to North America. Of 2,749 Russian and Polish Jews entering Britain in 1882, the year of major pogroms and the enactment of anti-Semitic laws in Russia, only 18 percent remained in Britain at the end of the year.[34] The US Congress imposed restrictions in 1882 on the immigration of anyone likely to become a public charge, a provision that is still in US immigration law to this day, which led to an increase in the numbers of Jews who stayed in Britain rather than sailing west. In response, the British Parliament passed its first wholesale restrictions on immigration in 1905. The 1905 Aliens Act reinstated the distinction between persecuted foreigners and other immigrants. The "destitute alien" was inadmissible unless he could prove "he is seeking admission to this country *solely* to avoid prosecution or punishment on religious or political grounds or for an offence of a political character, or persecution, involving dangers of imprisonment or danger to life or limb, on account of religious belief."[35] Note the strict standard of banning admission of foreigners seeking to enter for mixed economic and religious/political motivations. The public debate was clearly about restricting the admission of impoverished Eastern European Jews.[36] In the decade after the law passed, the annual number of asylum grants in Britain fell from 505 to 5.[37] A systems approach highlights that the closure of asylum in Britain was not just the product of local processes. Rather, it was created in interaction with immigration restrictions reverberating from the United States and persecutory policies in countries of origin like Russia.

The first multilateral agreement to grant territorial asylum was the 1889 Congress of Montevideo, whose Article 16 guaranteed that "political refugees shall be afforded an inviolable asylum." Seventeen Latin American countries then signed the 1933 Conference of American States treaty that created extensive obligations to grant territorial asylum. Just as states throughout the Americas were tightening their immigration laws, they crafted exceptions for people fleeing political persecution.[38] The pathbreaking regional instruments around asylum in Latin America enacted between 1889 and 1933 have been ignored by standard Eurocentric accounts that date modern refugee law to "legal and institutional initiatives taken by the League of Nations" in the 1920s and 1930s or the idea that the "different treatment of refugees and migrants in the international arena" began in the period immediately following World War II.[39]

The Euro-Mediterranean regime

Russian imperial expansion in the nineteenth century forced hundreds of thousands of Muslims from the Caucasus and Crimea into the Ottoman interior in what was, at the time, "the worst incident of mass flight in European history."[40] The splintering of the multiethnic Ottoman empire's Balkan provinces into the independent nation-states of Greece (1821), Serbia and Montenegro (1878), Romania (1881), Bulgaria (1908), and Albania (1912) created further flows of refugees as nationalists ethnically cleansed their claimed territories.[41] Twelve million people across Europe and the Middle East were displaced after World War I and the collapse of the Ottoman, Hapsburg, and Romanov empires.

New multilateral institutions, international humanitarian organizations, and groups of exiles developed extensive networks to provide refugee relief.[42] After the war, the newly founded League of Nations created the first multilateral agreements to manage stateless refugees. West European powers dominated the interwar refugee regime. The system was based on prima facie grants of refugee status, which is a *group*-level designation applied to a nationality or ethnicity. Prima facie recognition differs from the assessments of an *individual*'s fear of persecution that became dominant in the 1951 Refugee Convention.

In April 1921, the League of Nations appointed Norwegian diplomat Fridtjof Nansen as its first High Commissioner for Refugees. He introduced "Nansen passports," which gave refugees documents allowing them to travel and work within a group of states participating in the program. These were the first specific, albeit nonbinding, international agreements for determining the legal status of stateless persons. Fifty-four states eventually joined the arrangement, which was originally created in 1922 for Russians who had fled the civil war.[43] Thirty-eight countries agreed to an arrangement in 1924 for Armenians displaced by the genocide in Anatolia. In 1928, Nansen passports were recognized for Assyrians, Assyro-Chaldeans, Syrians, Kurds, and 150 Turks who were "Friends of the Allies."[44]

The 1933 Convention Relating to the International Status of Refugees, ratified by eight European states, was the first binding multilateral treaty to prohibit refoulement and to grant refugees the rights to travel documents, work, and education. Only the groups already under League protection qualified. Many member states joined with reservations that they did not accept the principle of non-refoulement or the treaty's application in their colonies, a precedent for the "colonial clauses" in the 1951 Convention.[45]

The League of Nations and the International Labour Organization (ILO) established a refugee regime based on relief and development as well as legal protection, although private agencies did most of the actual work of assisting refugees.[46] In 1923, the League of Nations helped organize the population exchange that expelled 355,000 Muslims to Turkey and 190,000 Christians to Greece. The Greek Refugee Settlement Commission, established by the League and financed by international loans, assisted the refugees in Greece in what was "the first major internationally sponsored refugee resettlement project."[47] The programs combined immediate relief and what would later be called development aid. Around the Balkans and Mediterranean, the League of Nations sponsored settlement projects for 800,000 refugees.[48] From 1925 to 1929, the ILO's Refugee Service operated a labor exchange to match around 60,000 refugees and employers, mostly in France and French-mandated territories, but also as far afield as South America.[49] The interwar refugee regime was most effective when it impinged least on sovereignty, which explains why the Nansen passports opened more doors than the asylum regime.[50]

Big power politics, rather than an objective assessment of which groups were most threatened by persecution, guided decisions about whom to include under the international refugee system's umbrella. While Nansen and his colleagues were instrumental in shaping the system, the geopolitical context limited their room for innovation. The Nansen passports only covered specific groups from the Ottoman Empire, which had been dismantled by the victors of World War I,

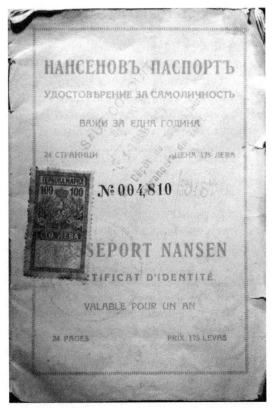

Figure 3.2: Nansen passports authorized recognized refugees to travel for work within a group of countries party to the agreement. Photo by Fine Art Images/Heritage Images/Getty Images.

and from what had become the Soviet Union, with which many states had refused to establish diplomatic relations. These groups could be safely declared refugees without serious foreign policy repercussions for League members. By contrast, the League did not recognize refugees from fascist Italy or Spain to avoid provoking these more powerful member states.[51]

The relative success of the League of Nations in protecting refugees from Russia and the post-Ottoman region in the 1920s was followed by its failure to protect Jews and others trying to flee Nazi Germany in the 1930s. Adolf Hitler took power in Germany in January 1933 and quickly moved to create a police state and persecute Jews. On October 12, the League approved the creation of a "High Commission for Refugees (Jewish and Other) Coming from Germany." The League initially made the new commission an independent agency in the hope that creating some distance from the formal League structure would soften a negative German reaction. The next day, however, Germany announced its withdrawal from the League. The High Commission and the Nansen International Office for Refugees were finally replaced in 1938 by a consolidated Office of the High Commissioner for Refugees under the Protection of the League.[52]

Negotiations outside the League framework also failed to protect European Jews. Thirty-two states participated in the 1938 Evian Conference on German and Austrian Jewish refugees. The conference produced a new Intergovernmental Committee on Refugees (IGCR) that negotiated with the German government over the terms of Jewish emigration and tried to convince other states to allow Jewish immigration. Liberal European states allowed few Jews to enter and became more restrictive by the late 1930s. Britain accepted 56,000 European Jewish refugees before the war began in 1939, in addition to 10,000 children sponsored by private citizens. The French government accepted antifascist dissidents and Jews fleeing Germany in 1933, but as fascism strengthened within France, it tightened controls.[53] British authorities exercising a League of Nations mandate over Palestine put quotas on how many Jews could enter in the face of opposition from Palestinians who feared they would be displaced and a Zionist state established at their expense.

Countries in the Americas mostly restricted the entrance of Jews, who were admitted under immigration provisions of the law rather than any special refugee status. The United States admitted 127,000 Jewish refugees between 1933 and 1940. Australia admitted around 10,000 in the 1930s. Canada admitted 5,000 between 1933 and 1945. Roughly 100,000 Jews reached Latin America in the 1930s, where the biggest host countries were Argentina, with 45,000, and Brazil, with 23,500. Throughout these countries, anti-Semitic restrictions reduced the number of Jewish refugees who would otherwise have been able to arrive under the provisions of immigration law.[54] The closing of the escape valve to the Americas, which had remained open to most Europeans in the nineteenth century, broke the weak international refugee system. Most Jews remained bottled up in Europe under expanding Nazi control, forced to be immobile and

Figure 3.3: German Jewish refugees look through portholes aboard the *St Louis* after it was turned away from Cuba, the United States, and Canada and arrived in the Belgian port of Antwerp in 1939. A quarter of the nearly 1,000 passengers aboard were murdered in the Holocaust after Nazi Germany conquered what appeared to be safe countries in Western Europe. Photo by Gerry Cranham/Fox Photos/Getty Images.

unable to become refugees. An international reaction against the murder of six million Jews in the Holocaust shaped a more robust refugee regime following the war.

The postwar regime

World War II displaced an estimated 175 million people.[55] An alphabet soup of international organizations focused on the 60 million displaced in Europe. The IGCR widened its mandate at a conference in 1943 from Jews fleeing Austria and Germany to include other refugees unable to return home. The IGCR's principal legacy was not its meager operations, but rather its model for defining refugees. The individualized definition of refugees included those from Germany or Austria "who must emigrate on account of their political opinions, religious beliefs and racial origin" – three grounds later included in the 1951 Refugee Convention. At least in principle, this move extended the refugee definition beyond Europeans and the Nansen passport refugees.

The Allies created the United Nations Relief and Rehabilitation Administration (UNRRA) in 1943 with greater resources to provide relief and organize repatriations. Allied military manuals in 1945 used definitions of refugees and DPs that were nearly the opposite of current usage. "Refugees" were defined as civilians living *in* their own countries who were uprooted by war and who wished to return home. Conversely, "displaced persons" were people who were *outside* their country and in need of repatriation.

The question of repatriations created new fissures in the fragile refugee regime. The Allies had agreed at the 1945 Yalta Conference that each state would repatriate the others' nationals at the end of the war. Between 1945 and 1947, more than 5 million Soviet citizens were repatriated, often through coercion. In one notorious incident in Austria, numerous Soviet officers committed suicide by hanging themselves or jumping off a bridge rather than be transferred to Soviet control by British soldiers.[56] Of the millions who returned to the USSR, more than a third were persecuted by arrest, internal relocation to special settlements, sentences to labor or army punishment battalions, banishment to the gulag, or execution.[57] As relations frayed between the Western Allies and the USSR, the US and British governments decided to end forced repatriation. In 1946 the UN General Assembly recommended that states avoid forced repatriation of refugees who "expressed valid objections," with the exception of "war criminals, quislings and traitors."[58] The principle of non-refoulement was taking shape under the UN framework.

The Allies closed the IGCR and UNRRA in 1947. Their replacement was the International Refugee Organization (IRO), which was founded in December 1946 by Western powers over the objections of a Soviet bloc that wanted to keep the resolution of the postwar refugee issue focused on repatriations that could be coerced if necessary. The IRO constitution emphasized protection for people subject, if they were repatriated, to "persecution, or fear, based on reasonable grounds, of persecution because of race, religion, nationality or political opinion."[59] Rather than use prima facie group-level definitions of refugees, its eligibility officers screened individual applicants. The IRO resettled more than one million Europeans and a token number of Asians.

By the late 1940s, most European refugees who could be resettled had already moved, leaving behind "the last million." Displaced persons camps housed a heterogeneous population that included stranded foreign laborers (many of whom had been enslaved by the Nazis), nationalists who had fled the Soviet domination of their homelands in Eastern Europe, Jewish survivors of the Holocaust, and Nazi collaborators from Baltic and other East European countries who had slaughtered Jews and then fled the Red Army's approach at the end of the war. Jewish DPs did not typically want to repatriate to their homes, from which they had been driven out and their families killed. Anti-Semitism sharply limited the number of Jewish DPs recruited for refugee worker schemes in West European countries and resettlement in countries such as Australia and Canada. President Truman wanted displaced Jews to go to Palestine, but when British Mandate authorities continued to limit their numbers, he eventually relented, and pushed the US Congress to accept some Jewish refugees. After Congress put obstacles in the way of resettling Jews, using a facially neutral date cut-off that was intended to exclude Jews who had been displaced twice from Poland, Truman threw his support behind the establishment of the state of Israel, which would be an alternative destination.[60]

Ethnic cleansing before and during the 1948 Israeli war of independence created the *Nakba*, the catastrophe, for Palestinians. As Hannah Arendt summarized: "The solution of the Jewish question merely produced a new category of refugees, the Arabs, thereby increasing the number of the stateless and rightless by another 700,000 to 800,000 people."[61] Anti-Semitic genocide and expulsions in Europe, and anti-Semitic immigration policies of the Western democracies, redirected displaced Jews to the Middle East. The formation of Israel came at the expense of the Palestinian majority population, millions of whom remain displaced in neighboring states more than seventy years later. Policies in one part of the refugee system, as far afield as Australia, Argentina, and Canada, shaped refugee movements in Europe and the Middle East.

The US government attempted to make refugee policy a more tightly controlled instrument of its foreign policy by creating two programs outside the United Nations. The Provisional Intergovernmental Committee for the Movement of Migrants from Europe, known by the glib acronym PICMME, resettled a million European migrants overseas between 1951 and 1960. Its mandate outside the UN system allowed it to include people displaced by violence as well as more strictly economic migrants. The committee and its successors eventually morphed into the International Organization for Migration.[62] The US Escapee Program, established in 1952, resettled those who fled from Soviet-dominated countries.

The United States only supported a temporary mandate for a new UN agency, the United Nations High Commissioner for Refugees, which would be limited to settling the last Europeans displaced by World War II. Like the IRO before it, the UNHCR would not include in its mandate the "transferred populations" of millions of ethnic Germans expelled from East European countries to Germany following the war, or other displaced people living in countries where they shared the same rights as nationals. The British, Benelux, and Scandinavian governments supported a permanent UNHCR mandate and a universal definition of refugees that was not restricted to Europeans. However, Britain and other metropolitan European states did not want the UNHCR involved in their colonies. The few countries that had recently decolonized differed in their support for Eurocentric or universalist refugee definitions, but several, particularly Pakistan and India, supported a broader mandate that would allow international relief for the 14 million people displaced by the 1947 partition of India. The Soviet Union viewed repatriation as the only legitimate solution to the refugee problem in Europe and refused to take part in the negotiations for a new agency.[63] The statute that defined the scope of the agency created by the UN General Assembly in December 1950 reflected a compromise among the negotiating powers. The agency was initially given a temporary mandate of only three years. The definition of a refugee was expansive in that it did not include the geographic or temporal limitations that were part of the Refugee Convention negotiated the following year. The UNHCR mandate included the groups of refugees previously covered by the League of Nations arrangements and the IRO.[64]

The 1951 Refugee Convention created the first binding, comprehensive international refugee regime. The Convention only applied to persons displaced by "events occurring before 1 January 1951," a provision known as the temporal limitation. Notwithstanding subsequent interpretations by many scholars, the Western powers that dominated the negotiation of the Convention did not intend to favor individual communist dissidents fleeing Eastern Europe during the Cold War, as these persons apparently would be excluded by the temporal limitation.[65] Unlike the UNHCR statute, which had no geographic limitations, the 1951 Convention allowed each state to choose between applying the refugee definition to persons displaced by either "events occurring in Europe" or "events occurring in Europe or elsewhere." Although scholars often suggest that "the Refugee Conventions prevented non-Europeans from being considered refugees until 1967," by the end of the 1950s, most European countries, Australia, Israel, and Tunisia had joined the Refugee Convention without the geographic limitations.[66] The Netherland and the UK signed without the European geographic limitations, but with reservations that excluded the Convention's application to their colonies. Four states (Congo, Madagascar, Monaco, and Turkey) chose the European geographic limitation. Canada did not join the Convention until 1969, because it did not want the UNHCR to pressure it to admit unwanted refugees.[67] The United States never became a party to the Convention per se, as it wanted a free hand to expel unwanted refugees thought to pose a security threat. Most countries in South Asia, Southeast Asia, and the Middle East never signed the Convention, even as they have consistently hosted a large share of the world's refugees, as described in Chapter 6.

The Convention excluded from its mandate "persons who are at present receiving from organs or agencies of the United Nations other than the United Nations High Commissioner for Refugees protection or assistance."[68] In practice, this meant that the Convention did not cover two major groups: (1) approximately 750,000 Palestinians aided by other UN agencies, and (2) about 4 million displaced Koreans aided by the United Nations Korean Reconstruction Agency (UNKRA) from 1950 to 1958. Palestinians and Koreans were the first two non-European groups recognized by the postwar international refugee regime, but they were not included in what emerged as the principal agency – the UNHCR.[69]

UN Relief for Palestine Refugees in 1948 began coordinating the League of Red Cross Societies and American Friends Service Committee to distribute relief supplies provided by the UN. In December 1948, UN General Assembly Resolution 194 resolved that Palestine "refugees wishing to return to their homes and live at peace with their neighbours should be permitted to do so at the earliest practicable date," and created the United Nations Conciliation Commission for Palestine (UNCCP) to find a solution to the conflict and the status of refugees. UNRWA was formed in December 1949 to take over refugee assistance in Gaza, the West Bank, Jordan, Syria, and Lebanon. Until 1952, UNRWA also provided assistance to Jews who had been displaced by the 1948 war. Palestinians in some ways enjoyed an initial advantage from other refugees by receiving services from UNRWA, which was better funded in the early 1950s than the UNHCR. However, the absence of a clear protection mandate under UNRWA, and the political inefficacy of the UNCCP, led to a long-term disadvantage. In 2021, more than 5.7 million Palestinians registered with UNRWA did not have access to UN-facilitated return or resettlement.[70]

Global expansion

The UNHCR's effective mandate expanded in the 1950s in response to four refugee crises: East Germans in West Berlin, Hungarians in Austria, mainland Chinese in Hong Kong, and Algerians in Tunisia and Morocco. All the policies were forged in the crucible of the Cold War. The Hong Kong and Algerian cases were further entangled with global processes of colonialism and decolonization. Policies developed in one context reverberated around the world to shape responses in new settings.

In 1953, as Cold War tensions raised fears among East Germans that crossing into the West might become restricted, tens of thousands of them hurried into West Berlin. Although East German refugees fell outside the UNHCR's legal mandate, its High Commissioner used the crisis to show powerful states that the agency could efficiently provide refugee relief and serve Western interests. In August, the United States passed the Refugee Relief Act, which provided 35,000 non-quota visas for German "escapees," among other groups, and in 1954 it co-sponsored a General Assembly resolution establishing the United Nations Refugee Fund, which would give the agency much more operational autonomy.[71]

In November 1956, Soviet tanks crushed the Hungarian Revolution. An estimated 200,000 Hungarians fled, mostly to Austria. On the face of it, these refugees fell outside the January 1, 1951, temporal limits of the UNHCR mandate, but the agency justified its involvement by claiming that a chain of events that began with the establishment of the People's Republic of Hungary nine years earlier had caused the refugee outflow in 1956. The UNHCR used prima facie determination of refugee status, in keeping with the older League of Nations model, rather than assessing each individual's claim to have fled persecution. For the first time, the agency was central to refugee resettlement efforts and helped displaced Hungarians move to the United States and Canada. The US government's original opposition to an expansive UNHCR further weakened as officials realized the organization could manage refugee emergencies in a way that promoted US interests in the Cold War.[72]

After the communist victory in China was consolidated with the establishment of the People's Republic of China in 1949, an estimated 700,000 refugees crossed the border into Hong Kong, then a British colony. Hong Kong had a tradition of selective asylum. After the Chinese nationalist government massacred a group of suspected Chinese communists in 1927, about 300 of the survivors attempting to reach Hong Kong were pushed back by Hong Kong's border guards. Although the colony's law had denied extradition for political offenses since 1889, the British Secretary of State for the Colonies stated the interpretation of the law "must to some extent depend on the degree of good relations existing between Hong Kong and Canton" on the Chinese mainland. The fact that those seeking asylum in 1927 were communists fleeing a government with which Britain had friendly relations doomed their attempt to find refuge in Hong Kong. On the other hand, colonial authorities reversed their reasoning when Vietnamese nationalist Ho Chi Minh was arrested in Hong Kong in 1931. His arrest was in response to a request from the French government, which had sentenced him to death in absentia for plotting to overthrow French rule in Indochina. Colonial authorities considered Ho Chi Minh's offense to be political and he was eventually allowed to leave the colony to go into hiding in China.[73] The UK signed the Refugee Convention in 1954 with a reservation that it did not extend to Hong Kong. The colony's precarious position, so far from the metropole and adjacent to the world's most populous country, motivated Hong Kong authorities to generally avoid using refugees from the PRC as a tool of anti-Communist propaganda.

Both the PRC and the Republic of China (ROC) based in Taiwan claimed to be the sole legitimate government of China. States that recognized the ROC argued that newly arrived Chinese in Hong Kong did not meet the refugee definition, because they were Chinese nationals owed protection by the ROC. The ROC promoted high-profile defections but discouraged ordinary people from trying to reach Taiwan, which had limited resources for resettlement and was already beset by tensions between the indigenous population of the island and newcomers from the mainland who had established the regime. The ROC only accepted 150,000 people for resettlement from Hong Kong between 1949 and 1954. Most of the refugees were former soldiers.[74] The UN General Assembly's solution in November 1957 was to allow the UNHCR to use its "good offices" to assist Chinese refugees in Hong Kong.[75] "Good offices" refers to the agency's ability to act as an impartial intermediary between parties in conflict. This mechanism introduced several advantages. First, it allowed the UNHCR to avoid answering messy questions about whether an assisted group fit the statutory definition of refugees. Second, it let the UNHCR provide humanitarian relief without blaming the government of countries of origin for persecution. Finally, the good offices approach could be applied to situations of a large, sudden influx where individual status determination was impractical.[76]

In 1957, the UNHCR discretely developed plans to assist Algerians fleeing from the war of national liberation from France. The fact that the initiative began at the request of newly independent Tunisia is critical for moderating the common argument that the refugee regime in the 1950s was exclusively Eurocentric.[77] Britain and the United States were ambivalent about France's war in Algeria. They allowed the UNHCR to organize ad hoc relief operations and to duck the issue of whether the French government's actions constituted persecution of Algerians and whether the war itself was a sovereign French matter.[78] In 1958 the UN General Assembly authorized the UNHCR to continue relief to Algerian refugees in Tunisia and to extend aid to those in Morocco. By the following year, the UNHCR was formally using the good offices concept, first deployed in Hong Kong, to legitimate its aid to an estimated 300,000 Algerians.

The UNHCR was able to expand the refugee regime beyond Europe through a sequence of justifications around its involvement with Chinese and Algerian refugees.[79] The agency could innovate within the boundaries of actions that were compatible with the foreign policy goals of powerful patrons. Expansion was not initiated in Washington, but the US government supported it and, in the 1950s, became the biggest UNHCR donor. It competed with communists for support in the decolonizing third world, while avoiding direct challenges to European allies that continued to be colonial powers. Providing relief to refugees through a Western-dominated, multilateral humanitarian agency that avoided naming and shaming persecutors was a way to balance competing US foreign policy objectives. From the perspective of decolonized African states, it was politically more convenient to receive US refugee aid channeled through the neutral UNHCR than through an embarrassing patron–client relationship. Political scientist Gil Loescher concludes: "In effect, the UNHCR became an indirect vehicle for US foreign objectives in Africa."[80] The good offices model spread throughout Africa and Asia in the 1960s as wars of decolonization generated new refugee flows.

By contrast, UNHCR involvement does not seem to have been considered during the persecution of ethnic Chinese in Indonesia from 1959 to 1961 – when 120,000 ethnic Chinese fled Indonesia for the PRC, including many whose families had lived in Indonesia for generations. While Chinese citizens returning to China would not have been considered statutory refugees, those with Indonesian citizenship would have met the criteria. The reason that the UNHCR ignored Chinese persecuted in Indonesia was because they were fleeing to, rather than from, a communist state. Thus, the UNHCR did not extend its mandate into a context where such an expansion would have cut against the major foreign policy goals of the United States and the other Western donor powers.[81]

As it became clear that new refugee emergencies would continue to erupt, and a legal way to impose obligations on states to provide protection was needed to move beyond the good offices mechanism for providing relief, the UNHCR successfully promoted a 1967 Protocol to the 1951 Convention. The Protocol abolished the Convention's temporal and geographic limitations, while incorporating the rest of its provisions. The United States, which never signed the 1951 Convention, ratified the Protocol in 1968 to demonstrate its compliance with international rights norms and to satisfy domestic religious and ethnic lobbies advocating for refugees. By 2011, 148 of the 193 UN member states had signed the 1951 Convention and/or the 1967 Protocol. Only Turkey and Madagascar maintained the European geographic limitations.[82] The Turkish government's 2005 National Action Plan on Asylum and Immigration stated that Turkey would only lift the geographic limitations when the EU shouldered its fair share of the "burden" and Turkey had developed the capacity to manage asylum-seekers.[83]

The UN General Assembly extended the mandate of the UNHCR in 2003 "until the refugee problem is solved."[84] The geographic and temporal limitations on legal definitions of refugees have increasingly fallen away, even as the particular groups and individuals offered protection still reflect inequalities of power and policy feedback around the refugee system.

In the context of rising displacements and European reactions against the arrival of large numbers of Syrians fleeing the civil war, the UN General Assembly in 2015 proposed a Global Compact on Refugees (GCR).[85] The final version of the GCR, released in 2018, included a nonbinding list of twenty-three objectives. The primary emphasis was on greater sharing of refugee relief and protection costs across host states and the inclusion of more stakeholders in policymaking, including nonstate actors and refugees themselves. As this chapter has shown, the GCR proposals have deep historical precedents going back to the reception of the Huguenots in the seventeenth century and the League of Nations framework after World War I. The unresolved dilemma is that, as Chapter 7 describes, powerful states have few incentives to share the costs of refugee hosting, which remains concentrated in poor and middle-income countries, as long as weaker countries can be paid or coerced to do the work.[86]

Regional regimes

In 1963 the Organization of African Unity (OAU) began drafting a convention to address the temporal and geographic limitations of the 1951 UN Refugee Convention and to create an instrument more responsive to the interests of states in Africa, where refugee flows were shaped by ongoing wars of decolonization and state formation. A refugee definition that did not require demonstration of individual persecution made it possible for states to protect refugees without incurring the diplomatic costs of naming fellow OAU member states as persecutors.[87] The goal was to complement the 1967 Protocol, whose drafts emerged in tandem with drafts for the OAU Convention and in cooperation between the UNHCR and the OAU.[88]

The 1969 OAU Convention expanded the refugee definition in several ways. Most importantly, it included people who fled from conflict due to "external aggression, occupation, foreign domination, or events seriously disturbing public order in either part or the whole of [their] country of origin or nationality."[89] The treaty allowed group designations in keeping with the prima facie recognition policy that the UNHCR had been using in practice, outside of the 1951 Convention definition, through the good offices mechanism. The disturbances of public order provision also opened the possibility of recognizing as refugees people who fled nonstate violence.[90] While some authors position the OAU convention in opposition to the Refugee Convention, they were explicitly designed to be complementary.[91]

Few Asian states were independent in 1951 during the drafting of the UN Refugee Convention. UNHCR officials hoped that states like Malaysia that had been decolonized later and states like India that had initially refused to sign the Convention would be willing to join the 1967 Protocol. Many Asian governments still refused to join, however, because they said they had not participated in drafting the Convention and could not afford the costs of caring for refugees. Instead, in 1966 the Asian–African Legal Consultative Organization, an outgrowth of the Non-Aligned Movement that sought to avoid siding with global power blocs, agreed to the Bangkok Principles.[92] The Bangkok Principles shared the 1951 Convention's principle of non-refoulement and the 1967 Protocol's elimination of temporal and geographic limitations, but they differed in that they were a nonbinding guide to how states should treat refugees, and they emphasized states' sovereign discretion to grant or reject asylum.[93]

Wars in Indochina created a major test for the regional refugee regime. Following the fall of Saigon in 1975, many Vietnamese fled by boat in the hopes of reaching other countries or being rescued at sea. The governments of Thailand, Malaysia, Indonesia, and Hong Kong often turned them away. Deaths from pirate attacks and dangerous ocean conditions created a major humanitarian crisis. In response, states of origin, transit, and resettlement negotiated the Orderly Departure Program in 1979. Under its terms, the Vietnamese government promised to prevent Vietnamese from leaving by sea. Southeast Asian governments agreed to temporarily host prima facie refugees until they could be permanently resettled to the United States, Australia, Canada, France, and a few other Western states. The agreement eventually fell apart as Vietnamese continued to exit, and it was replaced in 1989 by the Comprehensive Plan of Action for Indo-Chinese Refugees, which created individual screening for asylum-seekers and forcibly repatriated those who did not meet the statutory refugee definition.[94]

Since at least the 1960s, Latin American states have often allowed people fleeing conflicts to stay on their territory. Yet they rarely defined these people as refugees.[95] Ten Latin American states signed the 1984 Cartagena Declaration, which was inspired by the 1969 OAU Convention. Latin American leaders were looking for a way to respond to civil wars in Central America that pushed out hundreds of thousands of people, rather than the small numbers of elites that their national and regional asylum systems had historically envisioned since the 1889 Congress of Montevideo. As with the OAU Convention, the UNHCR took the lead in convening and shaping the regional Cartagena process.[96] In addition to those covered by the 1951 Refugee Convention and 1967 Protocol, the Cartagena Declaration included "persons who have fled their country because their lives, safety or freedom have been threatened by generalized violence, foreign aggression, internal conflicts, massive violation of human rights or other circumstances which have seriously disturbed public order."[97]

Although both the Bangkok Principles and the Cartagena Declaration were nonbinding, the latter has been more consequential, as fourteen states incorporated its expansive definition of refugees into their national laws by 2013. The massive displacement of Venezuelans in the 2010s, "the largest international forced displacement of people in Latin American history,"[98] put the expanded Cartagena refugee definition to the test. The UNHCR estimated in 2021 that 5 million Venezuelans were outside their country. Latin American states accommodated large numbers of Venezuelans without granting asylum. As discussed in Chapter 6, the legal instruments of refugee protection that had been widened under Cartagena were less important than the use of other kinds of employment, humanitarian, and temporary visas that give states more control over Venezuelans without forcibly returning them.

Internally displaced persons

According to the 1951 Convention, a refugee is, by definition, "outside the country of his nationality" or stateless and "outside the country of his former habitual residence."[99] In late 1950, there was a debate about whether "internal refugees," now known as IDPs, should be included under the 1951 Convention. The final treaty reflected the argument that sovereign states had sole authority over their own citizens in their territory.[100] Subsequent efforts to involve the UNHCR in IDP relief and protection faltered. In 1967 the UNHCR refused to become involved in the Biafran crisis when rebels seceded from Nigeria. "Since 'Biafra' is not recognized as a separate state, the displaced people from other parts of Nigeria into Eastern [sic] Nigeria do not fall within the mandate of the Office, and therefore, there is nothing that the Office could do for them," High Commissioner Aga Khan told a delegation of Biafran rebels seeking UNHCR intervention.[101] Such reasoning changed over time.

Five years later, the UN Secretary-General asked the UNHCR to coordinate relief and repatriation for refugees and IDPs in southern Sudan.[102] The UNHCR took a long stride toward work with IDPs when the UN Secretary-General designated it as the lead humanitarian agency in the former Yugoslavia in 1991 during the civil war. According to the UNHCR Working Group on International Protection, the principle in Bosnia was that the UNHCR was "to bring safety to the people, rather than to bring people to safety." Yet in practice, the agency delivered material supplies rather than safety. The agency also worked with IDPs in Iraq, while rejecting proposals to work with IDPs in Zaire and Cambodia.[103] The UNHCR began including IDPs in its displacement database in 1993. By 2021, two-thirds of displaced people in its records were IDPs.

Intensified UNHCR involvement with IDPs is due to several factors, including weakened notions of sovereignty that now allow greater external intervention, competition with other humanitarian groups for scarce resources and expanded organizational mandates, the decreased willingness of states to host refugees, and remote controls that prevent would-be refugees from leaving their countries.[104] As international relations scholar Phil Orchard summarizes, "increasing the protections available to IDPs fits in with the broader containment agenda" of powerful states.[105] Several regional legal instruments

Figure 3.4: A family of internally displaced Syrians walks through the UNHCR's Atme camp in Idlib province near the Turkish border in 2013. Bülent Kılıç/AFP via Getty Images.

provide some level of recognition of IDPs, including the 1984 Cartagena Declaration and the 2009 Kampala Convention of the African Union that entered into force in 2012.[106]

Conclusion

The claim that "no legal definition of the refugee concept existed" before the twentieth century is mistaken.[107] The refugee concept did not emerge *ex nihilo*. Distinct bodies of law and softer norms that regulate exit, slavery, extradition, asylum, refugee relief and protection, and refugee resettlement were precursors to elements of contemporary refugee law outlined in the 1951 Refugee Convention. This history reveals deliberations surrounding who should be given sanctuary and how religious, political, and economic reasons for displacement have been considered. Historical examples echo contemporary debates as state officials distinguished between those who fled "for the cause of liberty" and those who may seek refuge for "hostile purposes."[108] This history also reveals how state officials practiced their discretion surrounding forcible return and extradition. Officials were not only "guided by considerations of humanity," but also took into consideration geopolitical interests and giving special deference to powerful states as they weighed the diplomatic costs of providing sanctuary. By the twentieth century, ad hoc practices governed by informal norms had evolved into an international regime. The establishment of international organizations such as the League of Nations and the UNHCR increased cooperation among states. The UNHCR's global influence grew through the "good offices" approach, supported by powerful states whose interests aligned with the agency's humanitarian interventions. This examination of refugee regimes is necessarily global in scope. Through the systems approach, it becomes clear how contemporary national policies were shaped by movements and policies in other places and in the past. Eurocentric interpretations that privilege the 1951 Refugee Convention and focus primarily on the aftermath of World War II discount vital contributions to the development of refugee regimes from other parts of the world.

4
Should I Stay or Go?

In the image of refugee decision-making reflected in the 1951 Convention definition of a refugee, a credible fear of persecution prompts refugees to flee their countries or avoid returning home. Researchers have attempted to quantify the weight of different drivers of refugee flight and the role played by violence. "All other things constant, people leave their homes when they feel that their physical security is threatened," concludes one study.[1] Yet why do some people in similar circumstances leave, while others stay? And for those who leave, how do they decide whether to stay within the country or flee abroad, and how do they choose among specific destinations?

Refugees who were able to cross an international border are privileged compared with those forced to remain home or who are forcibly moved (recall Figure 2.4). Movement can be restrained by detention of individuals, internment of whole populations, or besiegement in times of war. Those facing enslavement, forced internal relocation, or expulsion may have no choice but death or submission to their enforced movement. State policies restricting exit (see Chapter 5) and a lack of admissions options in other countries (Chapters 6 and 7) make it more difficult to become a refugee in the first place. For those who face a threat but are not caged or transported against their will, "the choice may be constrained and dreadful, but it is ultimately up to the civilian whether or not to leave."[2]

The first question is, "Can I go?" – but choices about leaving a country of origin do not tell the entire refugee story.[3] Refugees *sur place* are people who left home voluntarily and became stranded abroad because of a change in circumstances at home during their absence. They cannot return without great risk. Syrian students who were studying abroad when the war began in 2011 and could not return for fear of persecution may be considered refugees *sur place* in an asylum hearing. Others end up outside their homeland, not because they crossed the border, but because a border crossed them during the dissolution of a state.

Forced migrants who fled their homes continue to make choices about moving within their home country or crossing an international border. How will they finance their trip, organize logistics, deal with legal barriers, and make a living in their destination? Which family members will try to join them? Should they stay in the first country they reach or try to keep moving to more desirable destinations? Should they try against all odds to win the resettlement lottery? Travel independently to a country where they can ask for asylum? Preserve their homeland ties by sending remittances? At every stage, the potential for return looms as well. As with decisions to leave, returns vary in their degrees of coercion, from deportation at gunpoint to a voluntary trip home. The permanency of return is never certain. All these decisions take place within changing policy contexts in countries of origin, transit, and destination.

This chapter describes patterns in how people facing violence make migration decisions. We begin by exploring how those decisions are shaped by the degree and kinds of violence and exit conditions such as transportation infrastructure and the availability of migration facilitators. Once refugees have left their home country, host state policies shape their judgments about staying or migrating onward. We introduce a model for refugee household decision-making that takes into consideration how families manage different kinds of risks and opportunities. The "new economics of displacement" builds on the "new economics of labor migration."[4] We develop this perspective first by drawing from studies of forced displacement to show the extent of family-level decision-making and the drivers of those decisions. We then present an original longitudinal case study of the Asfour family from the Syrian governorate of Daraa where the civil war began in 2011.[5] We explore how the Asfours have navigated obstacles that constrained their movement and how they took advantage of unexpected opportunities that gave them hope for a better future.

New economics of displacement

While the 1951 Convention privileged individual status determination to assess whether a person fits the refugee category, refugeehood is often based on family decisions. We adapt the "new economics of labor migration" framework to help explain decision-making among families facing violence, which we call the "new economics of displacement."[6] The starting point of the new economics of labor migration framework is that *households* – not just individuals, as asserted in most contemporary economic theories of labor migration – make decisions together. Households allocate labor to different markets to manage risks of unemployment, losses to small businesses, crop failure, and other economic problems.[7] Families diversify their income streams by matching members to markets where they are most likely to thrive. The "new economics of displacement" returns to the most ancient and classical concept of economics as *oikonomia* or "household management."

Economics has historically been underrepresented in the field of refugee studies because the entire refugee category has been based on the idea that refugees are not (at least primarily) moving for economic gain. The insistence of some advocates that refugees are not migrants, or claims by restrictionists that "mixed migration" is illegitimate, reduces understanding of the economic considerations of people with a credible fear of persecution. The sociological realist perspective elaborated in Chapter 2 views refugees as a subset of migrants and recognizes that people threatened with violence and persecution also face risks to their economic well-being. Decisions about migration incorporate economic considerations as well as strategies to avoid physical harm. Once they have reached a place of relative safety and survey their options in host states, refugees continue to take into account restrictions on work or owning businesses, as well as opportunities for economic betterment. For a lucky few, resettlement abroad may provide a pathway to family reunification, stable employment, higher education, and full rights of citizenship. On the other hand, resettlement poses new risks, including a hostile reception from nativists and the specter of resettling into poverty, such that families must collectively mobilize their resources to survive.[8]

The effort to mitigate economic and physical risks can incur new perils. In contexts of violence and persecution in the home country, the risks for those who attempt to leave include arrest and imprisonment, confiscation of assets, physical injury, and death. The very act of attempting to leave identifies dissidents to the authorities and becomes enhanced grounds for persecution. Clandestine movement exposes migrants to drowning, hypothermia, heat stroke, and attacks by bandits or border guards. When attempts to circumvent border controls by contracting smugglers fail, migrants may be left with debts that further sink the fortunes of the family. Rather than sending remittances back home, migrants may be forced to rely on reverse remittances from home just to survive. These harms ripple through a household and community.[9]

By focusing on family-level decision-making, the new economics of displacement highlights the shortcomings of siloed approaches that are focused on an individual's movement across state borders. The systems approach shows how spaces of displacement are simultaneously connected through family ties. No single refugee is likely to experience all of the potential types of entrapment and displacement, such as forced immobility, internal flight, crossing an international border to seek sanctuary, resettlement abroad through a formal program, independently seeking asylum, and repatriation. Yet if we shift our focus from individual experiences to decision-making within a family, it becomes clear how each of these types of immobility and mobility is related.

Entire communities sometimes flee together at the same time.[10] Yet even particular households do not always collectively escape the threat of violence or persecution. Individual members of a household may realize they are targeted for persecution and run while the others stay behind.[11] In contexts of generalized violence, not everyone who can leave always does so. Families manage the risks of violence at the same time as they manage economic risks, such as losing their assets if they all flee at once. During Nazi persecution of European Jews in the 1930s and 1940s, some families sent their children to different countries, which consequently reduced the risk of the whole family being killed.[12] Tutsi families facing *génocidaires* in Rwanda in the 1990s sometimes hid their children among Hutu friends.[13] Formal programs have brought refugee children to safety even as their parents stay behind. The many historical examples include the *Kindertransport* program that brought 10,000 Jewish refugee children from Europe to Britain between 1938 and 1939 and the Soviet program that took in 3,000 children from the Spanish Civil war from 1937 to 1938.[14]

The household is a unit of analysis in that it often functions as an economic and decision-making entity, but, as with other entities, decision-making can include bargaining, resistance, and impositions. Age affects the capacity to make autonomous decisions.[15] A 1953 study of Polish, Hungarian, and Czech defectors to the West found that they tended to be young and have few obligations to care for family members.[16] In 2017, most unaccompanied child migrants in Greece had come from war-torn countries such as Syria and had made a joint decision within their family, while most of those in Italy were from African countries and had taken an individual decision to move.[17]

Household decisions are deeply gendered. Men are often in greater jeopardy of being viewed as security threats when crossing the border, and, partly for that reason, may bring female family members and children with them so the authorities do not classify them as single men.[18] On the other hand, it is expensive to travel as a whole family unit, and irregular travel can be dangerous. Syrian men have often been pioneer migrants to Europe, moving first with the expectation that they will send for their family members once settled abroad, preferably through family reunification channels.[19] States have undermined refugees' plans for family reunification to deter them from seeking asylum. In 2015 the Danish government took out Arabic language ads in Lebanese newspapers that read, "foreign nationals granted a temporary residence permit will not have the right to have their family brought to Denmark during the first year."[20] In times of war, an international border is a way for some families to separate the sites of fighting and reproduction.[21] Families may send "women and children to refugee camps so the men are free to fight," notes political scientist Myron Weiner.[22] The fear of sexual violence targeting women, and unmarried daughters in particular, is a further incentive for families to send women to places of safety first.[23] However, gender-based discrimination does not stop when women cross an international border. Refugee women who ostensibly have reached a sanctuary have faced a greater risk than refugee men of harassment, violence, and exploitation.[24]

The new economics of displacement's focus on household risk management offers important lessons for refugee return. Ensuring that there are different household members in different locations is a way to hedge against the risk that the situation will deteriorate for the whole family at once. Risks include economic downturns as well as physical insecurity or an increase in persecution. As anthropologist Laura Hammond explains, refugees' "engagement in multiple places helps them to also manage the risks of return; if conditions turn out not to be as safe and secure as they had hoped, they can relocate to join their relatives in other countries."[25] For the same reason, most heads of household among Eritrean refugees in Sudan planned to first send a representative of the household back to the home country to assess conditions and make arrangements for others.[26] This strategy was in tension with a UNHCR policy of only promoting whole family repatriations to avoid the same person accessing benefits in both Eritrea and Sudan. Return decisions are not just produced by an assessment of conditions in origin and host countries; they are shaped by international organizations as well, which often act in support of host state interests (see Chapter 8).

People contemplating flight or who have been displaced make decisions within sharp structural constraints. Variations in the type of violence they face influence where they will go, especially when there are safe alternatives inside the home country. When wars drag on, social institutions break down and resources become scarce. Violence intertwines with economic push factors. Multifactorial deliberations take into consideration the availability of economic opportunities, relief assistance in different areas, and the financial and social capital needed to circumvent immigration controls. The vast majority of refugees remain in countries in the Global South, often seeking refuge across the border. As with other types of movement, the decision to return can be difficult and reflect the pressure of host and home states, even if the return does not constitute obvious refoulement. Shifting the lens from the individual to the family unit shows how refugees are connected throughout each stage of their journey.

Violence

How intense must violence get before civilians flee? A 2016 survey of Syrians and Iraqis who stayed at home, were internally displaced, or moved to neighboring countries found that as violence substantially worsened, people were more likely to seek information about destination country options and policies.[27] Other studies have found that, while many Syrians fled at an acute moment when the conflict started, just as many others fled over time only as life became intolerable.

Lack of access to work, education, and health care, in addition to the physical threats of chronic violence and lost hopes that the conflict would be resolved, pushed them to escape abroad.[28] Some refugees fled generalized violence, such as sniper fire against civilians, shelling, and "barrel bombings" in which government aircraft indiscriminately dropped explosives on neighborhoods. Others left because they were individually targeted for repression because of their humanitarian work, journalism, political dissent, or fighting on the side of anti-government militias. Young men approaching the age of conscription had an exceptionally strong incentive to escape abroad.[29]

Nonstate violence is a further reason to flee. Murders, extortion, and kidnappings for ransom that are perpetuated by gangs, or by state agents acting unlawfully, are push factors (see Chapter 5).[30] Criminal violence can provoke major flows of IDPs as well as refugees. Violence and economic factors drove internal displacements of African Americans from the Southern to the Northern United States from 1910 to 1930 during the Great Migration. During that period, Black people "were more likely to abandon counties where the number of black lynchings was relatively high."[31] In Colombia between 1951 and 1964, higher levels of political murders in a district were associated with increased internal outmigration. Between 1980 and 1985, Colombians tended to migrate from areas with high levels of violence to areas with low levels.[32] In Mexico, more than a quarter of a million residents fled from their *municipios* (counties) of origin between 2006 and 2010 because of drug-related murders or the threat of extortion. Areas of Mexico with high homicide rates between 1990 and 2018 had higher levels of outmigration to other parts of Mexico even as they had less unauthorized migration to the United States. The higher prevalence of murders in northern Mexico became an obstacle to people in southern areas of the country who might otherwise have migrated to the United States had they not feared passing through the north.[33]

How do people in conflict zones make choices about trying to reach domestic versus international destinations? Forced migrants faced with genocide between 1965 and 1995 were more likely to flee across the border and become refugees rather than IDPs.[34] The option of safe internal relocation reduces flows across an international border. For example, few refugees left Pakistan despite the separatist conflict in the province of Baluchistan in the 1970s in part because of the possibility of moving to more pacific areas of the country. Internal relocation possibilities also explain why displaced groups have typically moved within post-partition India rather than abroad. Armed conflict has not spread throughout the state's territory. Displaced groups can move to other parts of the country with concentrations of coethnics.[35] An internal relocation option is thus not only a legal consideration for authorities assessing whether to grant asylum, but also a sociological variable that explains why some countries produce higher levels of refugees than others.

Economic factors

Researchers have examined economic conditions in countries of origin to determine whether refugee flows are larger from poorer countries. The findings of these studies vary. A global study covering 1964 to 1995 and a study of asylum-seeking in Western Europe from 1982 to 1999 found refugee flows tended to be smaller from countries with low per capita income.[36] Yet a global analysis covering 1964 to 1989 argued that economic factors do not predict refugee migration.[37] This finding was generally repeated in studies of UNHCR data from 1981 to 1999 and 1971 to 1990, though the latter found that genocide and politicide produced smaller refugee flows from countries with higher levels of energy consumption per capita.[38] Studies of international labor migration consistently show the poorest do not migrate because it takes money, or at least access to credit, to move.[39] Poverty is also a constraint on movement for potential refugees.[40]

Over time, the composition of refugee flows usually changes and becomes more like labor migration, though each context has its own idiosyncrasies. For example, the first group of Vietnamese who left their country in large numbers in 1975 was dominated by elites and those who had collaborated with the United States. The second wave was dominated by Hoa ethnic Chinese. The third group mostly comprised the middle and working classes. A similar socioeconomic transition characterized flight from Haiti between 1957 and 1986 and Iraqis after the US-led invasion in 2003.[41] The movement of roughly 1 million Cubans to the United States in the decades following the 1959 revolution saw a great deal of variation in composition, but there was clearly a major shift from the initial wave dominated by the upper classes and supporters of the fallen Batista government and later waves that increasingly incorporated middle- and lower-income people.[42]

Detailed case studies of countries of origin typically find that levels of violence interact with economic and other considerations. Scholars have attempted to assess whether Russian Jews moving to the United States in the late nineteenth century, at a time when US policy did not include a special category for refugee admissions, should be considered unrecognized refugees, economic migrants, or both. The argument for their classification as unrecognized is that, at home, they faced serious state persecution against their religion that would meet the 1951 Convention's standard. Russian police and soldiers participated in the 1881 pogroms. The Provisional Rules of 1882 introduced legal discriminations against Jews that restricted their places of residence, professions, education, and land tenure. The numbers leaving spiked after 1905 when more pogroms broke out.[43] Economist Leah Boustan argues that a combination of labor market conditions in the United States, the rapid population growth of Russian Jews, as well as episodic anti-Semitic violence in Russia, explained the timing of migration flows during this period.[44]

Both violence and economic factors have generated displacement from Central America. A study of internal migration in Guatemala between 1976 and 1981 during its civil war concluded that, "at low levels of violence, a standard economic migration model – without violence variables – explains migration adequately. At high levels, violence itself begins to play a major role in shaping migration flows."[45] When conflicts endure, "political and economic factors come together to shape the experiences of those living in times of war" and it becomes difficult to untangle them.[46] In El Salvador, an analysis of temporal variation in military sweeps and the numbers of Salvadorans apprehended at the US border found that "fear of political violence [was] probably the dominant motivation" for Salvadorans trying to reach the United States from 1979 to 1983.[47] In Nicaragua, "the intensification of the Contra War itself was much more powerful in predicting migration to the United States than the related deterioration of the Nicaraguan economy," while economic factors were more important in shaping migration to Costa Rica.[48]

Surveys in other areas, such as Nepal, find that destruction of livelihoods and property were the main mechanisms that pushed people out. Destruction of a village's industry, destruction of one's home, seizure of one's land, and loss of crops or animals were all associated with increased levels of displacement.[49] In Colombia, economists Stefanie Engel and Ana María Ibáñez found that economic considerations affected household displacement decisions amid violence, but that the weight of economic considerations lessened as violence worsened. An anticipatory movement before violence reached critical levels allowed households to avoid the material losses of a sudden departure and to make better choices about exit and possible destinations.[50] "When households displace preventively, the decision-making process is less hasty," observed Ibáñez and Carlos Vélez. "As a result, traditional migration variables are more important for preventive displacement."[51] Where levels of violence were low, land-ownership was a deterrent to displacement, presumably because owners did not want to lose their major asset by fleeing. For households confronting high levels of violence, land-ownership increased the probability of fleeing, most likely because landowners were targeted for extortion. Households that owned more livestock were also more likely to be displaced, potentially because they too would have been targeted for extortion, but also because livestock can be converted into liquid capital to finance a move.[52] Each situation has its own complexities, but there is widespread agreement among researchers that economic factors and conflict interact to shape forced migration.

Finding a way out

How do refugees escape? Transportation infrastructure matters, but the greatest opportunities have not been enabled by jet-age technologies. Rather, nineteenth- and early twentieth-century advances in railroads, passenger shipping, vehicles, and roads have made the most significant difference. The advent of a global migration industry, including but not limited to people smugglers, and other institutions to aid refugees also facilitate movement that an individual's social networks cannot accomplish alone.

Transportation

Experts often assert that the spread of modern air transportation has enabled flows of "jet-age refugees" to new destinations in the Global North.[53] In the past, "Third World refugees were simply too distant to move directly in any significant numbers."[54] As Rey Koslowski summarizes:

> The dramatic expansion of passenger air travel in the 1970s meant that asylum-seeking was not necessarily limited to neighboring countries from which refugees might then be resettled to states much further away, but rather asylum seekers with sufficient resources could fly directly to countries such as the US, Canada, Australia, and New Zealand, which have a long tradition of large-scale refugee resettlement, as well as to European countries, such as Germany, which had exceptionally liberal asylum policies.[55]

The average distance between refugees' countries of origin and residence increased more than 40 percent between 1980 and 2018, rising from approximately 1,000 to 1,500 kilometers.[56]

On the other hand, many of the refugees whose arrival was met with a sense of crisis in Europe and the United States in the 2010s crossed the Mediterranean in rubber dinghies and old fishing boats, or traveled overland in buses, taxis, or on foot. It hardly requires cutting-edge technology to reach Greece from Syria or the US/ Mexico border from Central America. A bus driving at a sluggish 63 kilometers an hour would cover the average total distance traveled by refugees in a single day.

Roads and rails allowed for much faster movement away from danger in the late nineteenth and twentieth centuries than at any previous period in human history. Railroad and sea transportation costs dramatically declined in the mid-nineteenth century. The result was to facilitate movement across Europe to ports of embarkation for transatlantic crossings. For example, the railway network in European Russia increased from 499 kilometers in 1850 to 29,063 in 1890, making it much easier for Jews to leave the discrimination they faced in the late nineteenth-century Russian empire. Economic historians have found that real "transport costs have declined only modestly since 1950, thus pointing to the nineteenth century as a special globalization episode" – more so than the jet age.[57] The price that potential migrants can afford, rather than absolute costs, determines access to destinations. For most of the nineteenth century, migrants from China and India faced exorbitant transportation costs relative to their low salaries. Because of these financial constraints, the only way they could migrate was as indentured servants or through the credit-ticket system. The credit-ticket system was only possible because of the narrow networks linking migrants from particular hometowns to particular destinations in North America, where Chinese were segregated by law into Chinatowns and could be easily policed by their creditors to avoid default. The theoretical point is that very few people in Asia or Africa facing violence would have been able to afford to migrate long distances to flee violence. Financial constraints were too great, and the various systems of credit and indenture were in highly controlled contexts designed for long-distance movement of laborers, not refugees.

By the mid-twentieth century, long-distance refugee migrations were common. Some Polish refugees in World War II made their way through Central Asia, East Africa, and Mexico before finally reaching the United States.[58] An estimated 18,000 European Jews passed through Shanghai, many of them continuing across the Pacific to the United States after the war.[59] Postwar refugee resettlements took Europeans to distant destinations in North America and Australia. Contemporary asylum-seekers from Africa and Asia often take similarly circuitous routes to reach North America, Europe, or Australia.[60] Still, long distances remain a deterrent, all else being equal, particularly for those traveling outside state-supported resettlement schemes. During the 1990s in Africa, for every increase of 1,000 kilometers between two states, there was a 12 percent reduction in the number of forced migrants moving between them.[61] A study of asylum applications between 1997 and 2014 in sixteen European countries, Australia, Canada, and the United States, which together accounted for 91 percent of all asylum-seekers in the world, found a steep decline in the likelihood of asylum-seekers moving to distant destinations, even when there were other migrants from their nationality already established there.[62] The bounds of geography have not been broken for everyone, even as transportation technologies, most of which date to the nineteenth and early twentieth century, have helped some refugees overcome long distances.

Communication technologies have become faster, more widely available, and greatly expanded the kinds of information available to potential refugees and people on the move. Migrants have always relied on letters from individuals in their social networks as well as information from governments, transportation companies, and migrant organizations.[63] The advent of smartphones has allowed potential refugees and those who have already left to share more quickly detailed information about border and policy conditions, transportation options, and the services of smugglers and NGOs. The ability to keep in touch in real time with social connections in places of origin and different destinations can also be a catalyst for continued movement, as people in the place of origin encourage refugees who reached an initial place of safety to continue moving and reach a country where they can earn a better living and send remittances home.[64]

The smuggling industry

There is nothing new about refugees being forced to use smugglers to reach safety. The earliest people called refugees relied on smugglers to break harsh laws prohibiting their exit. Under Louis XIV's policy, Huguenot women caught trying to escape from France were sent to prison and men were sentenced to row in the galleys.[65] A clandestine network moved Huguenots from the French city of Lyon to safety in Geneva.[66] In the late nineteenth and early twentieth centuries, Jews leaving Russia en route to transatlantic European ports often traveled clandestinely because official Russian travel documents were expensive and difficult to acquire.[67] Refugees from the Russian Civil War, the first group to be recognized by an international treaty, often paid smugglers to reach Western Europe.[68] The *New York Times* estimated in 1924 that there were 17,000 to 200,000 "bootlegged immigrants" entering the United States each year by boat, plane, or on foot. Some fraction of these would have been unrecognized refugees.[69]

States routinely blame people smugglers for promoting irregular movement and putting migrants in danger. During World War II, British authorities charged that "unscrupulous tourist agents" were responsible for the plight of 2,000 Jewish refugees stuck on the frozen Danube River.[70] Yet states sometimes promote smuggling themselves. The US government's War Refugee Board financed false identity documents for Jews in France, smuggler fees to help Jews across the border to neutral Switzerland and Spain, and compensation for Germans who hid Jews in their homes.[71] After the war, East Germany imposed harsh penalties on those who attempted to emigrate illegally and used lethal force to prevent exit. East German secret police hunted illegal emigrants, the same individuals treated as heroic refugees if they reached the West.[72]

People-smuggling enables migration for those who cannot acquire visas, a process that, as we detail in Chapter 7, is made deliberately difficult for most potential asylum-seekers. The only way to migrate for those who do not have liquid assets is to get credit from several possible sources. Where the smugglers are the creditors, the migration tends to be coercive for long periods, and slides into trafficking as smuggled persons must pay off their debts. Credit can also come from employers, often operating through official or quasi-official schemes, but these programs are designed for labor migration, which often takes place in highly controlled "total institutions" such as a plantation, mine, or construction site. Credit can come from friends and family, but potential refugees may not have social networks linking them to distant destinations, and their network contacts may be too poor to share their limited resources to pay for the journey. Smuggling is only a realistic option for refugees who have some capital, which has sharply limited who can migrate both historically and today.

Where do I go?

Most refugees continue to live in their home region.[73] Three-quarters live in countries that neighbor their country of origin, though the share living in adjacent countries declined from 95 percent to 77 percent between 1987 and 2017.[74] The policies of neighboring states, which today are mostly in the Global South (see Chapter 6), as well as the policies in powerful hosts (Chapter 7), shape families' decisions about whether and where to migrate. A closing door in one potential destination reroutes refugees elsewhere in the system.[75]

Resources and relief

Economic opportunities are not the ultimate pull factor. While neighboring countries with higher wages tend to attract more refugees, richer countries that *do not share a border* with refugees' homelands attract slightly fewer refugees, and the richest countries attract even fewer. This finding "directly challenges the popular Western image of refugees as economic opportunists."[76] The authors attribute this outcome to the high costs of relocation to distant countries with high wages. Countries with high wages are also likely to impose strong border and remote controls.[77]

Meanwhile, access to assistance is a pull factor that shapes decisions to flee internally, cross into a neighboring country, or return home. The provision of aid for Afghans in Pakistan during the Soviet–Afghan War encouraged refugee flows rather than internal displacement. Since the UNHCR became much more deeply involved in IDP relief in the 1990s, many displaced people have stayed in their home country who otherwise might have left. Refugees also flee to areas where there are coethnics who they expect will show ethnic solidarity by sharing their resources. Zolberg and colleagues attribute the magnitude of the Afghan refugee population in Pakistan, constituting one-third of all Afghans during the war with the Soviet Union, in part to the presence of the Pathan community on the Pakistani side of the border who shared the ethnicity of many Afghan refugees.[78]

Colonial ties and migratory pathways

Decisions about where to seek asylum are strongly shaped by colonial histories and ties formed by trade, labor migration, and military intervention – all in keeping with the expectations of world systems theory. In Europe, asylum-seekers from former colonies and protectorates are usually overrepresented in the metropoles.[79] Preferential visas for nationals of former colonies, particularly before the EU's harmonization of short-term visas, made travel easier. Metropolitan countries spread their languages to their colonies, and speaking a common language facilitates refugees' integration. Previous migration networks link colony and metropole.

Refugees often rely on members of their social networks who blazed an earlier path. People in these networks provide practical resources and information needed to travel and establish a new life elsewhere. At a more diffuse level, these networks can generate aspirations to migrate and to reach particular destinations.[80] Huguenot refugees followed commercial and family networks between French and English ports.[81] Refugee flows in these cases become integrated into commercial and labor migration systems. Contexts in which some persecuted groups are part of established migratory networks and flee, while others who are similarly persecuted stay home, highlight the importance of established paths and social connections. For example, in the 1980s, Sikhs stood out from other persecuted groups in India for seeking asylum outside India; they often did so as part of a long tradition of labor migration to Anglophone countries like the UK and Canada.[82]

One might expect that with information available to anyone with an internet connection, the information-sharing function of social networks would become less important for migration decision-making. However, a study of Syrian asylum-seekers in the Netherlands found they used social media at all stages of their migration to verify the validity of information gathered from institutional sources.[83] Sociologist Milena Belloni shows how Eritreans throughout the diaspora are in regular contact by cellphone using video chat, text messaging, and calls. Many Eritreans who left their home country but remain in the region stay in contact with family in Eritrea, as well as those who have reached the most desirable destinations in Europe and Canada. Communication technologies shape their migration in important ways – not simply to tie migrants to their places of origin, as transnationalism scholars emphasize, but also to channel social pressure for further movement. Members of social networks try to convince those who left to keep going to more prosperous countries. Eritreans are constantly being reminded about their familial obligations back home, opportunities farther away, and the opportunity costs of staying wherever they are. Belloni's ethnographic account shows a refugee system evolving in real time.[84]

When asylum-seekers arrive in Europe, North America, or Australia, they have often traveled through transit countries along the way. However, it is impossible to determine in advance whether a given person is in transit through that country or if that country is the final destination. Surveys of asylum-seekers in Europe in 2016 found that more than a fifth of arrivals in Greece had left their country of origin more than eighteen months earlier. Nearly half of the Afghans surveyed had left home more than five years earlier. For many of these people, the countries they reached first were initially perceived to be permanent destinations. They lay down roots during long sojourns. As Heather Crawley and Dimitris Skleparis report:

> People experienced some degree of integration into local social systems: they married, had children and made a life. Many never intended to continue onwards to Europe but decided to leave due to a combination of political and economic factors sometimes allied to severe discrimination and a lack of access to rights and/or citizenship.[85]

There is rarely a single decision that guides a refugee's migration trajectory. Geographer Michael Collyer emphasizes the fragmentation of experiences, "broken into a number of separate stages, involving varied motivations, legal statuses and living and employment conditions. It is often not the case that entire journeys are planned in advance but one stage may arise from the failure of a previous stage, limiting future options and draining resources."[86] As we have emphasized, resettlement is rarely a realistic option for most refugees. There are far fewer resettlement slots available than demand for them. Most research on resettlement glosses over which refugees seek resettlement, how they make their decisions, and the process of selection.[87] Refugees are not passive agents in resettlement. Trying to make the case that one has a viable application, staying in contact with the UNHCR, and making sure not to miss an important phone call takes time and energy. As explained in Chapter 6, refugees must first make the decision and achieve the means to put themselves in a place where resettlement is possible, and then be willing to wait indefinitely in the face of long odds against success. These odds grew even worse during the Covid-19 pandemic when much resettlement was suspended.

Should I return?

While questions about how and why people leave their country of origin have received much attention, how and why people return is less understood. Yet voluntary return is one of the UNHCR's durable solutions – a possible conclusion to the experience of displacement. The UNHCR verified the return of 135,000 Syrian refugees between 2016 and 2018. Between 2017 and 2021, the percentage of surveyed Syrian refugees in Egypt, Iraq, Jordan, and Lebanon who said they hoped to repatriate varied between 51 percent and 70 percent.[88] Certain types of refugees were more likely to express their wish to repatriate than others. Those who hope to return have stronger attachments to family members, land, and houses left behind. Younger refugees, men, and those with higher levels of education were less likely to state their intention to return.[89] Refugees weigh the hardships of living outside their home country, without secure legal status, subject to economic precarity, and separated from their family members left behind, against the dream of return. "Home," as they once knew it, may no longer exist. Political, social, and economic factors change their communities of origin. The longer refugees are displaced, the more difficult it becomes for them to return home.[90]

International law and widespread norms protect refugees from refoulement, meaning the forcible return of refugees to their home country when they have a credible fear of persecution. Policies pressuring refugees to return raise the perennial question of when it is safe enough. Political scientist Stephanie Schwartz describes "return without refoulement," in which host and home states coordinate to coerce refugee return with little regard for refugees' preferences.[91] Return that on the surface looks like a refugee's choice has mostly been pushed by states.

The assumption that the end of a conflict makes repatriation safe is called into question when conflicts overlap. Some Iraqi refugees fled the US-led invasion in 2003 for neighboring countries. Many later returned home only to face renewed displacement. The US military declared an end to the Iraq War in 2011, yet more than 6 million Iraqis became IDPs between 2014 and 2017 due to conflict between ISIS and the state.[92] Overlapping refugee and IDP populations complicate an assessment of the beginning or end of displacement.[93] What might seem at the time to be the definitive end of the "refugee cycle" – a return – can only be understood with hindsight as one of many displacement decisions in a growing series.

Even if returnees are not met with violence, they can face social hostility. Following the civil wars in Guatemala and the former Yugoslavia, those who stayed behind sometimes claimed that refugees were cowards or traitors who should have stayed to fight for their cause, thus creating tensions with returnees and a disincentive for those still abroad to come back.[94] For a small minority, an ongoing conflict can be an incentive to return. Able-bodied Syrian men in Jordan have sometimes returned to Syria to fight for ideological reasons or to earn a salary they are unable to equal, given restricted access to labor markets in Jordan.[95]

Decisions to move are not always definitive even if armed conflict subsides. Chapter 8 describes the many types of cross-border connections, including long-distance interactions and circular migration, that refugees may pursue. Even refugee resettlement, generally considered the most permanent form of displacement from a home country, can eventually incorporate return. Resettled Somali refugees in the United States with full rights of legal citizenship still face racist and religious discrimination in their new home. Once they have a US passport as an insurance policy enabling them to re-enter the United States if necessary, some return to those areas of Somalia where levels of conflict are low.[96] Return is thus shaped by the interactions of factors throughout the refugee system.

The Asfour family

The Asfours are among the millions of people displaced by the Syrian civil war. A longitudinal case study using the framework of the new economics of displacement shows how members of one family have attempted to manage the risks of the conflict over a decade. Since the war began in 2011, the family has been displaced multiple times within and across several international borders. As of 2021, half of the Asfour family was still in Syria, while the other half had become refugees. They have endured barrel bombs dropped by Syrian–Russian alliance forces, targeted repression, and the scarcities that war brings as the cost of food, medicine, and basic goods rises. We explain how the Asfour family has experienced each type of entrapment and displacement and what they tried to do to mitigate the risks and improve their circumstances. Arar conducted repeat interviews with members of the Asfour family, primarily Wajih Asfour, in Jordan, and remotely with family members in Canada and Jordan between 2016 and 2021. As the Asfours describe the painstaking decisions they have made over the last ten years, several issues show particular importance. The Asfours have taken into consideration their family members' gender, age, individualized threats and abilities, and income and earning potential as they make decisions about who among them will migrate and where that person will go.

Figure 4.1 depicts a pedigree of the Asfour family. The parents, Mona and Tareq, have nine children: four sons and five daughters, many of whom are now married with children of their own. From left to right, the names of the adult children and their spouses are Wajih and Hala, Imad and Sawsan, Mostafa, Shireen, Tamara, Rami and Neda, Rula and Hani, Lana and Fadi, and Nisreen. The circles are female family members; the squares are males. Overlapping shapes signify a spousal relationship among the adult children. The left side of the pedigree with white and grey shapes shows family members who fled Syria, while black shapes are Asfours who remain in Syria.

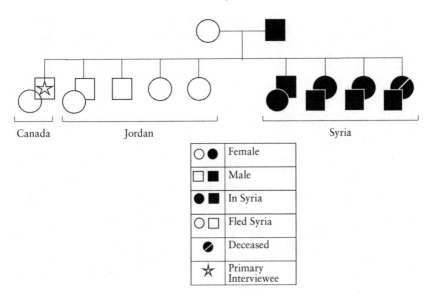

○ ●	Female
□ ■	Male
● ■	In Syria
○ □	Fled Syria
⊘	Deceased
☆	Primary Interviewee

Figure 4.1: The Asfour family's pedigree.

The star denotes Wajih, the primary interviewee. The Asfour family's story illustrates how a household facing a lethal conflict weighs competing considerations around violence, economics, network ties, and the effects of changing policies in multiple states in the refugee system.

The Syrian civil war began in the southwestern town of Daraa – near the home of the Asfours – within the context of the Arab Uprisings in 2011. A teenager named Naief Abazid spray-painted graffiti on a wall of his school calling for the ouster of Syrian president Bashar al-Assad. "It's your turn, doctor" was a clear threat against al-Assad, who had worked as an army doctor before his father bequeathed him the presidency after three decades of rule.[97] The toppling of Egyptian and Tunisian presidents earlier that year inspired dissidents and worried authoritarian leaders throughout the region. Syrian secret police arrested and tortured twenty-three boys in connection with the graffiti and refused their parents' pleas to see their sons. Anger and frustration around the plight of the captured boys grew into a broader protest against the regime. On March 18, 2011, about one month after the graffiti incident, police in Daraa fired bullets into a crowd of protestors, killing two residents.

Figure 4.2: The Syrian city of Daraa, shown here in August 2017, was devastated by the civil war, which began there as a protest in 2011 against police abuse. Photo by Mohamad Abazeed/AFP via Getty Images.

Subsequent funeral marches were met with gunfire from security forces. A cycle of protests and state violence grew into a full-fledged civil war. The internal conflict then became a proxy war through the interventions of numerous other countries – predominantly Russia, but also including the United States, Turkey, Iran, Israel, Iraq, Qatar, Saudi Arabia – and civilian fighters from foreign countries. After a decade of war, more than half of Syria's pre-war population of 23 million was displaced. The vast majority, approximately 7 million, fled to neighboring towns or villages within the country, while approximately 5.5 million Syrians became refugees in the Middle East; and 1 million Syrians found asylum in Europe. More than 150,000 Syrians moved to states in the Global North through resettlement programs.[98]

2011: Recognizing the threat

Wajih Asfour lived with his parents and eight siblings in a small village a few kilometers from Daraa. He grew up with the warning – "the walls have ears" – whispered or delivered through silent, wide-eyed stares directed at anyone who opened a mouth best kept shut. Everyone knew that people who ignored this maxim disappeared or were imprisoned. The secret police threw political prisoners into crowded, filthy prisons, where they endured hunger, disease, and torture.[99] On the other hand, people who stayed out of politics could enjoy free education through college, which was available for all Syrians before the war.

The transition from an ordinary life to the start of the war happened quickly. The violence started on a Friday. As Wajih recalls, he had stayed up late the night before, talking and joking with his friends. They misinterpreted the first sign of trouble.

> We didn't know anything was happening. Then, all of a sudden, there were planes overhead that passed by our village … We started to wave at them … like we always did. We thought the planes were part of a celebration. Within an hour, we heard that there were protests in Daraa.

Wajih could not believe his eyes as the news station reported the death of protestors and that even police officers were killed. "Something like this to happen here? Impossible." He reasoned that Daraa was more allied with the regime than other parts of Syria and that their living situation was "relatively good." At seventeen, Wajih was more committed to honing his soccer skills and graduating from high school than getting involved in politics. But when young people began to take to the streets, Wajih joined them. His brother Rami was away at college, but came home as soon as Wajih told him the news. The young men did not realize the government was filming the protests. Rami would be added to a wanted list that police perused at check points and border crossings.

Because they lived in the governate of Daraa, members of the Asfour family were among the first people affected by the violence and displaced in the Syrian conflict. Their challenges and opportunities were shaped by this coincidence of timing. As the war stretched on, borders that once had been open were closed. Some Syrians who could have become refugees in the first few years of the war missed their chance to cross into a neighboring country. Opportunities that were available to the first refugees fell out of reach for later arrivals. Refugeehood is defined by the fragile possibility of displacement.

Early 2012: Temporary internal flight

In 2012 the Asfour family, including Wajih's grandparents, took a bus to a neighboring village in search of a safer place to stay. Wajih's maternal grandmother lived there before she married and still had family connections. While Wajih's small village was under the control of the Free Syrian Army, a rebel group that stood with the protestors, the Syrian government still controlled the neighboring village. While "there are advantages and disadvantages to each option," Wajih explained, they quickly realized the dangers of staying in an area under government control. The family did not want to be recognized by government agents. Wajih and Rami had been filmed protesting. Imad, another brother, was nearing his eighteenth birthday and faced conscription.

> The moment we got to that village, military guys came and said, "We need all the people who came from other villages. We just need their names." We were so scared; we didn't want to give them our names. We stayed less than forty-eight hours. We got there, they asked for our names, the day after, we left. We couldn't stay.

The Asfours chose to live in a place where bombs were falling rather than a place with targeted persecution that would jeopardize several of the male children. This decision was gendered. The entire family, including the elderly Asfour grandparents, made a choice based on the individualized repercussions that the young men would likely face if they stayed in the neighboring village. The internal displacement option now seemed like a trap that was riskier than taking their chances with indiscriminate violence at home. Instead of being forcibly displaced, the Asfours were forcibly contained (see Figure 2.4).

2012: Imad flees to Jordan

Imad, who is one year older than Wajih, celebrated his eighteenth birthday as the violence in Daraa escalated. If conscripted, Imad might have to fight against his family, friends, and neighbors. Some friends had already fled to Jordan and, through messages on WhatsApp, a smartphone application that allows people to communicate through an internet connection, they encouraged Imad to cross the border. The Asfours agreed that fleeing to Jordan was the best possible option for Imad, and he became the first member of the family to seek refuge abroad. As Wajih put it: "We [the family] sent him to Jordan to claim asylum." For Imad, becoming a refugee was a family decision.

When he crossed the border into Jordan, Imad was placed in a refugee housing center called Bashabsha in the border city of Ar-Ramtha, less than fourteen kilometers from Daraa. He was then moved from Bashabsha, which was primarily reserved for refugee families, and taken to a soccer stadium called the Al Ramtha Club with other single Syrian refugee men. They camped on the field in tents. As a single man, Imad was subject to increased scrutiny by Jordanian authorities. After a few weeks, he was taken to the newly opened Za'atari camp. He stayed there until he could find a Jordanian *kafeel*, or sponsor. A *kafeel* enters into a formal agreement with the state to take responsibility for a refugee, allowing that person to leave their forced encampment. In other words, the *kafeel* pays a small fee to "bail out" a Syrian refugee from the camp. Imad's *kafeel* was a friend of his father's. In Wajih's words:

> For us, there is a relationship between Daraa, Syria, and Ar-Ramtha or Irbid in Jordan. The lines of communication were always open, always. We have many friends in Jordan and they have friends in Syria. And we traveled back and forth, so there were relationships. When my brother got to Jordan, my dad called his friends. And they took [Imad] out of Za'atari camp, and [Imad] went to go work there with them.

Imad relied on his family's existing networks across the border to make his way in the host country.

2013: Half the family flees deadlier bombing

Wajih, his mother Mona, and his sisters Shireen and Tamara, fled to Jordan in January 2013. The Asfours delayed the decision to leave as long as they could, but the violence escalated when the weapons became deadlier. This in turn changed the Asfours' stay-or-go calculation.

> It used to take 30 seconds [for the bombs to fall] ... If I was in the street, or somewhere outside, I had time to run and hide. And when it landed, the blast wasn't so bad. I mean, it would kill you, but if

someone heard it, that person could still run and hide, take cover. On January 15, there were stronger bombs. We would hear the bomb, and then, within *three* seconds, the bombs would land. With three seconds – you don't have time to do anything ... All I could do was clinch in my seat. There was no opportunity to run, or get down, or anything ... And, [the bomb] was much stronger when it landed.

The Asfours felt they no longer had a reasonable chance of protecting themselves from being killed. At the same time, they had competing concerns. Shireen and Tamara were still in school. Their final exams were scheduled for January 17. If the family fled on the 16th, the sisters would fail their classes. The family decided to take the risk for just one more day. On January 17, Shireen and Tamara completed their exams in the morning. That evening their father Tareq drove half his family to the Jordanian border in a car he borrowed from his brother. As of eight years later, this was the last time that Wajih saw his father.

Deciding who would leave was excruciating. Half the Asfour family stayed in Syria. How did they decide who would flee to Jordan and who would stay behind? First, the family agreed that Shireen and Tamara, as unmarried daughters, needed to leave because young women were at risk of sexual violence during the conflict. But given that they were only fourteen and fifteen years old, the sisters also needed a parent to go with them. Mona agreed that, as their mother, she would be best suited to take care of them. Mostafa, the eldest brother, also joined them to escape the war. Mostafa was shy and awkward around new people. Although he did well in school, the family believed he would not be adequately suited for the physically and socially demanding duties along the way to Jordan and in the camp if he were by himself. Tareq felt strongly that either Wajih or Rami should go with the group to Jordan as well. Rami refused outright. He was deeply committed to the resistance movement. "There was no way he would leave the revolution," Wajih said, "So, I went." Wajih intended to return to Daraa after having helped his family settle in Za'atari camp. "You have to know that everyone who came to Jordan would say it was just going to be one week, maybe two weeks, and then they are going back home," Wajih explained. But Wajih never made it back to Syria.

The married daughters, Rula, Lana, and Nisreen, also stayed in Syria with their husbands. Leaving was more complicated for them for several reasons, including their husbands' occupations and affiliations. Rula was married to Rami's best friend Hani, who was also a part of the resistance movement and wanted by the government for taking part in the protests. He would not be able to exit Syria without risking arrest by Syrian forces at the border. Lana's husband had a government job, which also meant that his affiliation would make it difficult for him to leave. Tareq decided to remain in Syria with his married daughters. "Even though they were married, they are still my daughters," he said.

With these decisions, the Asfours were separated again. Tareq stayed with four of his children (Rami, Rula, Lana, and Nisreen) and their spouses. Wajih sought refuge in Za'atari refugee camp with his mother Mona, and his siblings Mostafa, Shireen, and Tamara. The entire journey took twelve hours, although in peacetime, driving from the Asfours' hometown to Za'atari camp would have taken just over an hour. Imad, who had left for Jordan months earlier to avoid conscription, was having a difficult time securing a job and decided to join his family in Za'atari after they arrived.

2014: Lana is stranded at the closed border

Lana tried to become a refugee in 2014 but was denied entry into Jordan. After being stranded at the Rukban border camp for one week, she decided to return to Daraa. Rukban is an unusual camp. It is located in "no man's land" along the northeastern border between Jordan and Syria. This liminal space is technically neither Jordan nor Syria, which means that forced migrants who arrive in Rukban are neither definitively refugees nor IDPs (see Figure 2.1). Unlike Za'atari, which is one of the most photographed camps in the world and toured by diplomats and celebrities like Angelina Jolie, international humanitarian support for people in Rukban is very limited.[100] Residents have restricted access to food and water. Rumors abound of encounters with rats and scorpions.

In response to a question about why Lana waited until 2014 to leave Daraa, Wajih explained: "Everyone was thinking the revolution will win. We will have the victory in one month, two months. But, after things aren't going well, people don't have money anymore." The commitment to wait out the war was undercut by the depreciating Syrian pound. Even families who managed to hoard savings lost 40 percent of its value when the currency depreciated in 2012.[101]

As the war dragged on, social institutions across Syria collapsed. Unemployment rose. Food prices soared. Electricity, clean water, and gasoline became scarce.

The push factors that motivated Lana to leave were tied to the cumulative effects of war and the poverty it created. Yet, despite these intensified reasons to leave, Lana could not become a refugee, because she was not permitted to cross into Jordan. As the violence escalated, Jordanian officers became more stringent about vetting potential refugees. Lana was turned away because her husband was employed by the Syrian government. She tried to explain that Fadi was part of the "civil police," was not involved in the fighting, and should not be considered dangerous. Still, Jordanian officials deemed Lana to be a security threat. Given the choice between staying in Rukban camp and going home, she decided to return home. By 2015, the border between Jordan and Syria was mostly closed to new refugees.

2015–16: Internal displacements and confinement

The Asfour family home is located along the main highway that connects Daraa and Damascus. Whoever controls their village also controls the movement of goods and people, making it an important strategic location for the Free Syrian Army and the Syrian regime, which was bolstered by Russian intervention in 2015. Between 2015 and 2016, the members of the Asfour family who stayed in Syria were internally displaced several times. For a few months, each of them lived in different places. Rula moved the least. She fled to a town called Umm Walad and was safe there for a while. When Umm Walad was attacked, Rula found refuge in the city of Suwayda. At the time, the majority of Suwayda's residents supported the Syrian government, and being from Daraa, Rula did not feel welcomed. She left when she could.

Large groups of people fled together when they were warned about an impending attack. "The Syrian Army never gave notice to the civilians ... They would tell the Free Army, you have twenty-four hours to leave this village and we'll be attacking it. Then, the Free Army will tell the village, you have twenty-four hours, you want to stay, you want to leave, it is up to you," Wajih explained. Civilians often did not have such warnings. At one point, Rami found himself running from one tree to the next in a wooded area to evade crossfire.

There were periods in which the Asfour family members on the west side of Daraa were moving every couple of weeks between villages and towns that were between ten and seventy kilometers apart. "They were moving between Tafas, Jillen, Dael, Al Yadudah, and they went once to Nafa'ah, that's where Rami's wife has some relatives. They were lucky to have them there, but then ISIS came." Rami was able to escape, but his father, Tareq, was left behind. Living under ISIS-controlled territory brought incomparable challenges. Women were required to wear *niqab*, which covers every part of a woman's body except her eyes, and were not permitted to leave the house without a male chaperone. As an older man, Tareq did not need to change how he dressed, but he was affected by the all-encompassing draconian policies. Any resistance was met with violent force, including lashings and executions. Tareq lived under ISIS for about four months before he could leave. Wajih does not know how his father escaped. "To this day, I cannot ask him on the phone." Such a topic is too sensitive to discuss on a phone line they must assume is tapped.

2017: Wajih resettles in Canada

Because the Asfours entered Za'atari camp around the time it opened, Wajih was able to secure a coveted opportunity working with an international humanitarian organization that ran programs inside the camp. Refugees were not authorized to work, but they could hold volunteer positions, which provided a small amount of monetary compensation. Wajih excelled, and within a year, was promoted to "Child Protection Officer." These leadership positions gave his life purpose and connected him to international humanitarian workers whom he befriended. Wajih was encouraged to apply for the World University Service of Canada's Student Refugee Program. The program is open to refugee students in select countries in the Global South and provides them an opportunity to be resettled and attend college in Canada. After years of working diligently to learn English so that he could pass the prerequisite exam, Wajih succeeded and was invited to begin a new life in Canada. "I didn't want to leave my mother, but my dad said, things aren't getting any better here [in Syria]," Wajih said. "So, I went."

Arar met with Wajih the day he left Jordan for a new life in Canada. "Today, I am no longer a refugee," Wajih said, pointing to his travel documents. The UNHCR's identification papers that he carried around for years in Jordan clearly identified him as a refugee. The day that Wajih stopped being a refugee according to the UNHCR's roster was also the same day that Canada officially invited him to enter the country as a recognized resettled refugee. Once in Canada, Wajih took college courses and worked to improve his English language skills. He made new friends both Canadian and Syrian, attended mosque, played soccer, and found a part-time job.

Canada has a private sponsorship program in which groups of five or more Canadian citizens and permanent residents can collectively sponsor refugees to resettle. Sponsorship costs depend on the size of the family to be resettled. An estimated CAN$16,500 would support one person, while a family of five would require an estimated CAN$32,000. Given his financial constraints, Wajih decided to submit the paperwork to sponsor one family member. Who would it be? Wajih called his family to help him make the decision. He would need to sponsor someone outside Syria. Syrian IDPs do not meet the qualifications to be resettled. If Wajih were to sponsor his mother, she would have to leave her daughters in Jordan. The family agreed that option was unacceptable. Wajih's brother Imad was now married with a family, so he could not leave them behind. As the eldest son in his mid-thirties, Mostafa did not qualify for the university resettlement program that brought Wajih to Canada, but he was living in Jordan and eligible for private sponsorship. After discussing all the options with his family, Wajih agreed that sponsoring Mostafa would be best. "Right now, I am one hand trying to clap alone," Wajih said. "If I can bring Mostafa here, we will be two hands clapping together." Wajih described how they could work in Canada together to send money back home. He submitted the necessary paperwork in 2019, but with delays due to the Covid-19 pandemic, Mostafa's paperwork was still pending in 2021.

2021: Diverging futures

Rami considered seeking asylum. He called his brother Wajih for advice and told him he was thinking of catching a flight from Syria to Libya. From there, he could hire a smuggler to make it to Italy. Once in Italy, Rami would be able to seek asylum in Europe and eventually bring his wife and kids over too. Wajih discouraged his brother from making the clandestine trip. "They traffic human beings in

Libya," Wajih warned. There have been numerous reports of refugees and asylum-seekers living in horrendous detention centers, being subjected to deportation, and sold into slavery (see Chapter 6). "Even if you were able to get asylum, you would still need to wait years before you could bring your family over," Wajih continued. Instead, he suggested that Rami and his family find their way to Lebanon and register with the UNHCR. Two of Rami's children have physical disabilities that limit their mobility. Wajih explained that families who are exceptionally vulnerable may be prioritized for resettlement. As of July 2021, his father Tareq and siblings Rami, Rula, and Lana were stuck in Syria. His sister Nisreen had passed away.

Wajih met his wife Hala in Canada. She had been resettled with her family as part of a special program to bring Syrian refugees to Canada. Following a promise made by Prime Minister Justin Trudeau, Canada resettled 25,000 refugees between November 2015 and February 2016.[102] Hala and her family started their new life in Ontario, while Wajih was placed as a student in a university on the other side of the country. Their meeting was not serendipitous. They are both from small villages in the Daraa governate. A mutual family friend in Syria played matchmaker. In 2021, Wajih and Hala looked forward to welcoming their first child, who would become the first Canadian citizen in their families.

Conclusion

As the story of the Asfour family illustrates, refugees make cost-benefit calculations about staying or leaving despite numerous unknowns, often in consultation with members of their family. Drawing on the new economics of labor migration approach, we introduce the new economics of displacement to explore how households manage risks associated with immobility, displacement, transit, resettlement, and return. UN-recognized refugees and other forced migrants are presented with an array of restrictions and opportunities that people who migrate primarily in search of economic opportunities are not likely to experience. Differences in push and pull factors are not only tied to the violence or threat of persecution that refugees face, but also stem from national and regional state policies, humanitarian intervention, and cooperation among states in the Global North and South to manage refugees' movement (see Chapters 6 and 7).

Variation in the type of violence that refugees experience influences their decisions to flee and where they may go. Generalized violence indiscriminately threatens people in a given geographic location. Targeted violence can be wielded against an individual or a group of people such as in cases of genocide and ethnic cleansing. When there are safe places to flee inside the home country, some forced migrants become IDPs. In cases of state-sponsored genocide and ethnic cleansing, there are no safe options inside the state. Violent places along the route to exit may also serve as a deterrent that stops potential refugees from leaving. The Asfour family story illustrates how generalized and targeted violence can intersect over the span of the conflict. Approximately 70 percent of displaced Syrians (9.5 million people) fled their homes due to aerial bombardment executed by allied Syrian–Russian forces.[103] Aerial bombardments forced most members of the Asfour family to flee across the border into Jordan and to neighboring towns and villages around Daraa. Imad was the first member of the family to become a refugee for fear of forced conscription. He crossed the border because he feared targeted violence, while his brother Rami *stayed* in his hometown to evade government efforts to register internal migrants, until staying was no longer an option. The fear of being imprisoned while attempting to exit also informed Rami's decision not to seek refuge in Jordan. People may choose immobility when there are restrictions on migration.

Variation across cases reveals that there is no single component that can predict how economic factors will shape forced displacement. Access to greater economic resources is not the primary pull factor for refugee migration, but resource scarcity at home can amplify the challenges of living in violent spaces. The breakdown of social institutions and the inability to access basic goods at home intersect, which is ultimately what motivated Lana Asfour to seek asylum in Jordan three years after the start of the war. As the living situation deteriorated in Syria, Jordan too faced monumental challenges as a host country that were reflected in more restrictive refugee reception policies. Some of the same escalating events that led to Lana's decision to migrate also shaped Jordan's new border closures and enhanced vetting. Had Lana migrated with other members of the Asfour family one year earlier, she would have likely been allowed to enter Jordan. Recognizing the complexity of Lana's experience interrupts deeply entrenched dichotomies between economic migrants and refugees and between refugees and IDPs. These categories of legal practice only partly reflect a person's lived experiences.

While flight is facilitated by advanced transportation technologies, most people leave on foot, in cars and buses, and on boats. Refugee movement is not random. Migratory pathways develop over long histories in which refugees may follow previous routes of laborers or seek refuge in places with colonial connections. As Mary Kritz and Hania Zlotnik note, "international migrations ... take place usually between countries that have close historical, cultural, or economic ties."[104] Social networks can also shape migratory pathways. While Wajih and Hala were resettled to Canada through formal resettlement programs, they became the connection between Canada and their extended network of family and friends in Syria and neighboring countries in the Middle East. Wajih hosts annual Facebook Live sessions to share his experiences of resettlement with other Syrian refugees in Za'atari camp and beyond. He is actively working to resettle his brother, Mostafa, through Canada's private sponsorship program. Mostafa can be resettled because he is a refugee in Jordan, but state policies do not allow for Wajih to support Rami's resettlement because Rami lives in Syria. With limited options and dismal prospects of a secure future in Syria, Rami is considering whether he should turn to smugglers to travel clandestinely and evade European immigration controls.

Decisions about how to live a safe and dignified life are shaped by myriad considerations. Over the span of a decade, the Asfours have moved numerous times inside Syria as IDPs, across the border to Jordan as refugees, and to Canada for resettlement. The family made strategic decisions with limited knowledge about when and how to leave Syria. Their deliberations illustrate the importance of understanding the decision-making processes of those who go and those who stay, as opposed to a count of final outcomes alone, which can only be grasped through in-depth interviews. As of this writing, the hope to be reunited in Canada seems more tangible than being able to return safely to Syria. The Asfours will continue to strategize with one another as they assess changes in state policies that create new restrictions or present new opportunities. The following three chapters lay out state logics of exit and hosting that have shaped the options for the Asfours and millions of other families.

5

Exit

"Everyone in Syria would have left if they knew what would happen. All 23 million."

Wajih Asfour, reflecting on how difficult it became to leave Syria

The option to leave home cannot be taken for granted. To cross an international border and become a refugee, one has to be able to both exit the home country and enter another. Most powerful states banned or regulated exit until what Aristide Zolberg called "the exit revolution" in the nineteenth century.[1] Although the 1948 Universal Declaration of Human Rights guarantees the right to leave one's country, the politics of containment remain a contemporary issue.[2] Shifting the focus from family's deliberations to "stay or go" described in the previous chapter, we turn to state logics of exit management to explore how states may prohibit, tolerate, encourage, or compel exit.

Governments make choices about whether and how to shape outflows of target populations to achieve nationalist and state-making goals. Bans on exit can be motivated by attempts to hoard human resources, to prevent dissidents from organizing abroad where they have greater freedom to maneuver, and to hold a population captive until it is eliminated. The reasons to tolerate exit include allowing the most troublesome dissidents to go into self-imposed exile, linking permission to emigrate to other foreign policy goals, and extorting people trying to leave. Rationales for encouraging exit include ridding the country of enemies as part of a nation-building project of genocide, forced removal, and/or population exchange. Policies toward exit are not always coherent, and they can swing radically over time. Diktats from distant capitals are ignored in the field. Local agents engage in contradictory practices. Even if policies are consistent, state capacity to enforce them and the robustness of their effort varies. Policies with other goals in mind often unintentionally promote outflows.[3]

This chapter offers a typology of state goals around exit and illustrative examples. A broad historical and global view reveals policy goals and other patterns that tend to be associated with the retention and expulsion of populations and the spectrum between these poles. The conditions that shape flows in a refugee system are interactive across borders, as exit from one country depends on access to another.

Studying conflict and migration in tandem puts the emphasis on what makes forced migration *forced*. By contrast, the causes and possibility of displacement fall out of many siloed accounts. For major humanitarian organizations dedicated to solving the "refugee problem," refugeedom is the starting point for their intervention. Publicly discussing the reasons why refugees left might be construed as blaming the state of origin, which could imperil access to IDPs to provide relief, or make return more politically difficult. Discussion of how foreign intervention is involved in a conflict could threaten funding from those same powerful donor states (see Chapter 1). The causes of exit and the interests involved are ignored. Current and potential host states are far more concerned with the effects of refugees arriving at their borders than the lives of people in dire straits in other countries. This perspective spills over into academic work that consciously or inadvertently adopts the view of the host state to study refugees as a social problem. As a consequence, the situation of immobilized people and IDPs fades from view, with important exceptions.[4] Scholars of conflict and humanitarian law are deeply concerned with the fate of civilians caught in conflict. However, these bodies of knowledge do not typically engage the experience of refugees after they leave their home country, unless the refugees continue to be involved in the conflict.

By shifting the parameters of inquiry to include not only refugees who cross the border, but also those who consider the option, try and fail, or flee internally, exit becomes an empirical question rather than a taken-for-granted starting point. The similarities between refugees and IDPs are made plain. A further advantage of asking whether, when, why, and how people exit is that it highlights those who are immobilized because they are imprisoned, besieged, or interned. The most extreme form of immobility is death. Killings of individuals and groups of people affect the decisions of surviving members of their community. A systems approach thus ties the causes of displacement, including ethnic cleansing and genocide, to refugeedom. Understanding the mechanisms linking violence and displacement requires taking the politics and strategies of the home state and nonstate combatants seriously.

Promoting exit

Refugees are sometimes caught in the crossfire as unintended casualties of generalized violence. They can also be targeted. Armies sometimes deliberately displace civilians for military advantage, as the German *blitzkrieg* into the Low Countries and France in 1940 perfected. Clogging roads and other transportation routes restricts an opponent's maneuverability. Dislocation of the population forces an enemy to spend resources and time caring for displaced people that might otherwise be used for military purposes.[5] Forcing civilians to flee can be part of a "scorched earth" strategy that deprives invading armies of potential labor.[6] Combatants can also seek to displace populations, whether internally or internationally, to intimidate their opponents, weaken social networks, and make it more difficult for their enemies to take collective action.[7] Pushing out IDPs and refugees can be a strategic weapon of war.

Revolutions

Any change of government involving violence can induce the flight of opponents. The more these changes are not simply coups, but revolutions seeking sweeping social transformations, the more likely they are to produce mass flight. Major historical examples of large flows include the French (1789–99), Russian (1917), Chinese (1949), Cuban (1959), and Ethiopian (1974) revolutions. Zolberg and colleagues argue that flight from revolution tends to peak quickly and then tail off. New regimes take time to establish the capacity to control exit and may even promote the flight of their enemies as a political escape valve. Rather than simply caging dissidents, governments sometimes

Figure 5.1: British armored vehicles maneuver around Belgian refugees on the Brussels-Louvain road on May 12, 1940, following the German invasion. Violence against civilians can be a deliberate tactic to slow enemy forces. Photo by Lt. L. A. Puttnam/Imperial War Museums via Getty Images.

expel them so they will not be able to organize opposition activities at home. Similarly, allowing the exit of individuals who supported the losing side is a mechanism to achieve stability, providing the opposition does not organize effectively outside the territory.[8]

Nation-state formation

Nationalism, the project of creating a particular state on a particular territory to represent a particular group of people, is the ideology most responsible for producing refugees. Nationalists try to homogenize diverse populations and/or eliminate those they consider to be inassimilable. Strategies to accomplish these ends include forced assimilation of despised groups, genocide, or forced removal, sometimes as part of a partition scheme to divide a territory along ethnic lines.[9] Nationalism has been especially likely to generate refugee flows in transitions from multicultural empires to nation-states.[10] There is nothing natural about nationalist ideology. Historian Michael Marrus observes that, before the nineteenth century:

> Europeans did not view [refugees'] calamity as a special kind of victimization, different from many other forms of oppression by the great and powerful. And as for the refugees themselves, the same was probably true. People were used to being ruled by foreigners of one sort or another in the days when the next valley or a nearby town was "foreign" in most respects.[11]

By the late nineteenth century, however, the spread of nationalist ideology meant that communities learned to abhor the prospect of being ruled by foreigners. Nation-state formation in the nineteenth and early twentieth centuries, as the Ottoman, Hapsburg, and Romanov empires collapsed, produced many of these flows. The disintegration of the Soviet Union, heir to the Russian empire, and its splintering in the 1990s into nation-states like Armenia, Azerbaijan, and Tajikistan, and separatist movements in places such as Chechnya, Abkhazia, and Transnistria, generated new refugee movements.[12] Russia's 2014 annexation of Crimea, a territory located within the Ukraine, and invasion of the eastern part of the country led to the internal displacement of hundreds of thousands of people. Russia's 2022 invasion of Ukraine generated the largest internal and refugee displacements in Europe since World War II.[13]

Ethnic cleansing is a form of forced removal in which a targeted population is expelled from a state's territory. Ethnic cleansing is often accompanied by genocidal violence.[14] The "ethnic" character of ethnic cleansing has been based on many different, sometimes overlapping, distinctions, including religion, language, race, or claims of a shared history. The expulsion of Jews and Muslims from the Iberian Peninsula beginning in 1492 is the first known example of this phenomenon on a mass scale. Unlike future ethnic cleansings, Jews and Muslims had the narrow draconian option to convert to Christianity, be expelled, or be killed.[15] Subsequent ethnic cleansings tended to adopt a harder concept of immutable racial boundaries, in which individual self-identification was irrelevant and conversion impossible. While some individuals might be able to pass as members of a protected group, persecutors expelled those identified with the target category.[16]

The goal of creating a homogeneous nation-state is often intimately tied to foreign interventions. Russian conquests of the Caucasus and Crimea in the late eighteenth- to nineteenth-century Ottoman Empire sent hundreds of thousands of Muslims from multiple ethnic groups fleeing into the interior of the Ottoman Empire in "perhaps the first full-scale ethnic cleansing, or genocide, of a region in our modern era."[17] An estimated 1.7 million people fled the Caucasus alone. At the same time, the Russian Empire claimed the authority to protect Slavic Orthodox Christians in Balkan territories controlled by the Ottoman Empire in a longstanding effort to weaken the Ottoman state.[18] In the "Bulgarian model" of state-seeking nationalism, Bulgarian nationalists in the Ottoman Empire used the Russian position to their advantage. Nationalists killed Muslims to provoke a Muslim counterreaction against Christians. Russia then intervened on behalf of Bulgarian Christians in the Russo-Turkish War of 1877–88, which led to the establishment of a de facto and later de jure independent Bulgarian state and mass expulsion of Muslims and ethnic Greeks. Other ethnic groups in the multiethnic empire sought autonomy as well and looked to the great powers and their diasporas abroad for support. Many Armenian nationalists in 1855 and 1877 supported Russian expansion in the Caucasus, hoping that, in exchange, they would receive Russian assistance to establish an independent Armenian homeland. When Russia was forced to withdraw from some areas populated by Armenians at the end of the war, many Armenians fled with Russian troops and were replaced by Muslims whose families had earlier been displaced by Russia. In 1915 and 1916, as the Ottoman and Russian empires faced off on opposing sides of World War I, Ottoman forces carried out a genocide of Armenians in Anatolia. Between 600,000 and 1.2 million Armenians were killed directly or died on forced marches into Syria.[19]

The Armenian genocide was shaped by previous forced displacements as well as geopolitics. "Memories of past interactions, however unreasonably interpreted, distorted Ottoman assessments of perceived threats, like that of a large-scale Armenian insurgency that, dangerous as it might have been, never took place."[20] Four out of ten of the highest-ranking officials in the late Ottoman Empire were from lost Ottoman territories in the Balkans and orchestrated the persecutions of Armenians. Talaat Pasha, the Ottoman Interior Minister who ordered the deportations of Armenians, was from a family whose hometown was taken by Bulgaria in the First Balkan War in 1912, prompting the mass flight of the Muslim population.[21]

Theoretically, the point is that refugee expulsions and genocide were part of a sequence of displacements and interventions by foreign armies, diplomats, and diasporic groups supporting autonomy. Decades of episodic conflict in which IDPs fled lost Ottoman territories, interventions by European powers, and the broader context of World War I, were part of a multi-decade system of displacement and geopolitical maneuvering. Such connections are lost in ahistorical solutions-oriented approaches to understanding refugees, which rely on characterizing contemporary refugees as *only* victims (see Chapter 2).

Nationalist ideology drove the many organized population exchanges and transfers in Europe between the end of World War I and the aftermath of World War II. The Treaty of Neuilly imposed on Bulgaria in 1919 included a provision for a population exchange with Greece. The exchanges between Greece and Turkey sponsored by the League of Nations after the 1923 Lausanne Convention transferred 189,916 "Greeks" to Greece and 355,635 Muslims to Turkey. Many "Greeks" in the exchanges did not speak Greek. Religion was the metric. The new Turkish republic took advantage of the opportunity to Turkicize its population by also expelling Serbs, Romanians, Russians, Roma, and Greek Orthodox Arabs. Greece tried to expel Albanian Muslims but was restrained by the Mixed Commission that oversaw the exchange. The exchange was obligatory, except for long-established communities of Turks in Western Thrace and Greeks in Constantinople.[22]

In Central and Western Europe following the 1919 Treaty of Versailles, France expelled 150,000 German speakers from its recuperated territory of Alsace-Lorraine. One of the provisions of the Geneva Convention on Upper Silesia in 1922 led to the transfer of 170,000 people from Silesia to either Germany or Poland. After the First Vienna Arbitration, around 300,000 Czechs were expelled from parts of Hungary, Slovakia, and the Sudetenland that had been ceded to Germany by the appeasement at Munich in 1938. Around 500,000 people were transferred between Romania and Hungary in the Second Vienna Arbitration in 1940 and the Treaty of Craiova between Romania and Bulgaria.[23]

After World War II, there were numerous population exchanges among neighbors, some of which involved land as well as population.

"There will be no mixture of populations to cause endless trouble
... A clean sweep will be made," Winston Churchill told the British
Parliament in 1944.[24] To better align a multiethnic sociological reality
with nationalist ideology, ethnic Poles and ethnic Ukrainians were
traded between Poland and Ukraine, for example. The Allies agreed
to forced population transfers at the Potsdam conference in 1945.
The primary group was 12 million ethnic Germans who had been
living, at the end of the war, in Poland, Czechoslovakia, and Hungary
– a mixture of people who had been settled there for generations and
colonizers invited by the Third Reich. By 1951, one out of five people
in West Germany was a transferee from the east.[25]

Organized population transfers and exchanges had several goals.
They were meant to increase political stability in Europe, along nationalist principles, in part as a reaction to efforts by states to intervene in
other states on behalf of "their" ethnic minorities. The capitulations
system of minority protections in the Ottoman empire, under which
foreign governments such as France provided diplomatic protection
for Ottoman Christian subjects, was highly destabilizing.[26] The
League of Nations Minority Treaties in the 1920s, which had given
designated ethnic minorities rights that would be protected by League
intervention, had inflamed domestic and international tension, and
were not afforded to groups without a nation-state that claimed to
speak for them, such as Jews, Armenians, Ukrainians, and Roma.[27]
Hitler justified taking the Sudetenland area of Czechoslovakia in
1938 to protect its ethnic German minority, thus highlighting the
potential for a geopolitical earthquake when states claimed to act
on behalf of coethnics abroad. The solution of the Great Powers
was based on a modernist conceit that it could manage populations
and geopolitical security by moving millions of people around on
a chessboard, often without taking their wishes into account. The
strategy generated enormous movements of refugees. They were not
just forced out by persecution in their places of origin. Rather, they
were caught up in geopolitical power struggles interconnected with
local experiences.

Frustrated attempts to coerce emigration can lead to genocide.
Until around 1941, the Nazis promoted Jewish emigration by making
conditions intolerable for Jews in Germany and other areas under
fascist control. The Gestapo sometimes "dumped" Jewish people
at the borders of neighboring states such as Poland.[28] Pressure to
emigrate continued until the Gestapo order of October 23, 1941,

banned Jewish flight, as the Nazis turned to a policy of extermination. The shift from a policy of expulsion to genocide was the product of two main factors. The first was the conquest of Poland in 1939 and the rapid advances against the USSR in Operation Barbarossa. Territorial expansion dramatically increased the numbers of Jews living under German control in a total war aimed at destroying what the Nazis falsely portrayed as the "Jewish-Bolshevik system." The second, related, factor was the entrance of the United States into the war in December 1941. The notorious Nazi meeting at Wannsee in January 1942 to "resolve the Jewish question" through genocide took advantage of a global war when it would be easier to ignore the international opprobrium that constrained the harshest policies in times of peace.[29] Ethnic cleansing by periodic expulsions and encouraging exit turned to genocide.

Ethnic cleansing campaigns can take place before, during, and after wars. For example, in 1948, even before the war began between the

Figure 5.2: "Arkan's Tigers," a Serbian paramilitary unit, kills Bosniak civilians in Bijeljina, Bosnia, on March 31, 1992. The unit was responsible for killing thousands of people during the Bosnian war, which displaced an estimated 2.7 million people. This was the highest number of refugees displaced in Europe since World War II until the 2022 Russian invasion of Ukraine. Photo by Ron Haviv/VII/Redux.

newly declared state of Israel and its Arab neighbors, Zionist forces began an organized campaign of forcing Palestinians from their homes that continued over the course of the war, followed by laws that prevented Palestinians who had been absent from returning, thus making them ethnically cleansed refugees *sur place*.[30] Since World War II, intercommunal civil wars, which often include some element of ethnic cleansing, as in the former Yugoslavia in the 1990s, are among the types of conflict most likely to generate refugees.[31]

Colonialism

Prominent theorists of refugee migration have positioned it exclusively within the framework of the nation-state because of the close relationships between nationalism and ethnic cleansing and the way that refugees disrupt the nationalist principle that each individual in a territory should belong to one nation and be protected by one state. "Without an international system there would be no refugees," posits Emma Haddad, who argues that refugees are "an inevitable if unintended consequence of the international state system."[32] While there is much insight in this approach, one casualty is to obscure the pre-national political processes, before the entire planet was carved into nation-states, that have shaped forced migration.

In North America, European settler-colonialists and their descendants pushed west, ethnically cleansing native populations as they went. White militias expelled hundreds of Delaware Indians to Spanish Louisiana in the 1780s and 1790s. Settlers drove out hundreds of Potawatomi families in 1838 from what is now called the state of Indiana, to what is now called Kansas, along the Potawatomi Trail of Death.[33] The Indian Removal Act of 1830 authorized the president to forcibly transfer Native Americans to lands west of the Mississippi River. The US military rounded up an estimated 15,000 to 21,500 Cherokee people in the southeastern United States, interned them in concentration camps, and then expelled them to Oklahoma in 1838 and 1839. A quarter to a third of them died along the Trail of Tears.[34]

Some indigenous people crossed an international boundary to seek refuge. After the Battle of Little Big Horn in 1876, Sitting Bull and his Lakota Sioux followers fled to Canada, where they were granted sanctuary for four years. Given the harsh conditions of their exile, Sitting Bull and 148 others returned to the United States. He was promptly arrested.[35] Indigenous people also escaped south across the border. In the 1880s, hundreds of Cree people fleeing the aftermath of the 1885 North-West Rebellion in Canada crossed into the US Territory of Montana, following trading and hunting routes. When Canadian and US authorities finally negotiated their deportation, the US Congress unanimously passed a bill to pay and provide for "the deportation of refugee Canadian Cree Indians." Three-quarters of the deported returned to Montana after their leaders, Lucky Man and Little Bear, were arrested in Canada.[36] Related stories of expulsions into spaces outside the nation-state system could be told in other areas of colonization, such as Latin America, Asia, Russia, Oceania, and Africa.

The modern obsession of distinguishing between refugees who crossed an international border and IDPs does not map onto pre-colonial experiences in much of Africa where political power "was exercised not over land but over people."[37] In general, a "ruler's territory [was] defined by the limits of what his subjects [were] occupying at any given time."[38] As Bill Gould summarizes,

> Discussion of international migration normally assumes the existence of states with fixed and internationally agreed boundaries and area, and movement between these states is recognized to be across these boundaries from one sovereign area to another. This essentially European concept of the nation-state as the framework within which international migration takes place was until about 1960 inapplicable in Africa. There were no nation-states, apart from Ethiopia and Liberia, but large areas of colonial territory, the antithesis of the nation-state. Nor were there many nation-states of the European type before the establishment of colonial rule, for tribal groups varying in size from a few hundred to over a million people occupied areas that were not always rigidly demarcated or universally accepted.[39]

In pre-colonial African states, the lack of institutionalized territorial borders and the low population density at their margins enabled large numbers of people to move away from the control of oppressive or rival rulers or to flee slavers.[40] In the early years of colonialism before European control was consolidated in Southern Africa, the rise of the Zulu kingdom under King Shaka led to mass killings in the 1820s that displaced hundreds of thousands of Africans into the interior and set in motion chain reactions felt as far away as modern Tanzania. The so-called *Mfecane*, "the crushing," was propelled by a combination of tribal conflict, raids by Portuguese slavers, and the expansion of the Cape Colony that sought African laborers.[41] For sociological realists (see Chapter 2), refugee flows are not predicated on a nation-state system.

Many colonial projects directly created massive forced migration by pushing the native African population off its lands. In the first genocide of the twentieth century, the German military in South West Africa began an extermination campaign against the native Hereros in 1904 and drove the "starving refugees" who survived into concentration camps or the desert. Three-quarters of the Herero people died.[42] In South Africa, white settlers expropriated more than 85 percent of the land, and the apartheid government forced 3.5 million African people into Bantustan territories with fictive sovereignty.[43]

Consolidated colonialism generally reduced the numbers of people fleeing armed conflict.[44] However, colonizers displaced native populations directly and indirectly to further their economic strategies. Colonial policies of taxation and forced labor generated migration. For example, between 1900 and 1950, an estimated 0.5 million people in Upper Volta (now Burkina Faso) fled French colonial policies of forced labor on cotton plantations and head taxes meant to compel Africans into working for colonizers in a newly monetized economy. Many of those who fled built villages in remote frontier regions of Upper Volta where state control was weak. Several hundred thousand people escaped across the border into the British colony of the Gold Coast (now Ghana). Similar movements took place in other French colonies. A 1902 report from a French administrator of Ubangi-Shari, now in the Central African Republic, lamented the "massive exodus" in which everyone "abandons his tribe, his village, his family and plantations, goes to live in the bush like a hunted animal, to escape from recruiters."[45] Mozambican men fled forced labor recruitment by colonizers in Portuguese East Africa by joining labor migration to British-controlled South Africa, while many women moved several days' travel away from their homes to work on hidden small-scale agricultural projects in the bush. A third strategy was flight into British-controlled Southern Rhodesia.[46]

European colonizers were keen to draw mutually recognized boundaries along the coast, which was easy enough to demarcate. Boundaries in the hinterland were ill-defined and barely policed. "The actual [interior] boundaries in Africa were less important to the colonialists than avoiding conflict among themselves in a part of the world that was of questionable value and far from home."[47] Consequently, as in much of Latin America, frontier regions long remained places where individuals or even whole villages could escape state control with little regard for migration status or subjecthood.

The forced displacements of settler colonialism continued in the twentieth century on a massive scale in Europe. The Nazis' General Plan East of May 1942 is the most ambitious and notorious example, which was influenced by the model of internments, expulsions, and genocide in German South West Africa.[48] Their plan, after an anticipated victory over the Soviet Union, was to expel to Siberia an estimated 31 million "racially undesirable" Slavs living in the Ukraine, Belorussia, the Baltic states, Poland, and western Russia. The 5–6 million Jews in the region would be murdered. The remaining population would be Germanized if they were assimilable or turned into slave laborers if they were not. Ten million ethnic Germans would colonize the conquered territories. Germany's defeat in World War II prevented much of the plan from being carried out, with the exception of the killing of 6 million European Jews and flows of millions of slave laborers to Germany and more limited German colonizations of conquered territories.[49]

Decolonization

Scholars commonly point to decolonization as a cause of refugee flows, but decolonization only stimulates exit under certain conditions.[50] Where colonial settlers gained independence from the metropole, refugee flows tended to be modest. In the twenty-two countries in the Americas that became independent by World War I, none involved indigenous groups gaining power at the expense of settlers and their descendants. With few exceptions, independence from colonial administration in the Americas, beginning in 1776 with the United States and generally complete outside the Caribbean by the end of the nineteenth century, was not associated with large numbers of refugees. In Haiti, the hemisphere's uniquely successful slave revolt and revolution (1791–1804) expelled white French enslavers and settlers and established the world's first Black republic. French settlers primarily fled to Cuba, where they were called *refugiados*, and to the United States, where Congress granted them special financial support.[51]

Decolonization in British North America only produced modest refugee flows. Around 40,000 to 50,000 Loyalists fled to Canada after the US Revolutionary War and smaller numbers of rebels moved south into the United States. The US Congress of the Confederation passed laws granting land to explicitly named "refugees" – Canadians and Nova Scotians who had supported the rebels in the Thirteen Colonies and their failed 1775 invasion of Quebec, and then joined the retreat back to New York.[52] The British loss of the thirteen US colonies prompted an accommodating stance toward Canadian and Nova Scotian demands for increased autonomy that led to a drawn-out, peaceful process of independence that did not produce refugees.

In Spanish America, decolonization was led by *criollos*, Spanish-descended elites born in the colonies. Armed conflicts during the struggles for independence did not result in large numbers of people crossing colonial boundaries to flee violence. The boundaries of incipient nation-states were ill-defined and changed even after independence, such as the fracturing of Gran Colombia into Colombia, Ecuador, Panama, and Venezuela, and the decomposition of the United Provinces of Central America into Costa Rica, El Salvador, Guatemala, Honduras, Nicaragua, and the Mexican state of Chiapas. Vast tracts of wilderness eroded meaningful state control at the margins. There was little incentive for a group to flee across a particular border line, with the exception of elite political dissidents. The new nation-states were not formed based on an existing idea of nationhood, and persecuted indigenous and Afro-descended groups in one state would have faced similar persecutions in the others. Only in Mexico did the independent government expel Spanish-born *gachupines* between 1821 and 1836, the result of the relatively prolonged conflict with Spain, which fought harder and longer to keep the crown jewel of its mainland American colonies. Brazil was unusual in that the Portuguese monarchy relocated there from Portugal in 1808. Independence from Portugal in 1824 was led by Portuguese and their descendants, and there was no major refugee flow out of Brazil.

By contrast, decolonization in Asia led to large forced migrations. In the subcontinent, the religiously heterogeneous British colony of India was divided into a Muslim-dominated Pakistan, geographically split into East and West Pakistan, and a Hindu-dominated but more secular state in India. An estimated 14 million people were displaced during the 1947 Partition as Muslims went to Pakistan and Hindus,

Sikhs, and other religious groups moved to independent India. The independence of Bangladesh from Pakistan in 1971 generated a further 9.5 million refugees in a war that was a continuation of nation-state formation during Partition.[53]

The Japanese empire's defeat in 1945 produced the division of Korea the same year, and, after the brief and ultimately failed restoration of French colonial control, the division of Vietnam in 1954. The wars in each country that produced millions of displaced people were the result of ideological divisions supported by Cold War military patrons (the Soviet Union, China, and the United States), rather than religious or ethnic divisions, even as Catholics were overrepresented among the 900,000 Vietnamese who moved from North to South.[54]

Decolonization in the 1950s through 1970s sometimes produced large refugee flows. Unlike in the Americas during the long nineteenth century, these were movements led by indigenous populations, rather than the descendants of European settlers.[55] In contexts where relatively large numbers of European settlers made compromise more difficult with national liberation movements and metropolitan governments, more violent conflicts and refugee flows tended to erupt.[56] The first major case was in Algeria. During the war, 300,000 refugees fled to neighboring Morocco and Tunisia, as related in Chapter 3. In cases with small European settler populations, decolonization usually produced fewer refugees, as independence was typically the result of a negotiated settlement rather than armed conflict, such as in Ghana, the Ivory Coast, and most Caribbean colonies.

Areas of the world that experienced large refugee flows during periods of state formation, such as in parts of Africa during the main decolonization period from the 1950s to 1970s, continued to generate large numbers of refugees decades after the states were created. In some cases, these movements were affected by legacies of state formation. Colonial powers drew borders with little regard for tribal, linguistic, or other ethnic divides. Approximately 44 percent of African states' borders are straight lines. The colonial borders established by the early twentieth century changed little over the next century, even after independence.[57] Only two separatist movements were successful – Eritrea in 1991 and South Sudan in 2011. Both successful and failed separatist movements, such as the Biafran independence movement in Nigeria (1967–70), created massive displacements.

Large numbers of European settlers and their descendants, many of whom had never lived in the European metropoles, moved to Europe from African, Asian, and Caribbean colonies during mid-twentieth-century decolonization. The extent to which European colonizers were forced out, anticipated persecution from newly independent states, or wanted to move for other reasons varies. An estimated 1.5 million settlers arrived in France from Francophone Africa after decolonization, including a million from Algeria, half of whom did not have any French ancestry and were descended from earlier settlers from Italy, Spain, Malta, and Gibraltar. Many had been born in Algeria during the 130-year period of French control. Around 0.5 million Italian nationals returned to Italy from Ethiopia, Eritrea, Somaliland, Libya, Albania, and the Dodecanese Islands after World War II. These *profughi nazionali* (national refugees) were eligible for Italian state assistance, but fell outside the international refugee regime.[58] Returns included 800,000 Portuguese from Angola and Mozambique, 312,000 Dutch from Indonesia, 380,000–500,000 British from Britain's many former colonies, and 38,000 Belgians from Congo called *réfugiés* in the Belgian press.[59] Similarly, an estimated 5 million Japanese settlers in Manchuria, Korea, and Taiwan were forced to return to Japan after its defeat in World War II.[60]

Cross-border conflict

What kinds of wars are more likely to produce large numbers of refugees? The scope conditions of scholarly answers are often narrow. For example, the argument that civil wars are more likely than wars between states to generate large flows of refugees would fall apart simply by including World War II or Russia's 2022 invasion of Ukraine in the cases considered.[61] However, a number of patterns emerge in analyses of the association between different kinds of war since 1945 and the number of refugees in UNHCR statistics.

Civil wars have become more prevalent than interstate wars in the post-World War II era. The absolute number of civil wars declined in the 1990s, before rising sharply in the 2010s, mostly as minor civil wars related to the expansion of ISIS and its imitators.[62] Civil conflicts are often strongly shaped by outside forces as well as internal dynamics. Myron Weiner describes regional effects in which "violent conflicts within one or more neighboring countries can ricochet into other neighboring countries when ethnic groups are divided by international boundaries, large numbers of refugees spill across the borders, and arms move across porous international borders."[63]

Internationalized civil wars – internal conflicts in which other states intervene militarily on one or both sides – rose from 4 percent of intrastate conflicts in 1991 to 40 percent in 2015. During that time, internationalized civil wars tended to last longer, cause more deaths, and create more refugees than other types of wars.[64] Between 1971 and 1990, the average number of refugees fleeing a civil war was 59,000 greater when there was foreign military intervention.[65] The involvement of great powers in a civil conflict can generate refugee flows through several mechanisms. Intervention sustains a local conflict longer than it would have otherwise endured, such as in French, US, Soviet, and Chinese involvement in the conflict in Vietnam.[66] Rebels or deposed government forces can recoup their strength from safe bases abroad to renew their fight. Foreign intervention often provides weapons that increase the destructive power of conflicts and thus drives out more civilians. Finally, foreign intervention can create pull factors of large-scale humanitarian assistance in "safe havens" within the conflict country or its neighbors.

Civil wars in which nonstate actors can earn money from international smuggling tend to last longer, as do those where resources can be easily looted, so that leaders of armed groups have trouble imposing discipline and peace agreements on their supporters. External markets for products such as illicit drugs tie rebel groups to the world economy and sources of funding, which allows them to sustain their operations even without external sponsors.[67] Military and economic links across borders help sustain conflict.

Since the 1990s, "state failure" has generated many large refugee flows, such as from Somalia, Afghanistan, and Syria.[68] Failed states are constituted by a breakdown in the state's monopoly over the legitimate means of coercion. Power is disputed by multiple armed groups. The result is violence that can generate refugee flows. Military interventions by neighbors and great powers have further destabilized these states. Wars are often prolonged or rekindle after periods of relative calm. Failed states have had great difficulty controlling movement across arbitrarily drawn borders, which run through remote regions where states have limited infrastructural power.[69]

Economic interests

States expel refugees, forcibly transfer people within territories they control, or allow them to leave for a mix of motivations that include economic interests. During Germany's military occupation of much of Europe in World War II, forced labor recruitments moved 2.8 million *Ostarbeiter*, mostly from the Ukraine, as well as millions of Soviet POWs. By 1944, 7 million foreigners, constituting a fifth of Germany's labor force, were coerced to work in Germany.[70] These movements ranged from moderate coercion using carrot-and-stick tactics to outright slavery. Nazi persecution of Jews and Roma involved a combination of extermination and transporting them from their home countries to Poland and other sites to be worked to death as enslaved laborers.[71]

Persecutors often combine economic and ethnic rationales for targeting groups. In caste-like systems, ethnicity and class position are tightly intertwined. In such contexts, there are fewer cross-cutting cleavages that moderate efforts by one group to eliminate another.[72] These caste-like divides were often hardened by colonial authorities, such as in Rwanda and Burundi during the German and Belgian colonial periods. Harder divisions contributed to ethnic violence and large-scale refugee flows beginning in 1959–64 and reached their heights in the 1994 Rwandan genocide.[73]

In states with "middleman minority" economies, an ethnic minority group is the primary commercial interface between a controlling minority and a marginalized majority, which makes these middlemen the target of popular ire. Political entrepreneurs and governments sometimes incorporate this persecution into state policy, leading to the expulsion of persecuted groups, such as when President Idi Amin expelled South Asians from Uganda in 1972.[74] The Vietnamese government encouraged the exit of ethnic Chinese people in Vietnam (the Hoa minority) in 1979 because communist officials considered them a despised class of merchants and potential allies of China, against which Vietnam fought a brief war.[75]

Encouraging the exit of people based on their position as class enemies rather than their ethnicity is clearer in the case of early flows of Cuban elites after the 1959 revolution.[76] Exit policies sometimes vary depending on the individual economic character-istics of members of a persecuted group. For example, in the 1970s, the Soviet Union eased exit restrictions for infirm and elderly Jews because the government considered them an economic drain. Yet the Soviet Union continued to sharply restrict the emigration of Jewish scientists to avoid losing human capital.[77]

Totalitarian governments have sometimes commodified refugees and offered them for ransom. In 1944, as the German war effort was failing, the Nazis came up with several plans to ransom groups of Jews. Adolf Eichmann's *Blut gegen Waren* ("blood for goods") plan promised to end the extermination of Jews in Europe and allow them to leave in exchange for enormous quantities of industrial goods, including 10,000 trucks, unspecified amounts of tungsten, and "two million cakes of soap, two hundred tons of cocoa, eight hundred tons of coffee, and two hundred tons of tea."[78] The motivation for a ransom offer that was never going to take place on those terms is not obvious, but US analysts at the time considered several possibilities. The scheme could continue the pre-war Nazi effort to publicly expose the hypocrisy of Allied governments that condemned Nazi policy toward Jews while generally refusing them sanctuary, open negotiations for a peace settlement, or drive a wedge between Allied governments taking different positions on the ransom. Small-scale ransoms did take place, such as the "Kastner train" that carried 1,600 Hungarian Jews to Switzerland in exchange for a payment of cash, diamonds, and gold.[79]

During the Cold War, the West German government quietly paid East Germany 3,436,900,755 deutschmarks and 12 pfennigs to allow 33,755 East German political prisoners to cross to the West.[80] In what cynics called the "Jews for wheat" program, Russian premier Leonid Brezhnev allowed some Jewish families to emigrate in the 1970s as part of a package that included the purchase of grains from the United States.[81] Refugees are sometimes allowed to leave through self-ransoming. In Vietnam after the communist victory, officials charged ethnic Chinese a ransom in gold as an extra-legal but systematic condition of exit.[82] In all these cases, whether ransom payments came from foreign governments, NGOs, or refugees themselves, allowing their departure was a means for the persecuting state to accumulate resources.

Tools of foreign policy

Political scientist Kelly Greenhill argues that weaker states and non-state actors have often encouraged refugee outflows to induce concessions from other states. She identifies fifty attempts at "coercive engineered migration" since 1951, more than half of which succeeded in their objectives. One common goal is to "overwhelm the physical or political capacity of a target state to accommodate an influx." A second goal is to blackmail the target country by exploiting differences among its political actors' interests. A third goal is to weaken a target state's international legitimacy by highlighting the hypocrisy between a public commitment to rights norms and a limited willingness to accept refugees in practice. Liberal states are especially vulnerable to this kind of strategy.[83]

An example of all three of these mechanisms took place in 1980, when Cuban president Fidel Castro suddenly eased exit controls and allowed 125,000 Cubans to leave the island in small boats. His goals included overwhelming the perceived US hosting capacity in Florida, driving a wedge between Cuban Americans eager to accommodate coethnics and other US actors opposed to their arrival, and provoking the US government to impose migration controls that would undermine its public posture as a sanctuary for people fleeing communism.[84] Castro episodically allowed Cubans to leave for the United States as a bargaining chip to demand normalization of relations, and achieved some success, including the first agreement with the United States during the revolutionary era – an arrangement to close the port of Camarioca in 1965 in exchange for organized flights between Cuba and Florida.[85]

The use of refugees to point out the hypocrisy of liberal democracies precedes the post-1951 refugee regime. As outlined in Chapter 3, few states were willing to accept Jewish refugees before and during World War II. Before the onset of the European war in 1939, the German government explicitly hoped that by pushing Jewish people into other countries after stripping them of their assets, public opinion in those countries would become more hostile to Jews and encourage their governments to acquiesce to Germany's anti-Semitic policies. A 1938 circular from the German Minister of Foreign Affairs to diplomatic posts abroad read:

> The emigration movement of only about 100,000 Jews has already sufficed to awaken the interest of many countries in the Jewish danger ... Germany is very interested in maintaining the dispersal of Jewry ... [T]he influx of Jews in all parts of the world invokes the opposition of the native population and thereby forms the best propaganda for the

Figure 5.3: A 1994 cartoon published in *The Miami Herald* shows Fidel Castro turning the floodgate on a dam to let out Cuban rafters heading for Florida. *The Miami Herald*/Tribune News Service via Getty Images.

> German Jewish policy … The poorer and therefore more burdensome the immigrating Jew is to the country absorbing him, the stronger the country will react.[86]

Pushing out, or allowing refugees to leave, has been linked to numerous other foreign policy goals. An interest in trade links relaxed the PRC stance toward Chinese trying to reach Hong Kong during the Cold War, as did the Soviet relaxation of controls on Jewish emigration in 1971 during the détente with the West.[87]

In 2021, President Alexander Lukashenko of Belarus encouraged asylum-seekers from the Middle East and Afghanistan to cross into Poland from Belarus in an effort to pressure the EU to lift sanctions on Belarus.[88] In these and other examples, it becomes clear that refugees are not always the unintended victims of war, or expelled simply because they are not wanted. Governments sometimes use refugees to try to accomplish specific foreign policy goals.

Limiting exit

Many states historically prohibited their subjects from leaving because it would deplete their populations and, in the zero-sum logic of mercantilism, increase the demographic and economic strength of enemy states.[89] For example, Louis XIV banned the exit of the Huguenot rank and file, who were disproportionately high-skilled. Given the limited capacity of the French state and the growth of a people-smuggling industry, the king was unable to prevent the departure of 200,000 Huguenots, but three-fourths of the Huguenot population converted to Catholicism and remained in France.[90] After the French Revolution, passport checks around Paris attempted to control the flight of counterrevolutionaries, but, again, many were able to flee into exile.[91] Exit controls were generally eased as states developed capitalist economies built on free labor and liberal ideologies that viewed exit as a right.

The exit revolution was not permanent even if it is the dominant, bumpy-line trajectory. Destination countries have, since the nineteenth century, periodically pressured countries of emigration to deter unauthorized outmigration.[92] Russian exit controls that had been relaxed in 1891 were reimposed by the USSR in the mid-1920s, culminating in a 1935 law in the death penalty for unauthorized exit.[93] Restrictions on particular ethnic groups were then eased in the 1970s and 1980s, beginning with Jews, followed by Armenians and ethnic Germans, until the dissolution of the Soviet Union in 1991 opened the possibility of exit to all its former citizens.[94] All major communist countries during the Cold War had strict exit controls, with the exception of Yugoslavia, which broke with Stalin in 1948 and promoted temporary labor migration to Western Europe beginning in the mid-1960s.[95] Cuba reduced its strict exit controls, which it had only episodically eased since the 1960s, on an apparently sustained basis in 2013.[96] As of this writing, North Korea stands out for its unusually restrictive exit controls, which impose sentences for up to three years of labor "re-education" for exiting without permission. Punishments range from seven years of labor re-education to forfeiture of all property and execution for "any person who escapes to another country or to the enemy in betrayal of his motherland and people."[97]

Totalitarian governments restrict exit for multiple reasons. The goal of preventing emigration, not immigration control, was the driving force behind the construction of the Iron Curtain in Eastern Europe and its most iconic section – the Berlin Wall. Efforts to control and transform a society through draconian means are weakened if dissatisfied citizens can simply leave.[98] Attempted exit draws targeted discrimination. For example, Haitian dictator Jean-Claude Duvalier secretly ordered his military and the Tonton Macoutes militia to jail anyone who returned to Haiti after leaving illegally.[99] States try to restrict the exit of dissidents who might share damaging information with foreign intelligence services or form nuclei of resistance abroad. Autarky, the goal of economic self-sufficiency, shares with mercantilism a bias against outmigration. Autarkic governments try to avoid the loss of human capital in which they have invested.[100] Countries with forced conscription, particularly if they rely on long periods of mass conscription like contemporary Eritrea, seek to deter the loss of potential recruits.[101] When citizens vote with their feet by walking away, the international prestige of the origin country is weakened as well. Prestige is especially important in the context of existential struggles such as the Cold War, when warring systems for organizing society competed for the support of a global audience.

Forced relocation and concentration

Coercive relocation within a country's borders is an alternative to state strategies of mass deportation or killing the members of an unwanted group. The USSR adopted this domestic strategy on an unprecedented scale under Vladimir Lenin and Josef Stalin by moving ethnic groups around its vast landmass. The Soviet government forcibly relocated nearly 12 million Soviet citizens between 1920 and 1952, including ethnic Germans, Ukrainians, Rusyns, Koreans, Estonians, Lithuanians, Latvians, Crimean Tatars, Greeks, and class-based groups such as kulaks.[102]

States commonly immobilize populations during times of conflict through the concentration of civilians in camps or other guarded areas such as "strategic hamlets" or "model villages." Nearly a third of the counterinsurgency campaigns since the Napoleonic Era involved forced relocation, including in South Africa during the early 1900s, Libya in the late 1920s and early 1930s, Mexico in the late 1920s, Algeria in the 1950s, Vietnam in the 1960s, Peru in the 1980s, Guatemala in the 1980s, and Burma in the 1990s. Forced relocation took place in a third of the 160 civil wars between 1945 and 2008 and was most common in rural and border areas, irregular conflicts, and conflicts in which the state had limited resources.[103]

Forced concentration of noncombatants has several goals. One is an effort to deprive rebels of their ability to hide among the civilian population, or, to use the Maoist expression, to swim like fish in the sea. Concentration is a way to "catch the fish by draining the sea."[104] The strategy also punishes disloyal communities and makes the population available for recruitment as soldiers, laborers, and informants. The most sophisticated goal is to chart the sea.[105] Putting people in camps makes their political affiliations and activities more legible. Those who are disloyal can be identified using "guilt by location" based on whether they have obeyed a relocation order.[106] Regardless of the precise goals of forced relocation, the strategy is an alternative to mass expulsions and makes it much harder for IDPs to flee across a border to become refugees.

Foreign pressure

Exit policies are shaped by the interaction of external and internal pressures. Foreign military interventions can end, sustain, or intensify wars that push out refugees. Diplomatic pressure also has cross-cutting effects on exit policies.

Even democratic destination states have sometimes tried to compel countries of origin to contain their persecuted populations.[107] For example, once large ships began leaving Vietnam carrying ethnic Chinese passengers, the UNHCR and Western countries claimed Vietnam was illegally practicing mass expulsion and that irregular departures by sea were putting refugees at risk. The UNHCR and Western states effectively pressured the Vietnamese government to deter irregular exit. The Orderly Departure Program was the result of this negotiation.[108]

Decisive foreign invasion sometimes ends the persecutions that generate refugee flows even if that is not the invasions' primary goal. The 1945 Allied victory over Nazi Germany in World War II ended the genocides of Jews and Roma. India's 1971 invasion of East Pakistan and the establishment of independent Bangladesh ended the flow of 9.5 million refugees from the conflict between the Bangladeshi self-determination movement and Pakistani government. The 1978 Vietnamese invasion of Cambodia ended the politicide of the "killing fields."

Interventions that stopped one kind of refugee outflows have also produced new ones, such as the expulsion of ethnic Germans from Eastern Europe after World War II, and the flight of deposed Khmer Rouge and their families from Cambodia to Thailand in the late 1970s. The Rwandan Patriotic Front operated from bases in Uganda to defeat the Hutu-dominated Rwandan Army and end the genocide against Tutsis in 1994. This phase, not the genocide itself, produced the most refugees.

> A massive exodus of people was engineered not by the victorious army of the Tutsi-led rebels, but by the leaders of the defeated and Hutu-dominated regime. As they lost their grip on power, these leaders persuaded and induced more than a million of the country's citizens to leave the country and to take up residence in internationally assisted camps located in eastern Zaire and Tanzania. The aim of this strategy was simple: to deprive the new administration of a population to govern, and to establish large concentrations of exiles on Rwanda's borders, where they could engage in a campaign of intimidation and destabilization.[109]

The factors that shaped displacement in Rwanda were thus formed by complex interactions among state and nonstate actors in multiple countries, legacies of colonialism and postcolonial conflict, and feedback mechanisms that blurred the distinction between people fleeing and perpetuating violence.

Conclusion

Siloed approaches in refugee studies take movement across a border as the starting point. A binocular view that includes the lenses of conflict and migration studies gives a clearer, three-dimensional image. State actors and nonstate combatants vary tremendously in their intentions and ability to impede or impel exit. Deliberately creating refugees can be a tool of military strategies to create a problem that opponents must resolve, or it can be the unintended, even if foreseeable, consequence of warfare.

Certain kinds of conflict are more likely to produce refugees. Nation-state building is a major cause of refugeedom, and one of the reasons that flows since the nineteenth century during the global spread of the ideology of nationalism have been so intense. Efforts to create homogeneous national populations can involve a mix of forced assimilation, genocide, forced expulsions, and population transfers. Settler colonialism creates displacement directly, but had even greater indirect effects on displacement in Africa, where the creation of a monetarized, racialized political economy based on taxation reshuffled populations. Forced labor schemes by colonizers generated pressures to move to avoid them. During decolonization, refugee outflows tended to be largest in colonies with large settler populations where the settlers and their descendants lost power. At least since World War II, civil wars that are internationalized have produced more refugees. Russia's 2022 invasion of Ukraine was a reminder that wars between states can also cause mass displacement. Decisive foreign invasions can end major refugee flows, though history is replete with examples of successful invasions that end the exit of one group only to generate the exit of others.

The policy toolbox includes promoting exit as a deliberate strategy. It is an especially useful strategy for weaker powers aiming to achieve concessions from liberal states by publicly revealing the gap between liberal pronouncements about following the rules of the international refugee regime and a general unwillingness to accept many refugees, as we discuss in detail in Chapter 7 on the policies of powerful host states. During the age of mercantilism, many states placed restrictions on the exit of their subjects, in large part to avoid competitor nations building up their demographic strength through immigration. These policies were rolled back during the nineteenth-century "exit revolution." History never ends, and totalitarian states in the twentieth century enacted extreme exit controls that took concrete form in the Berlin Wall. Many states have created forced immobility during armed conflicts by concentrating civilians in camps or communities they cannot leave. These encampments cage people who might otherwise become refugees or IDPs in other parts of the country.

Exit policies are closely linked to admissions policies, especially around asylum. For example, Castro's efforts to open and close the exits from Cuba were only effective to the extent that the US government was willing to accept Cubans attempting to reach the United States without visas. Once the United States refused to accept most Cubans intercepted at sea, beginning in 1994, and extended that policy to Cubans who reached a US land border or beach in January 2017, the Cuban government lost much of its leverage. As we will discuss in Chapter 7, the willingness of states in the Global North to accept refugees from communist countries during the Cold War was shaped by the small numbers that communist states allowed to leave. Whether people flee their countries to become refugees is not simply dependent on conditions at home. State exit strategies are formed in interactions with potential destination countries. Chapters 6 and 7 explore the determinants of refugee hosting around the world.

Seria

IDPs → Refugees

Jordan

6

Hosting in the Many Global Souths

"The registration mechanism [at the Jordanian border] was very weak with only one or two people doing the registrations. Syrians were coming in the thousands. You would have to wait five or six hours in the cold, and we were not dressed for that. Our situation was much better than the people around us. We came just one family by ourselves. When we got to the border, we could see twenty or thirty families. Those families had children, babies who are breastfeeding, elderly people, so their situation was very hard. I mean, we could tolerate the cold, but what about a child that's one or two days old? That's very, very hard."

Wajih Asfour, describing the day he entered Jordan

Scholars and practitioners often begin their assessment of refugee reception by indicating whether a state is party to the 1951 Refugee Convention and its 1967 Protocol. Of the 193 UN member states, 148 are party to the Convention, the Protocol, or both. These legally binding commitments are central to most understandings of how and why states host refugees. Yet many non-signatory states host large numbers of refugees.[1] Experts who acknowledge this fact suggest it is surprising. "Although not a signatory to the 1951 Convention Relating to the Status of Refugees, Jordan has historically offered protection to refugees," reads an article in the *Lancet*.[2] Some mentions of non-signatory states recognize that they have made other commitments to refugees through national or regional law, yet even these acknowledgments continue to rhetorically elevate the Convention. "Although Iraq is not a signatory of the 1951 Refugee Convention, the Iraqi Constitution upholds the right to seek asylum," stated UNHCR representative Bruno Geddo at the 2016 signing of a memorandum of understanding between the UNHCR and Iraqi government.[3]

Public rhetoric is deferential to the Convention even while recognizing the reality of refugee reception that is not dependent on it. In 2020, at least 40 percent of UN-recognized refugees lived in non-signatory states. Some of the most celebrated signatories, including Canada, the United States, and Australia, received only a small fraction of the world's refugees – in many years, fewer than 0.5 percent combined. Knowing whether a state is a party to the Convention would be an unreliable basis for predicting whether it hosts large numbers of refugees and how it treats them in practice.

The global system of refugee management is fundamentally dependent upon non-signatory states and refugee hosting in the Global South more broadly. Southern host states are home to the majority of UN-recognized refugees and manage the movement of asylum-seekers, resettling refugees, and returnees. Refugee groups are often displaced for protracted periods and even generations. Millions of refugees reside in Southern states indefinitely. We argue that, in addition to being the final destination for most of the world's refugees and providing territorial space for Northern resettlement operations, Southern states are the foundation of the contemporary system of refugee management. Across the world, rights-oriented refugee reception, including adherence to the Convention and the protections outlined in national asylum policies, depends on mechanisms of immigration control that limit the number of individuals seeking refuge.[4] The current configuration of Northern refugee reception – even in the most generous states – is only possible because Southern states contain and control most refugee movement.

Social scientists warn researchers not to select on the dependent variable, meaning that, to understand an outcome, one should avoid observing *only* cases in which the outcome appears, while simultaneously excluding cases in which it is absent. We heed this call by examining Southern cases of mass reception as well as cases of deterrence, rejection, and limited hosting. Southern states discriminate among refugees and asylum-seekers at their borders much like their Northern counterparts discussed in Chapter 7. The challenges of reception are tied to global hierarchies among states, fueled by inequalities rooted in histories of colonialism, and developed through feedback mechanisms. We invite the reader to consider the many Global Souths as we illustrate variation among these states.

Conceptualizing the Global South

The preamble of the 1951 Refugee Convention states that accepting refugees "may place unduly heavy burdens on certain countries." This insight remains true decades later. In 2020, 85 percent of the UN-recognized refugees lived in developing countries such as Lebanon, Pakistan, and Iran, and 27 percent lived in the world's least developed countries, including Bangladesh, Tanzania, and the Democratic Republic of Congo.[5] Designations such as "developing" and "least developed" are relational and imply a comparison to "developed" states. These terms are used by the UN to describe a state's economic capacity and reveal that the poorest countries in the world receive the largest number of refugees. We use the terms "Southern" or "Global South" to reference a similar group of states, while avoiding the normative hierarchy and teleology that is implied by "developed" and "developing."

The terms Global South and Global North are not intended to capture a strict geographic divide. We operationalize the Global South at the time of this writing to include Africa, most of Asia, Latin America, and the Middle East, while the Global North includes Europe, the United States, Canada, Australia, New Zealand, Japan, Singapore, and South Korea. The countries of the Global North are rich democracies that include states that colonized most of the planet. The Global South is made up of countries that tend to have histories of being colonized and are less powerful. Admittedly, these classification grounds do not consistently overlap. A country might move from one category to another over time, and there is variation within particular countries or regions. Global North and Global South are relational terms, such that Bulgaria is in some ways a Southern state relative to much richer and more powerful European states like Germany. Any dichotomization of the nearly 200 countries in the world is a simplification that loses its analytical utility at the margins. We nevertheless use these categories to highlight the power differentials and histories of intervention that are key concepts in the refugee system.[6]

The Global North remains the focus of scholarly investigations despite a burgeoning literature on Southern refugee management. There is a broad recognition of the need for more scholarship about refugee hosting in the Global South. Yet beyond the empirical neglect of particular contexts in the Global South, the Global North bias appears in the ways that research questions are posed and generalizable claims are asserted. Scholarship that focuses predominantly on the United States, Canada, Australia, and Europe does not require the terminology of "Global North" to establish its scholarly relevance. The importance of these cases is simply implied and accepted. Moreover, scholarship about Southern hosts tends to treat them as a monolith. The academy incentivizes making generalizable claims, which collapse differences among Southern states for the sake of theorizing the Global South. This tendency is advanced by the study of humanitarian organizations that operate throughout the Global South (most notably the UNHCR and its private partners), which can further conceal variation among states when the study of humanitarian management is prioritized over the examination of local practices. Finally, when the scholarly focus is on a region or state in the Global South, the point of comparison often remains states in the Global North, not in small part so that scholars remain in conversation with canonical academic works.[7] Analyzing variation within the Global South helps to fill theoretical and empirical gaps in the study of forced migration.

Displaced people in Southern states

Most refugees flee from countries in the Global South and find refuge elsewhere in the Global South. In 2019, two-thirds of UNHCR-mandate refugees came from just five countries: Syria, Afghanistan, South Sudan, Myanmar, and Somalia.[8] More than 52 percent of UN-recognized refugees live in the Middle East and North Africa alone.[9] The rest of Africa hosted 6.3 million refugees (24 percent), while Asia and the Pacific host 4.1 million refugees (16 percent). These percentages change over time, but one consistent pattern is that refugees usually flee from their home state to neighboring countries. The patterns reflect Southern reception as well as the fact that conflicts in the Global South induced most displacement between the breakup of Yugoslavia in the 1990s and the Russian invasion of

Ukraine in 2022. The top countries of reception in 2020 were Turkey (3.9 million), Jordan (2.9 million), Colombia (1.7 million), Pakistan (1.4 million), Uganda (1.4 million), and Lebanon (1.4 million). Germany is an important anomaly. As a Northern state that also hosted 1.2 million refugees in 2020, Germany was the exception that defied the broader trend in global reception patterns. The mass flight of refugees from Ukraine in 2022, mostly to European neighbors such as Poland, represented a further divergence from the dominant trend in recent decades.

Refugee reception often becomes a long-term commitment for states, which factors into every aspect of refugeedom. Approximately 82 percent of UN-recognized refugees live in "protracted situations," a term used to reference contexts in which a refugee group of 25,000 or more people is displaced for five or more years. There is no shorthand to reference smaller groups of refugees that have been displaced for decades, such as the thousands of Liberian refugees who fled to Ghana after the civil war in 1989. Their refugee status was revoked in 2012, making them ineligible for resettlement, and many are stuck with the option of local *non*-integration or coerced return.[10] The intergenerational transfer of refugee status means that most children born in exile do not have access to citizenship in their host state. Many do not remember or have never set foot in their home country. Conservative estimates suggest that 1 million children were "born into a refugee life" between 2018 and 2020.[11]

Refugees from Syria, the largest nationality of contemporary refugees, were displaced by the war that began in 2011. By 2021, 6.6 million Syrians were recorded as refugees, and an additional 6.7 million were internally displaced.[12] Palestinians were the second largest refugee nationality in the world. Together, Syrians and Palestinians accounted for 47 percent of UN-recognized refugees.[13] Most Palestinians are stateless refugees whose displacement has spanned seven decades. Between 700,000 and 800,000 Palestinians became refugees as a result of the creation of Israel in 1948. An additional 300,000 Palestinians were displaced following the 1967 Arab-Israeli War. The majority of Palestinians are registered with UNRWA, a UN agency that administers relief and humanitarian aid in the West Bank, Gaza, Jordan, Lebanon, and Syria. Many Palestinians found opportunities in Arab states outside UNRWA's operations. Their stateless status, however, extended their precarity despite access to labor markets. Most notably, Kuwait expelled

300,000 Palestinians after the 1990–1 Gulf War, illustrating the generations-long insecurity of stateless refugee status.

Southern states also host refugees who are not counted in humanitarian reports or scholarship that relies primarily on UNHCR data. Forcibly displaced Venezuelans largely fall outside the scope of recognized refugees. Between 2014 and 2019, approximately 4.5 million Venezuelans were displaced, 3.6 million of whom sought safety across state borders. Venezuelans fled economic collapse after government mismanagement led to hyperinflation and a shortage of basic goods. While the Venezuelan exodus was catalyzed by extreme poverty, the country also has a documented history of human rights violations, including arbitrary arrests and torture. Were Venezuelans refugees or economic migrants? Drawing on the 1951 Convention definition of a refugee, Peru only recognized 1,200 Venezuelans as refugees between 2014 and 2019.[14] Nearly 500,000 cases were pending as of 2021.[15] By contrast, Brazil applied the refugee definition outlined in the 1984 Cartagena Declaration, a non-binding regional instrument that has been incorporated into national law throughout Latin America, as described in Chapter 3.[16] Following the more expansive Cartagena definition, Brazil recognized tens of thousands of Venezuelans as refugees. However, millions of Venezuelans who were not legally recognized as refugees were allowed to stay in Latin American countries under other categories, such as visitor and worker. A fixation only on Venezuelans who received refugee status might lead one to conclude that states in Latin America have done little to support Venezuelans. In fact, Latin American countries have done far more to support Venezuelans than most countries in the Global North that grant small numbers of Venezuelans some kind of humanitarian status.

The UNHCR estimates there were 45.7 million IDPs in 2019, most of whom lived in the Global South. The largest populations of IDPs lived in Colombia (7.9 million), Syria (6.2 million), the Democratic Republic of Congo (5 million), Yemen (3.6 million), Afghanistan (2.6 million), and Somalia (2.6 million).[17] Many IDPs would become refugees if given the chance to cross the border. For example, between 2008 and 2021, the 2 million Palestinians in Gaza experienced four wars and indiscriminate Israeli airstrikes across the tiny territory. Eleven days of Israeli airstrikes in May 2021 internally displaced more than 100,000 Gazans.[18] When asked about the mental health consequences of such violence, psychiatrist Samah Jabr explained:

"In Gaza, there is no 'post' [traumatic context] because the trauma is repetitive and ongoing and continuous."[19] Gaza's residents, approximately 1.4 million of whom are registered as refugees with UNRWA as a result of their families' earlier displacement in 1948, cannot seek refuge in neighboring states due to a land, air, and sea blockade upheld by Israel and Egypt.

Other potential refugees remain IDPs when border guards or immigration officials block them from crossing. In many parts of the Global South, "the borders of most receiving states are porous, vaguely delineated, and inadequately policed, and the crossing of thousands of people within a short period can seldom be prevented."[20] On the other hand, many Southern states have developed an extensive capacity for control. Individuals who flee North Korea have sought safe haven in China or South Korea. As described in Chapter 5, leaving North Korea without official authorization is a criminal offense, punishable under some circumstances by execution. Prioritizing their diplomatic interests, Chinese officials have refouled North Koreans despite being party to the 1951 Convention.[21] Southern states are not always helpless when it comes to controlling refugee movements. As in the Global North, Southern states wield a range of tools to control their borders and populations, though their capacity and will varies over time and place.

The numbers game

Refugee statistics are created through a political process rather than simply reflecting an objective reality. Many Southern hosts strive to make their refugee hosting contribution legible through the numbers game.[22] State officials benefit when they present a sizeable number of refugees to the international community and establish the toll of the "refugee burden." From Ethiopia to Somalia, UN refugee counts are considerably lower than state estimates, which can be explained by competing incentives.[23] Counts by the UN include only those who are registered as persons of concern, while state counts include registered and non-registered nationals from a particular country. From the perspective of the host state, those who cannot return to their country due to conflict, but are not registered with the UN, should be considered in assessments of the refugee burden.

The politics of refugee counting also appears in estimates of the number of refugees and their share of the population. Turkey hosts

4 million refugees in a population of 82 million. While Turkish officials boast their country hosts the largest *number* of refugees, Lebanese officials claim the largest *percentage* of refugees in any country's population (20 percent).[24] Yet moving from the national to the subnational level, the Turkish city of Gaziantep located near the Syrian border is home to nearly 500,000 Syrians, and it equals the Lebanese national record of a jurisdiction in which 20 percent of the city's inhabitants are refugees.[25] Counting refugees is a political project that involves negotiations among state and humanitarian leaders. "We used to exaggerate the numbers with the Iraqis, but we do not do that anymore," said one Jordanian government official. "We are not exaggerating the Syrian numbers."[26] In 2007, the Norwegian research institute FAFO estimated there were 161,000 Iraqi refugees in Jordan, while Jordanian government estimates claimed a population of between 750,000 and 1 million Iraqis.[27] The Iraqi numbers remain unverified almost two decades after the US-led invasion in 2003.[28] Regardless of how closely refugee population estimates correlate with the sociological reality, the appearance of large numbers of refugees allows Southern hosts to emphasize their contributions to the global system of refugee management.

Hosting large numbers of refugees allows Southern officials to justify requests for increased international support, development aid, trade concessions, and access to freer travel for their nationals. An acknowledgment of the uneven demographic distribution of refugees makes for a pithy retort to quell accusations that Southern states are not doing enough to support refugees. In a 2016 interview with the BBC, King Abdullah II of Jordan responded to criticisms that Jordan was closing its borders to Syrian refugees:

> We've already taken in 1.4 million people ... If you are going to take the higher moral ground on this issue, we'll get them all to an airbase and we're more than happy to relocate them to your country ... If you want to help the refugee problem, 16,000 refugees to your country, I don't think is that much of a problem.[29]

Leaders in the Global North trying to keep out most refugees buy into the argument that they should not be too critical of Southern mass host states. When the Associated Press questioned German President Frank-Walter Steinmeier about the mistreatment of Syrians in Jordan, he responded that "much can be improved, much needs to be done through international aid, but I believe it's not justified to come with big complaints against Jordan ... I believe we should show restraint with complaints about countries like Jordan, which truly carry the biggest burden of the refugee influx from Syria."[30] By using refugee statistics to point out the asymmetry between the large scale of refugee hosting in the Global South and small numbers in the Global North, an imbalance that the Global North wants to preserve, states in the Global South avoid criticism of their own violations of refugees' rights.

Rate of movement

A snapshot of Southern hosting captures the distribution of the world's refugees but usually does not address the rate of movement. The rate of refugee movements – which includes initial displacement as well as reception across state borders, resettlement, and return – shapes how state and humanitarian officials coordinate their responses. Fast flows require great organizational capacity to provide basic resources such as food and shelter. When organizational demands go unmet, rapid reception may compound the challenges that refugees and their host communities face. As a result of the 1994 Rwandan genocide, approximately 2 million people fled to neighboring Tanzania and the Democratic Republic of Congo, crossing at a rate of 10,000 people per hour on some days.[31] Overcrowding became a public health emergency when infectious diseases began to spread. A cholera epidemic claimed the lives of 50,000 Rwandan refugees in eastern Zaire (now the Democratic Republic of Congo). While the rate of Rwandan displacement was extreme, it was not unique. The mass displacement of Rohingya refugees from Myanmar's Rakhine State beginning in August 2017 was described by the International Rescue Committee (IRC) as the "fastest refugee exodus since the Rwandan Genocide."[32] The majority of 742,000 Rohingya refugees fled to Bangladesh within three months.[33]

Rwandan displacement was also characterized by rapid return. On December 5, 1996, the Tanzanian government released a joint statement with the UNHCR stating that "all Rwandese refugees in Tanzania are expected to return home by 31 December 1996." At least 400,000 people were expected to return within twenty-six days. Fearing for their lives, many Rwandan refugees did not want to return. Hundreds of thousands fled toward Kenya and Uganda to circumvent Operation Return Refugees.[34] Armed Tanzanian troops set up roadblocks to force refugees to turn back. With financial and logistical support from the UNHCR, the military continued to repatriate Rwandan refugees through the end of the month. Sometimes rapid return is engineered.

The rate of movement has long-lasting effects on refugeehood. Legal scholar Kirsten McConnachie describes the slow growth of refugee camps along the Thai-Burmese border as Karen and Karenni refugees arrived in the 1980s and 1990s. The gradual increase in the number of refugees contributed to the emergence of stable local governance, giving refugees more opportunities for self-reliance despite their inescapable dependence on international humanitarian support. While the camps were settled gradually, outbound resettlement was rapid. Emptying the camps of more than 100,000 refugee residents, including leaders like teachers and medics, posed a challenge for self-governance. In Mae La Oon, one of the nine camps along the border, 40 percent of teachers applied for resettlement to the United States in 2009–2010. Resettlement contributed to a decline in "camp management capacity," which was built over many years of community organizing.[35] The cumulative effects and secondary consequences illustrate how the challenges of mass hosting are not only measured in the number of displaced persons, but accumulate depending on the speed with which people move.

Humanitarian governance

States depend on humanitarian institutions to support and manage refugee populations. The UNHCR is the primary international agency that champions refugees' needs, although 5.7 million Palestinian refugees are excluded from its mandate. The logistics of managing aid and providing protection requires leadership, cooperation, and organizational capacity. The UNHCR operates in 134 countries and partners with more than 900 organizations, including NGOs, government institutions, and other UN agencies.[36] This humanitarian infrastructure strives to assist refugees by securing access to nutritious food, cash-based interventions, suitable housing and shelter in camps, hygienic living spaces including clean water and toilets, and medical care with an emphasis on public health and psychosocial support. The UNHCR also spearheads protection efforts, which include addressing and preventing gender-based violence and violence against children and youth, refugee registration and identity management, and facilitating refugee status determination.

The UNHCR depends on wealthy donors who channel most of their funding into particular earmarks. The majority of the agency's funding comes from states in the Global North. In 2020, the top five donors were the United States, the European Union, Germany, the United Kingdom, and Japan. Southern states and private donors from Southern states also contribute to the UNHCR, with significant resources coming from states in the Gulf Cooperation Council and private donors in Qatar, China, Lebanon, Brazil, and Thailand.[37] The international facets of humanitarianism are not reserved to spreadsheets for UN accountants to peruse; they become part of the daily landscape for many refugees. In Jordan's Za'atari refugee camp, a Syrian refugee may live in a shelter funded by Saudi Arabia, attend a school built with donations from Norway or Bahrain, write articles and short stories for a magazine produced with Japanese funding, and seek medical attention in a field hospital established by France or Morocco. Through humanitarian engagement, the UNHCR becomes a liaison among Southern host states and donor countries.

Figure 6.1: Housing in Jordan's Za'atari refugee camp in 2016 is stamped with the Saudi Arabian national emblem of two swords crossing under a palm tree. Photo by Rawan Arar.

Financial commitments from donor states are not guaranteed. The need for support is consistently greater than annual pledges made to the UNHCR. In 2020, contributions totaled $5.4 billion, leaving 41 percent of needs unmet in a total budget of $9.1 billion.[38] This annual cycle of appeals and pledges ushers state interests into refugee management.

The earmarking of donations reveals the influence of other states in refugee governance. When donors give money to the UNHCR, they usually specify how those funds can be spent by limiting support to a designated region, situation, or theme (softly earmarked), to a specific country (earmarked), or to a specific sector or project in a specific country (tightly earmarked). Figure 6.2 illustrates the percentages of earmarking categories for 2020. While the UNHCR has made appeals for unearmarked funds because they can be better used to "kick-start an emergency response, bolster efforts in underfunded crises, [and] scale up programmes in a coordinated and efficient way," in 2020 only 10 percent of all contributions were unearmarked.[39] The impact of donations on Southern hosts cannot be measured only by sum totals. Restrictions placed on how funding is spent influences who receives aid and what kind of aid they receive.

There are important limitations to humanitarian interventions. As anthropologist Barbara Harrell-Bond explained, "assistance to refugees is conceived of in terms of charity rather than as a means of enabling refugees to enjoy their rights."[40] Comparisons of human rights with humanitarianism emphasize that humanitarianism is fundamentally not about expanding refugees' access to rights, but about "expanding architecture whose purpose is to save lives at risk."[41] The UNHCR has made a strong commitment to non-political intervention, despite the known limitations of this position, because the agency needs states' support to operate. Across the Global South, the UNHCR only operates with the permission of host governments that exercise control over the extent of humanitarian interventions.

At the same time, UN involvement in a country's affairs may erode state sovereignty, especially when that country abdicates basic aspects of governance to international organizations.[42] Scholars have theorized the emergence of a UN "surrogate state" in which the UNHCR takes on "state substitution roles" and UNRWA acts with "phantom sovereignty" in host states.[43] State authority may also be

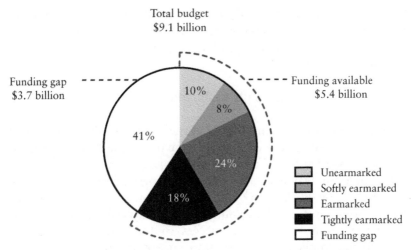

Figure 6.2: Percentage of funds earmarked in UNHCR's 2020 budget.
Source: UNHCR Funding update 2020, https://tinyurl.com/5n95st2h.
Percentages may not add up to 100% due to rounding.

undermined when refugees approach the UN to reverse government decisions. For example, Vietnamese whose claims to refugee status were rejected by Hong Kong authorities in the 1990s could appeal to the UNHCR for a "mandate review," which allowed the UNHCR to grant asylum independent of Hong Kong's Refugee Status Review Board.[44]

Southern hosts sometimes deliberately relinquish authority over refugee governance to benefit from international aid. Political scientist Kelsey Norman describes how officials in Egypt, Morocco, and Turkey practice "strategic indifference," in which governments invite international humanitarian organizations to provide services that benefit refugees and citizens while the state avoids directly managing refugee populations.[45] In other cases, states have deliberately limited UN operations to maintain control over the refugee response. Among states that were on the humanitarian frontlines at the start of the Syrian conflict, Turkey, Lebanon, and Jordan accepted various degrees of UNHCR involvement. Lebanon avoided creating formal refugee camps, which were established in Jordan and Turkey.[46] The UNHCR stopped conducting refugee status determination in Turkey as of 2018, following "the assumption of full responsibility by the

Government of Turkey."[47] Even in cases where UNHCR's humanitarian influence seems comparable, variations in national policies create consequential differences for refugees.

Assessing costs and benefits

Southern-led forms of care often fall outside the traditional humanitarian frames associated with international agencies.[48] In her study of the reception of Syrian refugees in Middle Eastern countries, historical anthropologist Dawn Chatty finds that coethnic and religious ties and the notion of "guests" help explain how and why states were willing to accept such large numbers of refugees.[49] Refugees' needs for safety from violence and access to food, water, and shelter pose urgent challenges for the state and partnering humanitarian organizations. Refugees can affect a state's economic performance and its societal and political stability. States guard their authority to maintain national security and manage demographics, especially regarding the ethnic and religious composition of the population. At the same time, states – and particular sectors of society – can benefit from refugee hosting, because refugees bring new sources of wealth and opportunities to their host countries.[50]

States have often exercised control over refugees through the use of camps, which segregate refugees from members of the host community. In 2021, approximately 6 million refugees (22 percent of UN-recognized refugees) lived in camps.[51] Camps have been used by state officials to keep a conflict from spilling over into the host country and to prevent hosted refugee groups from taking up arms (see Chapter 8).[52] Although humanitarian organizations espouse a commitment to political neutrality, the UNHCR has aided state officials by equipping and training police forces in various host countries. Tanzania negotiated a $1 million security package with UNHCR in 1995. In Kenya's Dadaab camp, police also benefited from training.[53] Refugee women in Ghana's Buduburam refugee camp who fled the Liberian civil war (1989–2003) organized social protests to demand greater rights, but were met with "compassionate authoritarianism" when UNHCR officials worked with the Ghanaian police to maintain ultimate control over the camp.[54]

Inflation and increased competition over employment, affordable housing, and good schools – or the perception that there are fewer opportunities for citizens – can lead to more hostile native reactions.[55] In an effort to generate goodwill from the host society, some international organizations make relief assistance and infrastructural improvements available to members of the local community. Organizations have worked to improve transportation, communication, electricity, water, and access to health care for everyone in a region regardless of their refugee status.[56] Southern officials note that, when refugees and hosts drive the same roads, attend the same schools, and seek medical attention at the same clinics, it is hard to distinguish the state's refugee response from its own development needs. Under the mantle of "resilience," Southern officials have strategically emphasized the effects of refugee reception on host communities, tying together the needs of refugees and hosts, and advocating for this relationship to be recognized when aid is allocated.[57]

Host communities are not uniformly affected by refugee reception. Even mass influxes of refugees can impose strains on one sector while creating new opportunities for others.[58] Economic activity often thrives in and around refugee camps. In some cases, the camps themselves have been strategically placed in locations to expand a state's infrastructure by paving roads and extending access to water and electricity to remote frontier regions. Farmers in many Southern states have benefited from hiring refugees and paying them lower wages, which can also be a detriment to the local labor force, therefore benefiting only a particular sector of the host society. The camp can become a hub for activity that spurs not only an internal market in which refugees buy, sell, and trade goods, but also leads to new partnerships with surrounding areas. Refugee reception has fueled trade in many local economies, which has introduced far-reaching benefits throughout a country. The presence of Congolese refugees in Rwanda, for example, ignited trade between localized economies and the rest of the country.[59] The influx of Burundi, Rwandan, and Congolese refugees in western Tanzania led to a surge in business among refugees and members of the host community.[60] Refugees engage in trade with members of the host community by bartering their UN-supported food rations and other goods. In her study of Vietnamese refugees in Malaysia in the 1970s, historian Jana Lipman describes an "inverted hierarchy" in which refugees become richer than their hosts, and their spending creates inflation. A black market emerged in which refugees were willing to pay three times the market rate for fish, which led to resentment among some locals.[61]

Camps provide opportunities for employment. International workers who are usually from wealthy countries, local humanitarian workers, and refugees may all earn money in exchange for their services to run the camp – albeit on vastly different scales. Many of the most coveted positions in aid agencies go to international staff members. Local residents are often charged with providing refugees with their daily needs and become the liaisons with international organizations. Refugee reception in Jordan created new opportunities for Jordanians who found employment in the humanitarian sector and were favored for their local knowledge.[62]

Refugee reception is likely to benefit some sectors of society while ushering in new challenges for others. Hosting refugees is costly in the sense that displaced people have needs for basic resources including shelter, food, medical care, education, and protection. Concerns for the state emerge from changing demographics and host community hostility toward newcomers whom they may perceive as getting better resources than citizens. On the other hand, refugees bring with them financial and human capital that generates economic activity in and around camps and can have far-reaching effects throughout the host country when refugees live among the native-born population. Humanitarian relief becomes another source of capital. Donor states invest in humanitarian responses, which not only address refugees' basic needs, but also create jobs for some local citizens. Streams of humanitarian revenue, however, disincentivize refugees' economic integration and limit their potential contributions. As Michael Kagan explains, "host governments have reason to keep refugees segregated and highly visible in order to maintain pressure on the international community to continue to support their care and maintenance."[63] Because many Southern host states are vying for humanitarian investments in the national refugee response, government officials often emphasize the costs of refugee hosting over its benefits.

What is the "refugee burden"?

The "refugee burden" is a term that encompasses many of the challenges associated with accepting large numbers of refugees. Some people reject the term for conflating the challenges of hosting with dehumanizing language that portrays refugees simply as problems.[64] Critics rightly point out that framing refugees as a burden neglects their real or potential contributions to their host communities. As captured by the title of a 2017 study called "Boon, Not Burden," refugees can play a constructive role in their host economies, not only through their skills and labor, but also as a magnet for the resources that come with international relief efforts.[65]

Empirical attempts to measure the costs and benefits of refugee hosting do not account for how the language of burden operates among politicians and humanitarian officials. First, it addresses an empirical reality in which states that accept mass influxes of refugees also confront the challenges associated with providing for their basic and long-term needs. Short-term emergencies develop into long-term struggles as humanitarian governance, schooling, housing, health systems, and social and economic sectors are strained for extended periods of time.

Second, officials invoke the "refugee burden" as they maneuver its geopolitics. Efforts to promote "burden sharing" are not intended to *equalize* state responses. Policymakers and world leaders acknowledge that a few Southern states bear most of the weight and will continue to do so. As hot debates unfolded in the headlines over the influx of asylum-seekers in Europe in 2016, UN High Commissioner for Refugees Filippo Grandi stated: "The most important thing is to help Turkey bear the burden, responsibility by taking people ... not in the thousands or tens of thousands but in the hundreds of thousands."[66] Yet Grandi's statement came as EU states were revisiting an agreement negotiated with Turkey a few months earlier. The EU–Turkey deal negotiations aimed to achieve the opposite of what Grandi suggests in the quote above; the deal was premised on *reducing* the number of migrants and asylum-seekers in Europe. The Turkish government pledged to limit the number of asylum-seekers who were traveling through Turkey to reach Europe and to accept the return to Turkey of new irregular migrants who reached Greece. Also included in the deal was a swap that ultimately failed. The EU agreed to resettle one Syrian refugee for every irregular migrant returned to Turkey. The resettlement commitment was capped at 72,000 slots. Between 2016 and 2021, approximately 28,000 Syrian refugees were resettled in the EU from Turkey, fewer than 40 percent of the agreed number.[67] In all, the EU committed to Turkey €6 billion and the promise of easing visa controls on Turks in exchange for its assistance in stemming the flow of migrants and asylum-seekers. There was never any question that Turkey would continue to host millions of refugees on its territory.

Negotiations such as the EU–Turkey deal reveal that new concessions continue to uphold the global distribution of the world's refugees, in which Southern hosting is indispensable. This dynamic helps explain how the challenges and opportunities of mass hosting are intertwined. To maximize leverage, major Southern hosts strive to make their contributions to the global system clear by highlighting the large numbers they host and the costs. Officials know that their refugee hosting exists within a larger system of refugee management. As one Jordanian official lamented in reference to what he understood to be a missed opportunity: "We should have blackmailed the EU like Turkey did."[68] Southern leaders emphasize the challenges of refugee reception to donor state representatives in a larger effort to advocate for Southern state interests. In doing so, Southern officials strengthen appeals for increased aid that are intended to offset the "burden," while also justifying development-related gains including trade concessions or easing visa restrictions for their citizens to travel to Northern states. History records similar negotiations between states of temporary asylum and rich donors, such as when Austria threatened to stop its support for Hungarians fleeing the 1956 revolution unless it received broad material assistance from the West.[69] The EU–Turkey deal is only exceptional in its scale.

In practice, the use of the "refugee burden" does not capture the full array of challenges faced by major host states in the Global South. Instead, it operates as an acknowledgment of the unevenness among major Southern host states and Northern hosts who strive to keep asylum-seekers away.[70]

Making resettlement possible

The global distribution of the world's refugees is not solely an accident of geography. States in the Global North fund refugee hosting in the Global South, and in exchange, Southern states keep most refugees away from the North. In fact, all Northern states combined accept fewer than 1 percent of the world's refugees through a process called resettlement that allows officials to select, vet, and invite refugees to settle on their territory. Legal scholar Mariano-Florentino Cuéllar describes this arrangement among states as the "grand compromise."[71] While Southern states may benefit from Northern financial support, housing large numbers of refugees is challenging.

Acknowledging the challenges associated with a rapid rate of refugee reception helps explain why powerful hosts depend on Southern countries to regulate the global movement of refugees. Southern states do not only contain refugee populations; they provide the space for Northern states to operate their resettlement programs. In 2018, twenty-seven countries ran refugee resettlement programs in partnership with the UNHCR. The following year, the UNHCR submitted applications for 81,671 individuals to resettle, but only 63,726 individuals departed for resettlement.[72] Approximately 0.25 percent of UN-registered refugees, or 4.5 percent of those whom the UNHCR has identified are in need of resettlement, were invited to resettle in Northern states.

Even when powerful hosts agree to accept large numbers of refugees, systematic and manageable reception remains paramount. Between 1980 and 1997, more than 623,000 Vietnamese refugees were resettled through the Orderly Departure Program, which negotiated the global management of Southeast Asian refugees (mostly Vietnamese, but also Cambodians and Laotians) between origin, transit, and resettlement states. The United States received more than

Table 6.1: Top departure countries for resettlement in 2019

Departure country	Persons
Turkey	10,558
Lebanon	8,359
Jordan	5,501
Tanzania	4,030
Egypt	3,995
Uganda	3,288
Rwanda	3,069
Burundi	2,928
Malaysia	2,850
Thailand	2,284
All others	16,301
TOTAL	63,726

Source: UNHCR Projected Global Resettlement Needs 2021. https://reliefweb.int/report/world/unhcr-projected-global-resettlement-needs-2021.

70 percent of refugees resettled through the program.[73] In the case of Vietnamese resettlement, the "country of first asylum" designation is fitting. Resettlement operations depended on regional hosts from which refugees were selected, including Malaysia, the Philippines, Indonesia, Singapore, Thailand, and Hong Kong. Southeast Asian hosts were able to exert pressure on the United States and UNHCR to change their resettlement practices, for example, by speeding up removing refugees from camps. On the other hand, in the early 1980s the Thai government successfully pressured the United States to make resettlement more selective, with the goal of deterring new groups of Indochinese from trying to reach Thailand in the hopes of resettlement. Under Thai pressure, the United States increased screening to prevent the resettlement of people thought to be primarily seeking to better their economic situation.[74]

Resettlement allows Northern states to vet and select refugees, who, as Chapter 7 describes, are generally preferred if they are considered "assimilable."[75] Pre-entry integration – state efforts to promote integration before an immigrant arrives in the territory of their destination – sometimes takes place in Southern host states.[76] For example, the United States funded programs in Filipino camps that hosted approximately 400,000 Indochinese refugees from 1980 to 1994. Many had been transferred from camps in Hong Kong, Malaysia, and Thailand, where there was stronger political pressure to remove them. Starting the integration process in the Philippines was less expensive for the US government. Refugees were taught English and tips for getting by in the United States. Classes taught how to search the want ads for employment, use US measurements such as gallons, cook US foods, and navigate the layout of US kitchens. The courses even addressed how Vietnamese refugees would experience racism in the United States.[77] Placed within a larger historical context, it is clear that the selection of the Philippines as a site of pre-integration was the result of legacies of the US occupation beginning in 1898, which ushered in the widespread use of English in Filipino schools and a massive US military presence that endured after Filipino independence. A cadre of English-speaking Filipino teachers and a government that was a Cold War ally of the United States created the conditions for temporarily hosting and attempting to acculturate US-bound refugees. Then, as now, integration begins for many refugees long before they step off the airplane at LAX.[78]

Figure 6.3: Burmese refugees at Mae La Oon camp in Thailand hoping for resettlement in 2007 view pictures about life in the United States. Photo by IOM/Thierry Falise/LightRocket via Getty Images.

Transit countries can help regulate the rate of reception without becoming mass hosting states. Sociologist Molly Fee describes the experiences of Iranian religious minorities, including Armenian Christians, Baha'is, Jews, Mandaeans, and Zoroastrians, who travel through Vienna as they pursue resettlement in the United States through the Lautenberg Program. Initially enacted to facilitate the resettlement of Jews from the former Soviet Union in 1990, the Lautenberg Program was amended in 2004 to create a pathway for Iranian religious minorities as well. Refugees experience material, emotional, and physical costs as they wait for US resettlement in Vienna – without any guarantees that they will be successful. In this case, the costs of orderly resettlement are shifted from the powerful host state to refugees. As Fee explains:

> [F]or these Iranian refugees, their intermediate stay in Vienna is compulsory, depleting, and symptomatic of their powerlessness. These refugees would never have travelled to Vienna if not for the Lautenberg Program. Humanitarian protection is conditioned on their transit

migration and the idleness that follows, creating impositions of mobility and immobility.[79]

A siloed focus on the security that resettlement provides to refugees neglects the unavoidable challenges of "pre-resettlement" and the cooperation involved in making resettlement possible.[80]

Resettlement allows Southern hosts and resettlement countries to exercise control over refugee communities – not only individuals who will be resettled – and influence national-level politics. Host states may cooperate with the UNHCR to support the resettlement of one group over another, depending on their preferences regarding long-term residence. For example, in cooperation with the Indian government, the UNHCR prioritized the resettlement of refugees who were not considered to be of "Indian origin" with the understanding that the government would consider naturalizing Hindus and Sikhs. Non-"Indian origin" refugees were more likely to be selected for departure. Resettlement in this case was a mechanism for ethnic engineering. From the perspective of the Southern hosts, the "promise of resettlement" may also have an effect on managing refugee populations. Resettlement has a disciplining effect when used as a "carrot" to manage refugees' behaviors. Resettlement applications can take several years. During that time, people hoping to win the refugee lottery are incentivized to keep them from complaining about conditions in their camps, to encourage them to pay their fees and fines to the host country government, and generally to present themselves as "deserving refugees."[81]

Northern deterrence, Southern containment

The practice of containment in the Global South is the result of coordination among states in partnership with humanitarian organizations. Through cooperation with Southern hosts, powerful Northern states work to curtail the movement of potential asylum-seekers even before they embark upon their journeys. These partnerships are not a one-way street. Southern states exercise their authority over the extent to which they are willing to serve as buffer states, and officials make strategic choices regarding how best to leverage their refugee hosting – and refugee containing – capacity.[82]

Mechanisms of "remote control" are written into bilateral agreements between Southern and Northern states. For example, a partnership between Italy and Libya to curtail the movement of irregular migrants, including asylum-seekers, has developed over decades. Libya's proximity to Italy and Malta makes its geographic position an asset to EU officials interested in restricting the movement of those who plan to travel through Libya to seek asylum in Europe. In 2000, Italy and Libya signed an agreement that addressed coordination on issues related to terrorism, organized crime, drug smuggling, and irregular migration. Over the next two decades, bilateral agreements expanded the partnership to include joint patrols in the Mediterranean Sea; the stationing of EU immigration liaisons at Libyan airports and seaports; a Libyan commitment to deport irregular migrants; a readmissions agreement in which Libya agreed to accept people deported from Italy; and the construction of immigration detention facilities funded by Italy in the Libyan cities of Garyan, Sabha, and Kufra. Italian officers trained Libyan forces in immigration control techniques and provided Libya with military vehicles, boats, cameras, night vision scopes, and kits to detect fraudulent documents. Outlined in the 2008 "Treaty of Friendship," the Italian government apologized for the damages that Libyans endured under Italian colonialism and committed to investing $5 billion over twenty-five years to build up Libya's infrastructure. Although the funds were characterized as reparations, hundreds of millions of euros were designated to surveil and police Libya's southern land borders. Beyond material and financial support, such commitments for coordination "opened the door to new relations between Libya and the West."[83] Italy entered into these agreements with the support of the EU, indicating that Brussels was also invested in bolstering the externalization of its borders.

The practice of Northern states deporting unwanted asylum-seekers to third countries in the Global South is not peculiar to Italy. Unlike agreements in which asylum-seekers are sent back to apply for protection in the "first safe country" through which they traveled, a scheme of deterrence employing a system of permanent transfer has emerged in which Northern states deport asylum-seekers to countries they never entered.[84] In 2013, Israel signed what was intended to be a secret agreement with Rwanda and Uganda to deport "infiltrators," a label that was applied to asylum-seekers from Eritrea and Sudan who entered through Israel's southern border with Egypt. The term "infiltrator" originated from a 1954 law targeting Palestinian refugee fighters (*fedayeen*), but its adaptation to securitize the framing of Eritrean and Sudanese asylum-seekers began in 2012.[85] Rwanda and Uganda received deported Eritrean and Sudanese asylum-seekers through what became known as the "Voluntary Departure" policy, although asylum-seekers themselves had little choice in what Israeli activists termed the "Rwanda or prison" policy. When the legality of this policy was adjudicated in the Israeli Supreme Court, government attorneys compared the policy to the EU–Afghanistan deal and the EU–Turkey deal to justify the removal of African asylum-seekers. Israel also called the "Rwanda or prison" policy a Safe Third Country agreement, which, as researcher Shani Bar-Tuvia explains, is misleading, because Rwanda and Uganda are neither homelands nor transit countries for the asylum-seekers who were subjected to transfers. The court rejected this distinction.[86]

Safe third country agreements were first legislated in Denmark in 1986 and adopted by Australia, the United States, and the EU in the decades that followed. The most recent deterrence scheme, which draws on earlier safe third country agreements as a justification, emerged in Denmark in 2021, an example of policy diffusing back to the source. Denmark signed a memorandum of understanding with Rwanda outlining an arrangement similar to Israel's deal, although it is unclear if Danish officials consulted with Israeli officials.[87] Stating that the current asylum system is "unfair and unethical" because it provides incentives for asylum-seekers to take "dangerous journeys" in search of safe haven, the memorandum stated that "Denmark is committed to finding new and sustainable solutions ... that affect countries of origin, transit and destination." Using Rwanda as a territory to which asylum-seekers can be expelled was one of these new solutions.

One state's refugee deterrence measure is another's opportunity to secure financial assistance. Such an arrangement is predicated on deep inequalities between Southern hosts and Northern states trying to evade the non-refoulement norm. Although the incentives outlined in the bilateral agreements between Israel and Rwanda remain confidential, legal scholar Ruvi Ziegler describes the policy as an "aid-for-asylum-seekers scheme," in which Rwanda has been rumored to receive financial and agricultural aid along with weapons and military training.[88] It is also believed that Israel agreed to pay $5,000 for each deported asylum-seeker. However, the Israel–Rwanda deal collapsed in 2018 after Rwandan officials responded to local and international protests.[89] Rwanda's contribution to the global system of refugee management gained new prominence in 2019 when it signed an agreement with the African Union and the UNHCR to receive up to 30,000 African refugees and asylum-seekers – primarily from Eritrea, Somalia, Ethiopia, Sudan, and South Sudan – held in Libyan detention centers. The UNHCR promised to continue to search for other countries that would be willing to host them.

The global connections in the cases described above illustrate competing control measures. The Israeli transfers of asylum-seekers (and potentially the Danish application of the same deportation mechanism) can undermine EU-backed Italian deterrence efforts to use Libya as a buffer between Africa and Europe. As a report entitled "Better a prison in Israel than dying along the way" explains, some Eritrean asylum-seekers who were subjected to deportation from Israel to Rwanda eventually made their way to Europe through the Libya-to-Italy route and were able to secure refugee status in Germany and the Netherlands. In fact, many of those who were deported to Rwanda only stayed there for a few days before migrating onward.[90]

Northern states that would like to use Rwanda as a legitimate place to contain refugees must support the claim that Rwanda is safe for deported asylum-seekers. The Danish-Rwandan agreement describes Rwanda's commitment to "providing life-saving protection" to refugees who have been "trapped in detention in Libya."[91] The critique of Libya's detention centers in the Danish-Rwandan agreement neglects the fact that the EU, of which Denmark is a member, has provided "hundreds of millions of euros to bolster the country's detention infrastructure" and support Libya's Department for Combating Illegal Immigration, which supervises Libya's detention system.[92] The same disassociation appears in a UNHCR press release that thanked the EU for donating $10 million to the Rwandan relocation effort and simultaneously noted: "Around 4,500 refugees and asylum-seekers continue to be held in detention centers in Libya, including people newly detained after being rescued or intercepted at sea by the Libyan Coast Guard."[93] These are siloed presentations of reality. They highlight Rwanda's role in providing a safe haven for refugees who are transiting through Libya while simultaneously neglecting EU-backed Italian efforts to enhance Libya's buffering capabilities. Such a characterization undergirds the EU's use of Libya as a buffer state because Rwanda can be used to alleviate the suffering of people in detention.[94] In turn, Rwanda also enjoys reputational benefits in the post-genocide era as a humanitarian refugee host state.

Variation across Southern states

The Global North/South framing invites scholars to consider the macro inequalities that perpetuate the contemporary refugee system. Colonial histories and their legacies become especially clear through the development of bilateral agreements such as those between Libya and Italy and through migration patterns that follow the "we are here because you were there" route described in Chapter 1. Following the money, the "grand compromise" illustrates that wealthy Northern states pay Southern states to host and contain refugees. On the other hand, dividing the world into only two categories conceals important variation among states.

Table 6.2 suggests an alternative lens through which to conceptualize the role of Southern states within the global system of refugee management. The table takes into consideration two variables: whether a state has signed the 1951 Refugee Convention and the extent of legal recognition of sociological (de facto) refugees. The examples in the table make evident connections between places of origin and hosts that fall outside the scope of standard humanitarian knowledge production. This approach incorporates groups who have fled violence but who are not labeled as refugees by their host states and not categorized as such by the UN. Four countries are included as ideal types of each category: Uganda is a signatory state that hosts more than 1.4 million UN-recognized refugees. Lebanon has not signed the 1951 Refugee Convention but hosts one of the world's highest proportions of refugees to non-refugee residents. Peru is a signatory that hosts fewer than 5,000 UN-recognized refugees, but is home to more than one million "unrecognized" refugees.

Table 6.2: Southern hosts by Refugee Convention status and recognition of sociological refugees

	Recognized refugees	Unrecognized refugees
Signatory	Uganda	Peru
Non-Signatory	Lebanon	Saudi Arabia

Saudi Arabia is neither a signatory nor does it host large numbers of UN-recognized refugees, but the country is home to hundreds of thousands of Syrian nationals who are "unrecognized" refugees. Each of these Southern states has approached refugee reception in a unique way, which not only includes how they label individuals who are fleeing violence and seeking refuge, but also shapes their relationship to the international system of refugee management. While there are important exceptions to these characterizations, the categorization scheme in the table invites readers to reconsider geographic and political groupings among Southern states in a way that provides insight into the relationship between signatory status and other state interests. We focus on variation among Southern states, as opposed to comparisons between the Global North and the Global South.

Uganda: A signatory state that hosts UN-recognized refugees

Uganda became a signatory to the Refugee Convention and Protocol in 1976 and in 2021 was home to 1,429,248 UN-registered refugees, the largest number of refugees in an African state. Uganda is one of fifty-five states that ratified the Organization of African Unity (OAU) Convention, which, as described in Chapter 3, was intended to complement the 1967 Protocol and was tailored to the needs of African states by expanding the refugee definition. South Sudanese refugees make up more than half of Uganda's refugee population (882,058) followed by Congolese refugees (418,369).[95] Others come from Burundi, Somalia, Rwanda, Eritrea, Sudan, and Ethiopia. Many refugees have lived in Uganda for more than three decades. Uganda granted South Sudanese and Congolese refugee status using a prima facie determination, while other refugees underwent individual refugee status determination. Uganda is often lauded as one of the world's most generous hosts, allowing refugees to move freely in the country, work, establish businesses, own property, and access health care and education.[96]

Lebanon: A non-signatory state that hosts UN-recognized refugees

Lebanon is not a signatory to the 1951 Refugee Convention, although it is home to approximately the same number of UN-recognized refugees as Uganda. The two largest refugee groups in Lebanon are Palestinians and Syrians, followed by Iraqis, Sudanese, and

Ethiopians. Despite being one of the world's largest hosts of refugees relative to its population, Lebanese officials have continuously rejected the notion of local integration and restricted refugees' rights. The Lebanese reception of Syrian refugees has been informed by Lebanon's experiences of hosting Palestinian refugees in camps, which were controlled by the Palestine Liberation Organization until its expulsion by Israeli invasion in 1982.[97] This contributed to the government's deliberate "policy inaction," in which it avoided creating official refugee camps for Syrians.[98] Lebanese officials have also taken a firm stance against local integration as a durable solution for Syrian displacement.

Legal scholar Maja Janmyr explores the non-signatory puzzle: why is Lebanon willing to host so many refugees when it has not signed the 1951 Refugee Convention?[99] Janmyr finds that Lebanon legitimizes its resistance to becoming a signatory in order to avoid refugees' permanent settlement. Such a stance has become politically expedient for politicians who tout restrictionist positions to win political favor. Another disincentive stems from Lebanon's reliance on the UNHCR and UNRWA as a "surrogate state," which provides refugees with education, health care, and access to livelihood support. As a non-signatory, Lebanon can also avoid labeling forced migrants as refugees, which supports the principle of "good-neighborliness" among Arab states. This allows Lebanon to avoid the impression that, by recognizing refugees, it is levying accusations of persecution against other Arab states. Finally, Janmyr reports that some Lebanese officials claim that signing the Convention would be redundant because the country has already established its commitment to refugees in other ways.[100]

Peru: A signatory state that hosts unrecognized refugees

Peru signed the Refugee Convention in 1964 and the Protocol in 1983. By the end of 2020, Peru had recognized 4,332 refugees, 60 percent of whom were Venezuelan.[101] In addition to these recognized refugees, Peru also hosted more than 1 million unrecognized forced migrants and asylum-seekers from Venezuela, making it the second largest host of Venezuelans in Latin America. Approximately 84 percent of Venezuelans in Peru held a migratory permit or were asylum-seekers, while the remaining group lived as irregular migrants with fewer protections. In 2017, the Peruvian government created a temporary work/study permit scheme exclusively for Venezuelan citizens that allowed them to stay for up to two years. Yet, as more Venezuelans arrived, the government discontinued the provisional work/study permits and introduced humanitarian visas with far greater restrictions, which resulted in more Venezuelan asylum claims.[102] Venezuelans' experiences in Peru have been shaped by xenophobia and being characterized as criminals.[103] Members of the host community fear that Venezuelans will hurt the economy and take jobs from Peruvians. Looking to Brazil as an example, refugee advocates have called on Peru to apply the 1984 Cartagena Declaration, incorporated into Peruvian law in 2002, which would extend greater protections to Venezuelans as people who have fled "generalized violence, foreign aggression, internal conflicts, massive violation of human rights or other circumstances which have seriously disturbed public order," as described in Chapter 3.

Saudi Arabia: A non-signatory state that hosts unrecognized refugees

Saudi Arabia is part of the Gulf Cooperation Council (GCC), which comprises six countries that are not signatories to the Convention.[104] Saudi Arabia, Kuwait, and Oman – all of which share at least one border with a major refugee producing country – have *not* become major refugee hosts in the traditional sense, which counts UN-recognized refugees and neglects unrecognized refugees. As Turkey, Lebanon, and Jordan hosted millions of Syrian refugees, and while European states confronted the challenges of receiving more than 1 million asylum-seekers, media headlines and humanitarian reports criticized the Gulf region for its lack of commitment to Syrian refugees. An Amnesty International report read that all GCC countries "have pledged 0 resettlement places" to Syrian refugees. Such assessments neglect what political scientist Alexander Betts calls the "refugee regime complex," in which intersecting mobility regimes create opportunities for refugee reception outside of the humanitarian framework.[105]

While Saudi Arabia did not receive Syrian refugees as *refugees*, Saudi officials renewed visitor visas for Syrian nationals. They also continued to accept new Syrian visitors. More than 670,000 Syrian visitors were residing in Saudi Arabia at the end of 2018, a number that closely matches that of UN-registered Syrian refugees in Jordan that same year. The 2019 UNHCR *Global Trends* report, with data that reflects the situation in 2018, lists Jordan among the top ten "major host countries of refugees," while Saudi Arabia is absent.[106] An overemphasis on the 1951 Refugee Convention would conceal Saudi Arabia's approach to Syrian displacement as a non-signatory state. To claim that Saudi Arabia has not received any Syrian refugees because those individuals have not been identified as refugees through a legal assessment is false.[107] This approach to refugee reception is shaped by the political economies of GCC states, which benefit from large numbers of refugee workers, but whose governments want to avoid providing refugees with the extensive rights enumerated in the 1951 Convention.

Which states protect refugees?

Signatory status to the 1951 Refugee Convention cannot be used to identify which states are willing to host refugees. The vast majority of Syrian refugees found safety in neighboring countries. A coalition of host states appears in the Regional Refugee and Resilience Plan (3RP) among five countries: Lebanon, Jordan, Turkey, Egypt, and Iraq. Only Turkey and Egypt are signatories to the Convention.[108] As Table 6.3 shows, the top five non-signatories in 2020 hosted more UN-recognized refugees than the top five signatories. This assessment is complicated by a few factors. First, Turkey maintains the geographic limitation to the 1951 Refugee Convention, which means that the state does not recognize non-European asylum-seekers. This was especially significant at a time when the vast majority of the world's refugees were non-European, and Turkey hosted the largest number of Syrian refugees. Political scientist Lamis Abdelaaty argues that Southern governance includes a balance of "discrimination and delegation" in which state officials choose which refugees to include, who to restrict, and when to delegate refugees' needs to the UN. Abdelaaty demonstrates that Turkish officials differentiate among refugee groups by providing more favorable treatment to some ethnic groups – such as Iraqi Turkmen, Bosnians, and Kosovars – over others, including Syrian and Iraqi Kurds, even after they have been permitted to enter Turkey.[109] Yet recognizing patterns of positive ethnic selection does not explain why Turkey maintains the geographic limitation while also hosting large numbers

Table 6.3: Top Southern hosts of UN-recognized refugees in 2020 categorized by signatory status

Signatories	Non-signatories
Turkey*	Jordan**
3,652,362	2,909,242
Uganda	Gaza and West Bank
1,421,133	2,348,243
Sudan	Pakistan
1,040,308	1,438,955
Iran	Lebanon
800,025	1,345,493
Ethiopia	Bangladesh
782,896	866,534
TOTAL	TOTAL
7,696,724	8,041,933

*Turkey maintains the geographic limitation of the 1951 Refugee Convention.
**Jordan hosts Palestinian refugees registered with UNRWA, most of whom also hold Jordanian citizenship.
Source: UNHCR 2020; UNRWA 2020, https://www.unrwa.org

of non-European refugees, which further reinforces the incongruent relationship between signatory status and refugee hosting.

Second, the separation between refugees' actual access to rights and a state's signatory status further breaks apart when recognizing that the majority of the 2.9 million UN-recognized refugees in Jordan have Jordanian citizenship. Notably, although the majority of Palestinian refugees in Jordan have citizenship rights, thousands of Palestinian Jordanians have had their citizenship arbitrarily revoked since 1998. Finally, general assessments of the world's top hosts are narrowly state-centric, and therefore neglect Palestine, which, since 2012, has been recognized by the UN as a "non-member observer state," which cannot be a party to treaties like the 1951 Convention. By combining UNHCR and UNRWA data, Table 6.3 illustrates that the Palestinian territories of Gaza and the West Bank host more UN-recognized refugees than most of the countries in the world.

Some African states are also included in other political geographies, such as the Arab League, which includes countries on the Asian and African continents. What new insights about the conditions of refugee reception may be gained from reconstituting relevant groupings of states? New patterns among signatory states emerge when comparing across Arab League states in Africa and Asia. The 1992 drafting of the Declaration of Refugees and Displaced Persons in the Arab World was ineffectual and ultimately only endorsed by Egypt.[110] Most African-Arab states are 1951 Convention signatories, while non-African states have not signed. Of all the African-Arab states, which include Algeria, Comoros, Djibouti, Egypt, Libya, Mauritania, Morocco, Sudan, and Tunisia, all but Comoros and Libya are signatories of the 1951 Convention.

A systems approach to displacement allows us to recognize variation across Southern states by exploring how sociological refugees are hosted throughout the Global South regardless of what they are called. By making comparisons among states in the Global South – as opposed to searching exclusively for distinctions between Southern and Northern hosting practices – it becomes clear that signatory status is not an accurate basis for understanding some core aspects of refugee reception. A signatory state can host more than a million "unrecognized" refugees, as the case of Peru demonstrates, while the Palestinian territories that are home to more than 2.3 million UN-recognized refugees are often excluded from UN assessments of top-ten hosts that make claims about all refugees but draw only from UNHCR data. Breaking away from siloed approaches to refugee displacement and reception invites readers to consider the interests of states in the Global South. States like Uganda and Lebanon may benefit from taking part in recognized refugee responses, while states like Saudi Arabia receive refugees as visitors or labor migrants, operating outside the UNHCR-led humanitarian and rights-based framework.

Conclusion

The contemporary system of refugee management depends upon the Global South. Southern states are not only countries of first asylum, they are *countries of final asylum* for most of the world's refugees. A survey of Southern refugee host states reveals that signatory status does not reflect a state's commitment to refugees. All states attempt some degree of controlling immigration across their borders, but the capacity to police state territory and officials' willingness to receive refugees varies across states. Variation also exists within a given state as restrictive practices can be wielded to discriminate among some refugees even while openly welcoming others.[111] Refugees' ethnicity, nationality, and year of displacement may affect their access to resources and protections.

Economic, political, and social considerations influence how Southern state officials make strategic assessments regarding refugee hosting, management, and return. The rate of refugee reception, coupled with the needs of overlapping refugee populations and protracted displacements, affects the cost and benefit calculations that Southern officials confront. Southern states with large influxes of refugees often depend on humanitarian support spearheaded by the UNHCR and/or UNRWA to respond to the needs of refugees. International organizations are tasked with providing refugees access to shelter, food, hygiene, education, and health care, but state officials often maintain final authority over security-related concerns. Because international humanitarian support is not guaranteed, many Southern leaders emphasize the value of their role as refugee hosts to the donor states in the Global North. Southern officials advocate for the indispensability of their refugee hosting capacity, sometimes even competing among one another for increased aid and valuable concessions. Some officials have worked to make their refugee hosting capacity legible through "the numbers game," which includes an exaggerated count of the number of refugees hosted, and rhetoric that they shoulder an unfair share of the "refugee burden." Because of this uneven arrangement between donors and hosts, the favor of Global North states has become central to the affairs of Southern host states.

In practice, Northern states' commitment to liberal rights for recognized asylum-seekers and resettled refugees are predicated upon limiting the number of forced migrants that are allowed to enter their territory.[112] A systems approach shows the role that Southern states play on a global scale as spaces of buffering and containment. Northern states also use Southern states to manage their refugee operations. Northern states depend on Southern states to run resettlement programs, asylum transfer and deportation schemes, pre-entry integration and ethnic selection, and a multitude of deterrence measures. One danger of framing the global system of refugee management as simply a story of Northern and Southern roles, however, runs the risk of collapsing variation across the Global South. By wrestling with diversity across the many Global Souths, we identify connections and feedback mechanisms that often fall outside the scope of legally oriented or humanitarian-focused knowledge production.

7
Powerful Hosts

"The first thing we [Syrians] were looking for was safety. Safety, and then, a place where the kids can have a future. There are a lot of friends who call me from Jordan and ask, 'Is there a way I can get to Canada? It is not for me, for me it is over. But it is just for the future of my kids.' He'll say 'I don't want them to live in a camp, I don't want them to be in a place that is not their country, and they don't have any rights.' Living in a camp is supposed to be temporary. Living in a place where you don't know what tomorrow holds for you, you can't even imagine the future. That's what is difficult. I just want to be in a place where I can sleep well, where I feel comfortable, and where I know my kids are safe."

Wajih Asfour, explaining the search for resettlement

Why do states accept refugees? The question is especially puzzling for powerful states with the capacity to turn away unwanted foreigners. One answer comes from theorists of the nation-state system. Emma Haddad observes that refugees disrupt the neat overlap of a state's national membership and the people in the territory over which it exercises sovereignty. All international migrants break these rings apart, but refugees break them more decisively because they have lost their state membership, de jure or de facto, and cannot fall back on it if potential host states deny admission. In her interpretation: "At the international level the society of states sees that the continued existence of international society as a whole is at risk without some attempt to reterritorialize refugees to a state."[1] This functionalist explanation does not identify the actors who would take concrete measures toward refugees for the abstract goal of upholding the nation-state system.

Governments have many motivations to promote or restrict the entrance of refugees.[2] There is a long continuum of policies that piles up on the restrictive side. No state allows infinite admissions. Many states do not accept any refugees, or only allow tiny numbers. Policies are shaped by expectations of whether there will be further demand to enter if the doors are cracked, perceptions of whether those seeking admission truly meet the refugee definition, whether arrivals are irregular or their movement is controlled, and ideas about whether particular groups have positive or negative characteristics that will benefit the host country. On the positive side of the continuum, some policies actively welcome admission of select groups through resettlement programs. Others only tolerate people who arrive at the border seeking asylum based on their fear of persecution.[3] States that host refugees may not have wanted them to come, but once the refugees have arrived, some states take whatever advantage they can of refugees' presence.

Understanding the motivations of states is urgent given that, while the international refugee regime prohibits refoulement, it does not create an affirmative obligation for states to resettle or host refugees. Policies are shaped by multiple agencies and individuals within states. Political scientist Randall Hansen condemns a tendency for migration scholars to adopt a state autonomy model that views states and politicians as acting outside public opinion, or always leading public opinion in highly manipulative fashion. "Such constructivist interpretations both give anti-migrant publics an undeserved pass and reflect a poor understanding of politics and the political process," he argues.[4] A further complication is that actors do not always have stable interests. They have goals which they hope their refugee policies will advance, but these goals are not necessarily fixed or deeply articulated. Political leaders are often highly reactive and driven by short-term crisis management thinking. These ad hoc reactions interact with more stable interests.[5]

Promoting refugee reception

What motivates states to admit and even seek out particular groups of refugees? The demographic reasons include increasing the size of the working population, using refugees as a tool of settler colonialism, and boosting the numbers of coethnics in a process of nation-state building. Economic rationales include using refugees to grow the human capital of an economy or attract refugees willing to do jobs that the native-born shun. Foreign policy rationales include attempts to increase national security by attracting refugees from international competitors, stabilize the interstate system, help defeated allies, prop up the stability of client states, publicly shame enemies, and brand a country as humanitarian. Demographic, economic, and foreign policy goals interact with domestic lobbying and public opinion. Even in the domestic arena, interest groups often reflect transnational interests that were created by earlier paths of international mobility, including ancestral immigration and "organizational migration" for humanitarian, missionary, and military purposes.[6]

During the age of mercantilism from the sixteenth to eighteenth centuries, the received wisdom was that a larger population created economic and military strength in competition with other powers. One of the reasons that Britain, the Netherlands, and some of the German states accepted large numbers of Huguenots was to increase the size of their populations to better compete against Catholic powers. Relatedly, war can generate demographic losses that refugees fill. The most prominent example is France in the 1920s. Many newcomers were refugees and even legally recognized as such under the Nansen passport system discussed in Chapter 3. After World War I killed 7 percent of the French male population, its government was eager to replace these losses. France accepted Russians, Armenians, and Jews at a time when the doors were closing in many traditional immigrant destinations. The French government even actively recruited Macedonian and Greek refugees living in Bulgaria and Constantinople to resettle in France.[7]

Settler colonialism is based on attracting settlers to displace the indigenous population and establish control. The United States, Canada, and Australia have deeply rooted histories of using immigrants, including refugees, to settle their vast lands. Britain's relative openness to asylum-seekers in the nineteenth century was due to "the very existence of overseas outlets that provided Britain with the physical space for what was fast becoming an expansive national moral commitment," argues historian Caroline Shaw. "Without the ability to offer long-term refuge elsewhere, the British would not have come to advocate refuge as a universal humanitarian norm."[8] Huguenots were especially useful to British and Dutch colonizers because these refugees could be used for colonial projects without sapping the metropoles of their populations. Dutch and British authorities sent 5,000–10,000 Huguenot refugees to their colonies.[9] Other Protestants fleeing persecution in Europe, such as Palatines and Lutherans from Salzburg, were also shipped to the American colonies.[10] Britain welcomed the migration of loyalists fleeing the American Revolution with grants of free land in Canada. The goal was to build up a loyal population that would resist further US invasions and to increase the ratio of anglophones to francophones to solidify British control over territory it had seized from France just a generation earlier.[11]

In the late eighteenth and early nineteenth centuries, Britain sent Black loyalists and slaves emancipated by British antislavery patrols to special colonies in Sierra Leone, where they developed agriculture and commerce in areas where it was difficult to attract British settlers.[12] Authorities in French Mandate Syria in the 1920s resettled Armenians who had fled the Ottoman genocide into ethnic enclaves with the goals of "further fragmenting the ethnoreligious landscape in postwar Syria, preventing the emergence of Communist sympathies among refugees," and creating "Armenian buffer zones in various areas where French control remained tenuous."[13] The British government, together with Theodor Herzl, the father of modern Zionism, developed the Uganda Scheme in the early 1900s to colonize British territories with Jews fleeing Russian pogroms. This "refugee colonialism" program in East Africa never materialized as efforts shifted decisively toward colonizing Palestine and establishing a Jewish state. The establishment and consolidation of Israel was made possible through the mass recruitment and settling of Jewish refugees from the Holocaust and other migrants.[14]

Refugees flee nation-state building that tries to rid itself of ethnic difference through forced assimilation, genocide, or mass expulsion. Recruitment and acceptance of refugees can also be a tool of nation-state building. The flipside of ethnic expulsion is ethnic attraction. Population exchanges, such as the Greek and Turkish 1923 exchanges, sought to align the borders of states with the populations those states claimed to represent.[15] Even after nation-state consolidation, certain groups are often preferred on nationalist or racist grounds. For example, after World War II, the British, French, Canadian, Australian, and US governments showed a preference for Balts whose independent countries had been swallowed, first by Nazi Germany and then the Soviet Union. As US Representative Frank Chelf (D-KY) reported after touring the displaced person camps in Germany, Baltic DPs showed "every sign of having come from good stock and good breeding."[16] Historian Philipp Ther notes that ethnic affinity eased the integration of millions of refugees in contexts as diverse as West Germany and India even if coethnics were not universally welcomed in a sustained way.[17]

Governments sometimes desire refugees with specialized skills. British and Dutch leaders were eager to attract Huguenot artisans and textile workers to improve their economies.[18] After World War II, several countries explicitly sought refugees to help them rebuild. The International Refugee Organization functioned as "an international employment agency," resettling more than a million displaced people between 1947 and 1951 to the United States, Australia, Israel, Canada, Britain, France, and Belgium. The Soviet Union, which insisted on the repatriation of its nationals by force if necessary, charged that DP "camps were being turned into a slave market" where "the capitalists of the beneficiary states" came to "recruit cheap labor."[19] Supporters of the program used less provocative language, but acknowledged its goal of filling the "need for manpower."[20] Skilled workers were more easily resettled, leaving behind people whose education, training, family situation, or physical ability made them less attractive candidates for recruitment.[21] Similar criteria have been part of many resettlement programs around the world.

Resettlement selection tends to favor refugees with certain language and occupational skills.[22] A 2020 survey experiment of local officials in the United States, who, under a Trump-era rule, had the authority to refuse to participate in the US refugee resettlement program, "found strong evidence that US local government officials are more receptive to refugees with a greater potential for a positive economic impact" as measured by their levels of education, English-language skills, and whether they were hypothetically sponsored by a business.[23] A 2016 survey experiment in fifteen European countries found that respondents were much more likely to prefer asylum-seekers who previously worked in high-skilled occupations like medicine and education.[24]

For all the talk of refugees posing a burden on countries that take them in, states have sometimes competed to entice temporary refugee workers. In 1946, Operation Black Diamond brought 32,000 displaced foreigners to the Belgian mines.[25] The cheerfully named Westward Ho! program attracted 82,000 displaced people to work in British mining, textiles, agriculture, and hospitals. Opponents of these schemes claimed that other countries were getting a better deal. An editorial in Britain's *Daily Mirror* fretted that "other countries had taken the cream and left us most of the scum." Refugee workers "must now be rounded up and sent back," the editorial concluded.[26] In France, observers bemoaned the British program's head-start on France's Metropolitan Scheme to recruit 38,000 displaced workers. The British "evidently want to reserve the best for themselves," wrote *Le Monde*. French industrialists grumbled that they were too late to the game, as "what remains available looks to be of bad quality."[27] As with the selection of migrant workers more generally, ideas about who made the right kind of refugee worker were riddled with racist assumptions of employers and policymakers.[28]

The international refugee regime resettles fewer than 1 percent of refugees. The current criteria for selecting them pay less attention to human capital endowments than in the period immediately following World War II. The UNHCR has developed several priority categories. One of the categories is medical need. Refugees are favorably considered under this category on several grounds, including if the "health condition and/or disability presents a significant obstacle to leading a normal life."[29] The logic of these resettlement programs is not driven by an effort to maximize the economic benefit of refugees for the host country.

Table 7.1: Top resettlement reception countries in 2019

Country of resettlement	Persons
United States	21,159
Canada	9,040
United Kingdom	5,774
Sweden	4,984
Germany	4,622
France	4,544
Australia	3,464
Norway	2,351
Netherlands	1,857
Switzerland	990
All others	4,941
TOTAL	63,726

Source: UNHCR Projected Global Resettlement Needs 2021. https://reliefweb.int/report/world/unhcr-projected-global-resettlement-needs-2021.

The United States, Canada, and Australia have hosted the majority of resettled refugees since 1980. In the United States, between 2009 and 2011, refugees were more likely to be employed than native-born Americans. Their use of public benefits fell sharply over time and, although their wages rose, they lagged behind those of the native-born.[30] Compared to other countries, the US resettlement program focuses more intently on a transition to employment within a few months, while other countries tend to take a more holistic integration approach that provides resettled people with housing, education, and health care over a longer period.[31] In Australia, a 2011 study found that people who entered the country with a humanitarian visa – a category that conflates resettled refugees and asylees – had lower labor force participation rates than native-born Australians, but they converged over time, and the second generation had higher participation rates than the native-born.[32] In Canada, resettled refugees catch up economically with other immigrants. Those who enter under private sponsorship fare better than those who receive government assistance, though it is not clear to what extent that is due to the selection of those in the private sponsorship program.[33] It can be difficult to predict which refugees will create extraordinary economic returns for the host population. No one could have forecast in 1956 that András Gróf, a twenty-year-old who fled the Hungarian revolution and barely spoke any English when he was resettled to the United States, would become Andrew Grove, the CEO of the multibillion-dollar Intel corporation and *Time* magazine's "Man of the Year" in 1997.[34]

Studies around the world find that labor migrants have better economic outcomes than refugees, even as refugees can make important economic contributions.[35] The logic of refugee admissions includes, but also extends far beyond, economic considerations.

Foreign policy interests

Immigration lies at the intersection of foreign and domestic policy. Refugee issues lean toward the foreign policy side even more than other forms of migration because of the expressive use of refugee policy in the international arena.[36] Where policymaking is relatively insulated from the public, it is more likely to emphasize foreign policy interests and to be more expansive than public opinion desires. The refugee policymaking process and implementation are often opaque.[37]

For example, the United States resettled more than 5 million refugees from 1945 to 2020, despite most Americans opposing the scale of admissions for the main groups in each period.[38] Congress has made no secret of its instrumental designs in accepting refugees. The 1962 Migration and Refugee Assistance Act gave the President funding to assist refugees "when the President determines that such assistance will contribute to the defense, or to the security, or to the foreign policy interests of the United States."[39] The US Refugee Admissions Program that began in 1980 is much less reliant on the UNHCR than programs in the other major resettlement countries,[40] which likely makes it more responsive to foreign policy uses.

Securitization

Framing refugees as a security issue is typically associated with restriction.[41] Yet securitization can also encourage programs favorable to refugees. "The potential for international conflict is increased when ambiguity exists about the allocation of, and responsibility for, either territory or populations of forced migrants," observes Andrew Shacknove.[42] The international refugee regime and national admissions policies increase the security of the interstate system over the long run. Protection for refugees is an "international public good."[43]

Security concerns can also drive targeted refugee admissions. During the early years of the Cold War in the 1950s, the US Escapee Program promoted defections from Eastern Europe that could provide intelligence information about conditions behind the Iron Curtain. Another explicit goal was to encourage a brain drain from communist countries, particularly the scientific and engineering prowess that supported military industries. Exiles can also be organized to agitate for regime change in their homeland, such as the Cuban exiles whom the US government supported in the failed Bay of Pigs invasion in 1961.

Helping refugees who are defeated allies may derive from a sense of obligation to former comrades in arms or an attempt to assuage the bitterness of defeat by enjoying the psychic rewards of projecting charity.[44] These efforts also send a message of solidarity to current and future allies. A commitment to rescue collaborators is intended to enhance long-term security. Declarations of such a special obligation was critical toward US, Australian, and French resettlements of Southeast Asian refugees after the Vietnam War ended in 1975 – though not for Canada, which did not take part in

Figure 7.1: Hungarian refugees in the US Escapee Program board a plane for the United States at Schwechat Airport, Austria, on January 1, 1957. Photo by Imagno/Getty Images.

the war and yet resettled 60,000 Southeast Asian refugees between 1979 and 1980. In the United States, the parole in 1976 of 11,000 Vietnamese, Cambodians, and Laotians into the country included preferences for those who had "worked closely with US forces on US missions" and certain former employees of the US government.[45]

Since the 1990s, small numbers of "special humanitarian concern" visas were offered to Iraqis and Afghans who had worked for the US military or State Department. The number of visas was tiny, as low as fifty per year, relative to the thousands of local translators and other employees and contractors. Bipartisan political pressure to open more slots in this case were only weakly successful. Backlogs grew. When the US military withdrew from Afghanistan in August 2021, the Taliban quickly took control. US and allied forces evacuated more than 124,000 people, many of whom had worked with the US government, in a chaotic last-minute mobilization.[46] The politics of refugee admissions are determined by multiple colliding interests and feedback loops from the military interventions emphasized by world systems theory.[47]

The ultimate goal of security undergirds the use of refugee policy to prop up the stability of client states and allies, which usually border refugees' countries of origin. In the Middle East, longstanding US financial support for UNRWA's operations to support Palestinian refugees' health care, education, and other services was primarily motivated by an effort to preserve the stability of states hosting Palestinians and to prevent Jordan and Lebanon, the two main hosts, from falling into the communist camp during the Cold War.[48] The United States resettled more than five times as many Iraqis as Afghans between 2001 and 2016. Nicholas Micinski explains that the logic of US foreign policy was driven in large part by a "politics of neighbors" rather than by policy toward the country of origin alone. For example, the United States sought to help Jordan from experiencing the establishment of Iraqi organizations that might carry out cross-border attacks in Iraq, and thus negotiated significant resettlements of Iraqis from Jordan. These fears were themselves feedback from the historical experience of Jordan hosting Palestinian refugees whose armed representatives sought to establish a state within a state, which Jordan's King Hussein repressed in 1970.[49] As Chapter 6 discussed, countries in the Global South that host large numbers of refugees are aware of the security motivations on the part of their patrons and leverage those to gain financial and material support and other advantages.[50] The security–refugee nexus encompasses countries of origin, mass hosting, and rich states in the Global North.

Shaming enemies

One of the classic uses of refugee admissions is to publicly shame a foreign government on the international stage by showing that its own people want to flee from the failures of their home state.[51] This logic guided refugee policy in the West during the Cold War. During the Korean War, the US government provided the UN Korean Reconstruction Agency with financial and logistical support for

Figure 7.2: A US Air Force C-17 transports approximately 823 Afghan citizens from Kabul, Afghanistan, August 15, 2021. Photo courtesy of US Air Force.

the 4 million displaced persons in Korea. Aid to 900,000 people who migrated from North to South Vietnam after their partition in 1954 was also designed to highlight communist deficiencies.[52] Of the 233,436 refugees the United States admitted between 1956 and 1968, all but 925 were from communist countries.[53] Despite the universalistic formulations of the refugee regime, in practice, Western countries gave asylum to people from communist countries and usually rejected the entreaties of citizens of authoritarian allied governments that often had equally poor human rights records.[54]

Often ignored in moralistic accounts pointing out Western hypocrisy during the Cold War is a more general lesson of why this kind of partial selection met Western foreign policy goals in a way that admitting refugees from other countries did not. Communist countries were an exceptionally useful target for using refugee admissions as a foreign policy tool because they met several conditions. The symbolic value of accepting refugees was tied to an issue of existential interest – in this case, a Cold War conflict of nuclear-armed foes who tried to undermine each other short of open warfare that would end in mutual destruction. The global nature of communism made refugee policies favoring individuals from communist countries an efficient means of exercising ideological power. The target was not just one country's government, but a whole competing ideology. The West used asylum for Soviet dancers and dissidents as a propaganda stick to beat the Soviet bear and to indict communism itself in its worldwide contest with capitalist democracies. By contrast, granting sanctuary to shame a government for persecuting a group on ethnic grounds or harassing dissidents does not itself advance a host state's existential goals. Promoting human rights is sometimes a foreign policy goal, but human rights violations are not usually seen as a geopolitical security threat.

The totalitarian nature of communist governments, which restricted exit to forcibly transform their societies, made possible the generous policies in the West for communist asylum-seekers. The attention to interactivity in a systems approach highlights the fact that it is politically easier to open the entrance to refugees when their exits are blocked. As Chapter 5 explained, the numbers of people leaving communist countries were strictly controlled by their governments, and thus manageable from the perspective of destination states. Once the fortifications of the Iron Curtain were completed, the potential numbers of asylees were limited. The symbolic function of shaming could be maintained without a serious financial burden or public backlash. Before the construction of the Berlin Wall and other fortifications between East and West Germany in 1961, 3.5 million East Germans, representing a fifth of the population, reached West

Germany.[55] Between 1961 and 1989, only 5,000 people crossed the Wall. The Orderly Departure Program limited the outflow of Vietnamese beginning in 1979. In Cuba, Castro's government restricted exit beginning in the 1960s and only periodically opened the sea and air gates to Florida. By contrast, many authoritarian governments often want to push out refugees, or at least tolerate their departure. Failed states such as Sudan, Afghanistan, and Somalia are unable to control exit.

The Western desire to reap the propaganda benefits of accepting refugees from communist countries only if their numbers could be kept low was highlighted in a 1979 meeting between US President Jimmy Carter and the de facto Chinese leader Deng Xiaoping. One of the topics on the agenda was a plan for the United States to conditionally grant China most-favored nation trading status. The 1974 Jackson-Vanik Amendment had pressured the USSR to allow the exit of Soviet Jews by denying normal trade relations to any country that restricted emigration. Deng Xiaoping quickly shut down any serious attempt by Washington to advocate for eased Chinese exit controls. As Carter related in his memoir: "Deng informed me that there was no equating China and the Soviet Union on the emigration question, and added, 'If you want me to release 10 million Chinese to come to the United States, I'd be glad to do so.' And, of course, everyone laughed."[56] The discussion moved on to student exchanges and other mundane topics because Deng Xiaoping had pierced the hypocrisy of US preferences to accept only symbolic numbers of communist refugees. Feedback from a Ford-era policy, meant to pressure the USSR on emigration, would distort the Carter administration's stance toward China if Carter pressed the point too hard. In 1996 Congress passed legislation with a provision aimed at China and its one-child policy that expanded the refugee definition to include those forced to undergo an abortion and/or sterilization, or who had been persecuted for resistance to a country's population control methods. Mindful of China's then-population of 1.2 billion, Congress initially limited the number of asylum grants to 1,000 per year.[57]

Generally ignored in Western-dominated accounts of post-World War II refugees are the occasions when Westerners moved to the East. Half-a-million Germans moved from West to East Germany, typically for family reunification or work, rather than because they were fleeing persecution.[58] After the communists lost the Greek civil war in 1949, 100,000 rebels and their families fled to Bulgaria and Albania.

Many were resettled to the USSR, Czechoslovakia, East Germany, Romania, and Poland as a gesture of Eastern Bloc solidarity.[59] While communist countries publicly celebrated these movements at the time for their propaganda value, they have been largely forgotten. Many more people voted with their feet by heading West. The propaganda damage to Western countries of origin was less severe as well, given that exit is considered a liberal right. Fleeing from a capitalist to a communist country was itself an exercise of core liberal values, unlike flight from East to West, which was labeled an act of treason.

International branding

Hosting refugees is a way for states to burnish their international brand. Governments gain positive publicity by showcasing their generosity through resettlements and avoid negative publicity by refraining from forcibly returning refugees. Accepting refugees from competitor states is doubly advantageous, because it highlights that refugees have "voted with their feet" *against* their own country's government and *for* the host.

Accepting refugees is one way for states to signal that they are relaxing a closed immigration policy. For the English-speaking settler societies, resettlement of small numbers of refugees from Asia was a way to telegraph to the world that they were relaxing their racist immigration policies that harmed their Cold War efforts to win the hearts and minds of people in the Third World. Policies in Canada, New Zealand, and the United States that admitted small numbers of Chinese refugees in the 1950s and early 1960s were the precursors to more fundamental shifts that later allowed large-scale Asian immigration.[60] For example, the US 1953 Refugee Relief Act included a quota for 2,000 Chinese refugees and 3,000 other Asian refugees in the Far East.[61] Although Australia did not allow the resettlement of Chinese from the PRC who sheltered in Hong Kong, a similar logic drove its opening toward Indochinese refugees in the 1970s. Accepting nonwhite refugees was a signal that it was ending the White Australia policy on immigration, which had hampered relationships with Asian countries.[62]

Liberal democracies seek soft power in the international arena through refugee admissions. As Australia's immigration minister Michael MacKellar explained in a typical formulation in 1978, "we are locked into international obligations towards refugees ... [and] Australia's credibility and status as a civilized, compassionate nation are under test."[63] States also compete for prestige using refugee resettlements as low-cost international public diplomacy. Canada and New Zealand copied small-scale US programs to resettle Chinese refugees from Hong Kong. Australia copied elements of Canadian refugee status determination procedures for Vietnamese.[64] The sources of a state's policies in the international diffusion of ideas, and one of their target audiences, global public opinion, extend far beyond a host country's borders.

The extent to which refugee policy has a strong humanitarian or human rights component varies over time. In the United States, the administration of President Gerald Ford established the Office of Human Rights and Humanitarianism primarily to resettle Indochinese refugees.[65] Human rights first became a major feature of US foreign and refugee policy in the 1970s under Carter, before a rollback under Reagan in the 1980s.[66] In a statistical analysis of asylum cases between 1983 and 1998, political scientists Marc Rosenblum and Idean Salehyan found that "human rights conditions within source states had no significant effect on US asylum during the 1980s," but "had a large impact on asylum approval rates, beginning in the 1990s."[67] They concluded that normative and instrumental factors predicting US asylum grants were roughly similar.

Domestic groups with transnational ties

The systems approach focuses on ties among and across countries, rather than dynamics exclusively within the domestic sphere. Many domestic interest groups advocating for expansion of refugee hosting grew out of transnational ties, however. In a world of restrictive immigration policy, the advocacy of these groups sometimes targets particular groups of potential refugees. "Partisan humanitarianism" guides much refugee policy in practice, even if the abstract humanitarianism legitimating the refugee regime is universal.[68] Historian Philipp Ther concludes: "Universal humanitarianism is apparently no substitute for the kind of religious, national, and political solidarity that has so greatly eased the hardships of massive flight since the late seventeenth century, and especially in the period following the Second World War."[69]

Interest groups sometimes try to increase admissions of coethnics and coreligionists. In settler societies like the United States, the presence of these groups is itself the product of earlier immigration.

Descendants of immigrants call for more refugee slots for "their" people in a multigenerational feedback mechanism linking earlier labor and refugee migrations with new refugee movements. After World War II, when US immigration law was still guided by national origins quotas, laws targeting people displaced by the war became a battleground over immigration more generally. Groups disadvantaged by the existing quotas inserted preferences, for Greeks and Italians, for example, in ways that had little to do with displacements by World War II. Pressure from the Student Struggle for Soviet Jewry was critical in pushing Congress to enact the Jackson-Vanik amendment to the Trade Act of 1974.[70] In the late 1980s, a coalition of Jewish, evangelical Christian, Ukrainian Catholic, and Ukrainian Orthodox organizations successfully lobbied for the 1990 Lautenberg Amendment. The amendment relaxed the standard of proof of persecution for specific religious minorities in the former Soviet Union by allowing them to demonstrate they were prima facie members of the persecuted category, without necessarily showing an individual fear of persecution.[71] Between 1990 and 2003, 470,000 refugees, representing more than a third of US refugee admissions, entered under the Lautenberg Amendment.[72] These groups were effective because their goals aligned with the consensus interests of the foreign policy establishment, making their effort among the most notable examples of successful ethnic and religious lobbying around US refugee policy.

Many apparently "domestic" groups attempting to expand assistance for refugees have strong ties across borders. In the United States, the primary umbrella organization is Refugee Council USA, which was created in 2000 and includes twenty-nine US-based NGOs. Most have strong transnational ties or form part of international NGOs. They include Amnesty International, the International Rescue Committee, Jesuit Refugee Service, Oxfam, and World Relief. Many of the organizations have a mission derived from religious values that now supersede exclusive advocacy for coreligionists, in keeping with the pattern of increasing secularization identified in Chapter 3. The slogan of HIAS, formerly the Hebrew Immigrant Aid Society founded in 1881, epitomizes this shift best: "Once, we helped refugees because they were Jewish. Today we help refugees because we are Jewish."[73]

Many strong advocates of expanded refugee protection have histories of international mobility, including humanitarian workers, missionaries, diplomats, and soldiers advocating for the resettlement of foreigners who served with them abroad as translators and in other support positions.[74] The experiences of "organizational migrants" who return to their home country with more internationalist commitments is another feedback mechanism linking earlier forms of mobility with refugee policy. A systems approach is attuned to how even domestic interest groups may be part of influential networks spanning countries of refugee origin and hosting.

Asylum and state autonomy

Resettlement and asylum policies follow logics that only partly overlap. Both involve protecting refugees. But resettlement lies outside any obligation in international law and raises questions of burden-sharing. By contrast, states that are party to the 1951 Refugee Convention and/or 1967 Protocol have a legal obligation not to refoule refugees, raising questions of whether and why states comply with international law.[75]

In the EU, many areas of asylum policy have been harmonized since the 1990s, culminating in the Common European Asylum System. Supranational courts, particularly the European Court of Human Rights, have limited the refoulement of asylum-seekers in many member states.[76] Yet member states still retain enough control over asylum policy that de facto procedures and grant rates for the same nationality vary widely across EU member states.[77] For example, in 2016, most major EU destination states granted some form of humanitarian protection to nearly 100 percent of Syrian applicants, but Hungary only recognized 8 percent.[78]

Constitutional laws can create more autonomous spaces for asylum adjudication. Germany's Basic Law, enacted in 1949, enshrined a right to asylum, unique among powerful countries, for people persecuted on political grounds.[79] The result was that Germany became the leading destination for asylum-seekers in Europe, and many were granted asylum despite public disapproval or any realpolitik German foreign policy interest. The fact that the law was constitutionally inscribed made it extremely difficult to change. The right to asylum endured until 1993, when it was removed from the Basic Law following an 8,000 percent increase in asylum applications between 1980 and 1993, the end of the Cold War that had given a strong political impetus for granting asylum to people fleeing communist countries, and the negotiation of the Schengen Agreement, which gave the German government the opportunity to erode asylum protections in the name of bringing German standards in line with those of other European countries.[80]

The extent to which asylum officers or judges have autonomy from the executive when deciding cases shapes their decisions. The greater their autonomy, the less likely they are to simply respond to the executive's foreign policy preferences. Asylum decisions are mediated by the structure of adjudicatory institutions, which vary even among countries that share many legal similarities.[81] In the United States before 1990, adjudicators from the Immigration and Naturalization Service (INS) would conduct interviews with asylum-seekers and then send the file to the State Department for its advisory opinion, which the INS followed 95 percent of the time. A reform in 1990 ended the advisory process and established a corps of asylum officers within the INS, thus weakening the link between foreign policy and asylum decisions.[82] Between 1983 and 1992, asylum applications in the United States were less likely to be granted if the applicant was a national of a country in a US military alliance, and more likely if the country was subject to US sanctions. Between 1993 and 1998, these two effects disappeared, though higher levels of bilateral trade were associated with lower recognition rates.[83] From 1999 to 2004, judges, who have more autonomy than asylum officers, were more likely than the officers to grant asylum to nationals of countries receiving US military aid, which reflects judges' relatively greater autonomy from the executive's foreign policy.[84] The extent to which world systems theory explains asylum recognition rates, as shaped by the host's economic and military interventions abroad, is mediated by the design of the asylum process.

Resettlement bargain

The UNHCR recognizes that resettlement can have a "strategic use" which carries benefits beyond the resettled refugee, to include benefits "to other refugees, the hosting State, other States or the international protection regime in general."[85] As Chapter 6 described, resettlement is one of the main goodies at stake in the "grand compromise" between hosting states in the Global South and the handful of countries of resettlement in the Global North. Powerful states have an incentive to use resettlement and funding so that other states will continue to host the much larger numbers of refugees in the Global South. Resettlement of even small numbers of refugees is a demonstration of solidarity that may encourage mass hosting states to improve their local integration by reducing encampment and dependency and improving access to labor markets, health care, and refugees' freedom of internal movement. The UNHCR prefers multiyear resettlement programs that can be part of iterative inter-actions among states to achieve mutually beneficial goals rather than short-term ad hoc bargains. At a regional level, resettlement is a way to "balance the burdens and responsibilities of receiving and hosting refugee arrivals."[86] The UNHCR warns that granting asylum or other forms of protection should not be contingent on resettlement, and that resettlement should complement rather than substitute other forms of protection.

Critics question the strategic uses of resettlement and argue that positive characterizations are "based more on hope and belief than actual evidence."[87] Yet there are historical examples of resettlements in a powerful country that encourage other states to do the same, even without a negotiated compact. By 1951, the "last million" displaced people in Europe were resettled after the United States ramped up its intake in 1948, followed by Australia, Israel, Canada, and countries in northwestern Europe and Latin America.[88] Many strategic uses of resettlement are not widely known or remembered. For example, the United States has long tried to convince friendly foreign governments to quietly accept small numbers of refugees who were intercepted at sea by US forces and passed the credible fear screening at its naval base in Guantanamo Bay. These governments may accept the requests to curry favor with the United States, but they do so quietly to avoid a backlash from their own restrictionist publics or from the refugee's state of origin.[89] During the administrations of US President Barack Obama and Australian Prime Minister Malcom Turnbull, the two countries agreed that Australia would resettle some Cuban and Central American refugees who had tried to reach the United States, in return for the United States resettling mostly South Asian and Middle Eastern refugees held on Manus Island and Nauru who had hoped to reach Australia. These resettlements were meant to serve the twin state goals of avoiding refoulement, while deterring future asylum-seekers by sending them to the opposite side of the planet from their intended destination.[90]

Resettlement often involves multiple foreign policy goals, including bargains with host countries and international branding. The Refugee Relief Act of 1953, which authorized nearly 200,000 US visas mostly for refugees in Europe and escapees from communist countries, included 2,000 visas for Palestinian refugees in the Middle East who were currently receiving assistance from UNRWA, 3,000 visas for East Asian refugees, and 2,000 visas for ethnic Chinese approved by the nationalist government in Taiwan.[91] Representative Walter H. Judd (R-MN), who had long been a champion of removing discriminatory provisions from US immigration and naturalization law, supported the Palestinian and Asian refugee provisions in the face of opposition from colleagues eager to keep the Eurocentric preferences in the US national-origins immigration quotas. In congressional hearings, Judd argued that if the proposed 1953 refugee bill only gave visas to Europeans, it would harm US Cold War interests by playing into a Soviet narrative that the United States was a "white man's club" that only cared about Europeans.[92] Judd acknowledged that the governments of Arab states hosting Palestinians did not want them to resettle abroad, and insisted on their return to territory that became the state of Israel in 1948, but said the measure was nonetheless an important symbol "for the political necessities of the Cold War." He reassured his more restrictionist colleagues that few Arab or Chinese refugees would actually reach the United States as they would also have to meet the other qualifications in US immigration law.[93] Representative Jacob Javits (R-NY) also supported the measure as an indirect way to support permanent resettlement *in the Middle East*. "You have to have an international plan for resettling the Palestine Arabs in the Arab countries," he explained in a congressional hearing. He had concluded from the experience of displaced persons in Europe that financial contributions were inadequate by themselves and that resettlement by the United States was a way to bring international attention to the issue and promote similar action by other countries. Resettlement of most Palestinians within Arab countries of the Middle East would promote core US foreign policy objectives, in the view of a Senate subcommittee, by avoiding "economic chaos, Communist penetration, or military hostilities." In short, the goal of accepting 2,000 Palestinian refugees was to promote two US foreign policy goals: (1) ducking Soviet charges that the United States was racially discriminatory toward people from the Third World and (2) promoting settlement, rather than return, of Palestinians in the Middle East.[94] Arab governments opposed the US effort but allowed the 2,000 resettlements from Palestinians in Jordan, Lebanon, Kuwait, and Egypt.[95]

One of the best-known examples of a resettlement bargain is the Orderly Departure Program, discussed in Chapter 3. States in the Association of Southeast Asian Nations (ASEAN) agreed to temporarily host Vietnamese refugees on the condition that they would be resettled to the United States, Canada, Australia, France, Germany, and other countries.[96] Because of Britain's control over Hong Kong, it was able to force the colony to receive Vietnamese asylum-seekers as a discretionary exercise in British humanitarian international branding, notwithstanding the fact that when Britain signed the 1951 Refugee Convention, it did so with reservations that excluded Hong Kong from the treaty's application. Historian Hong-kiu Yuen calls this logic "proxy humanitarianism."[97] As Hong Kong moved toward the transfer of its sovereignty to mainland China, the colonial government in 1988 instituted asylum screening for arriving Vietnamese. Hong Kong officials could not be too concerned with the anticommunist functions of accepting Vietnamese refugees when the colony itself would soon return to PRC control. However, forced repatriation of Vietnamese who did not pass the screening was sharply criticized on the international stage. Under pressure from Hong Kong and Southeast Asian states, individual screening for resettlement became part of a new 1989 Comprehensive Plan of Action for Indo-Chinese Refugees, in which all state parties agreed that those who did not pass screening in Southeast Asian countries and Hong Kong would be forcibly repatriated.[98] The status of Vietnamese people held in camps in Hong Kong became the object of high politics spanning the globe. Britain and China supported the closure of the camps before Hong Kong's transfer to China in 1997.

The United States re-established diplomatic relations with Vietnam in 1995. To promote the resolution of the refugee issue, the US government created a new program, the Resettlement Opportunity for Vietnamese Returnees (ROVR), to convince Vietnamese asylum-seekers in other Southeast Asian countries and Hong Kong to return to Vietnam, where they were then eligible to be interviewed by US officers for the resettlement program. In 1996, 6,000 Vietnamese people accepted repatriation from Hong Kong to apply for ROVR. The program eventually was extended to returnees' family members, and 20,000 Vietnamese were admitted into the United States under its provisions.[99] The theoretical point is that US and Hong Kong refugee policies were not just determined by the objective characteristics of individuals seeking sanctuary. Under ROVR, individuals who had escaped from the state that was putatively persecuting them had to openly return to it, and only then apply to resettle in its former wartime enemy. Resettlement policy in the Global North is intimately linked with policies of exit, transit, and hosting in the Global South.

Restricting refugees

Powerful states have many reasons to reduce the number of refugees they accept. Fiscal costs and the perceived economic effects on native-born citizens drive much resistance. Security concerns can also point toward restriction, as do ideologies of racism, ethnocentrism, and xenophobia. Harsh asylum policies aim to deter others who might follow.[100] The goal of restricting the number of refugees overall is sometimes combined with logics promoting the admission of a small select group. Many policy goals around branding are apparently met by allowing in symbolic numbers of refugees. States often try to promote certain groups of refugees while restricting or banning others.

Economic costs

Avoiding the perceived economic costs of hosting refugees is a major goal of most states.[101] These perceived costs may be fiscal; the results of economic competition between refugees and native workers, professionals, and businesses; or due to the very presence of refugees in suppressing economic activity such as tourism.[102] There is a long precedent of fears concerning the economic costs of taking in refugees. In the 1600s, British weavers rioted against Huguenots whom they accused of taking British livelihoods.[103]

As with migration more generally, the economic costs of providing sanctuary to refugees are often framed in a zero-sum way. For example, the "lump of labor fallacy" assumes that a labor market is a given size – a lump of labor – and that any newcomers will necessarily take jobs from natives. Whether refugees substitute or complement the existing labor force, and how much refugees grow an economy by becoming producers and consumers of goods and services, is the subject of controversy among researchers.[104] The issue of aggregate costs versus benefits in a given context cannot be resolved simply by more accurate accounting. An economic cost for one sector of society is an economic benefit for another. If businesses can hire refugees to produce goods more cheaply, the businesses and consumers of those goods benefit. Displaced native workers lose if they are forced into unemployment or lower-wage jobs, but the native workers benefit if they are pushed up the economic ladder into higher-paying jobs. The time scale over which these effects are measured predetermines many conclusions about the economic costs or benefits of refugee flows. Initial arrivals often incur resettlement costs, whereas many of the economic benefits are realized over a longer, even intergenerational, time frame.[105] All these nuances are typically lost in the public debate about refugee policy. Note that the polemical assertions that unemployed refugees are soaking up welfare benefits or stealing jobs contradict each other. Those who are working or forming new businesses are less likely to be able to access public benefits. Regardless of the empirical reality, perceptions of the economic effects of refugee admissions are a major driver of refugee politics.

The charge that providing sanctuary to refugees is too costly has a long history. Many Huguenot refugees in England required temporary assistance from the government and charities. Some natives protested that economic assistance programs favored refugees over Britons.[106] Fundamental changes in the political economy over the past 200 years in both countries of origin and destination have made the welfare issue even more salient to refugee politics. In subsistence societies, it is difficult for most people to move very far on their own. With no surplus, access to credit, or organizations offering support, long-distance travel becomes difficult on a large scale. Exile is only an option for a few hardy souls or an elite that can take their surplus with them. As a result, nineteenth-century exiles in Europe or Latin America tended to be rich, or at least middle class. Their numbers seldom rose above a few thousand in any given country. It was easier for the state to accommodate them as well, given that refugees often arrived with some resources, and states barely provided a social safety net for anyone, including their own citizens. When later waves of exiles in the latter part of the century included a greater proportion of workers, liberal European states grew more hostile.[107] Economic downturns create an especially hostile environment for refugees.

In Western Europe, North America, and Latin America, the crises of the 1930s hardened attitudes toward refugees in potential host countries. Almost all states sharply restricted immigration and made no exception for people fleeing persecution.[108]

Refugee inflows have become more contentious in part because of the growth of welfare systems.[109] Public assistance programs are not themselves a strong pull factor for refugees. Rather, the presence of those programs is a reason why the politics of refugee admission bend toward restriction in countries with strong welfare systems. Most refugees are hosted by states with extremely weak welfare provisions. The ILO measures the percentage of each country's GDP that is spent on social protection programs for their populations. The global median for such programs is 6.9 percent of GDP. The median in the top fifteen countries hosting refugees under the UNHCR mandate is only 2.3 percent. Two countries – France and Germany – are the outliers, respectively spending 31.7 percent and 25 percent of their GDP on social protection. Much more common are hosts like Uganda (2.2 percent) or Sudan (2.3 percent).[110] Several prosperous welfare states have attempted to dissuade refugees and ostensibly make them pay for welfare services by seizing their assets. In January 2016, Switzerland and Denmark announced that arriving refugees would be forced to turn over assets, with some exceptions, worth more than 1,000 Swiss francs (US$1,000) or 10,000 kronor (US$1,455), respectively.[111]

The notion that migrants are trying to gain admission for economic gain under the guise of persecution is as old as the refugee regime. This claim has continued, regardless of the strength of the economy, as massive wage differentials between countries have become structural features of the global economic system. A 2019 survey of adults in twenty-six countries found that 54 percent agreed and 31 percent disagreed with the statement: "Most foreigners who want to get into my country as a refugee really aren't refugees. They just want to come here for economic reasons, or to take advantage of our welfare services." The percentage of those agreeing varied greatly by country, with 60–70 percent agreeing in India, Turkey, South Africa, Russia, Malaysia and Peru; 50–59 percent in Germany, Mexico, Italy, Poland, Belgium, Hungary, Argentina, the UK, France, Saudi Arabia, Sweden, and Serbia; 40–49 percent in South Korea, Chile, Australia, the United States, Canada, Spain, and Brazil; and 37 percent in Japan.[112] Large segments of the public make a realist distinction between refugees and economic migrants (see Chapter 2), and this distinction informs how they assess the costs and obligations of providing refugee protection.

Security concerns

Scholars often assert that refugee policy has become more securitized. Stephen Castles argued in 2003 that "refugees and migrants have been increasingly linked to security concerns since the end of the Cold War."[113] However, worries that refugees pose a security threat, or the pretext of worries, are nothing new. Whether these fears have been empirically justified or not, the idea has driven many policy responses.

One claim is that refugees will undermine security by working on behalf of a foreign entity as spies, fifth columnists, or terrorists. As sketched in Chapter 3, British asylum policy during the French Revolution was based on distinguishing political exiles from foreign agents. During the parliamentary debate of the 1793 Aliens Act that authorized expulsion of foreign agents, Member of Parliament Edmund Burke "brandished a dagger on the Commons floor, dramatizing the danger now in this midst."[114] The following century, Belgian refugees from the German invasion in World War I found sanctuary in the Netherlands, France, and Britain. The 200,000–250,000 Belgians who arrived in Britain during the war represented the greatest refugee influx in British history. British security services were worried that spies for Germany hid among them.[115] Reception policies included both protection and special registration requirements and residence restrictions.[116] When Jews fled Nazi Germany beginning in 1933, French and US officials portrayed them as a security threat.[117]

Security fears were endemic in the displaced persons policy debates after World War II. The US government did not sign the 1951 Refugee Convention because it wanted a free hand to forcibly return refugees later determined to be communists. The powerful Senator Pat McCarran, author of the 1952 Immigration and Naturalization Act, led a sustained effort to show that displaced persons had faked applications and were probably communist "sleepers" acting on behalf of the USSR.[118] A US intelligence officer told a hearing of the Internal Security Subcommittee that, of adults claiming to be refugees reaching West Germany in 1954, 30–40 percent were Soviet sleepers sent to infiltrate the US resettlement program.[119] While the evidence for such claims was thin, they had serious consequences. Two years after the 1953 Act passed with a provision for 214,000 visas, only 21,000 had been issued as intensive security screening bogged down the process. Months of vetting to root out communists and spies continued in the process to resettle Hungarians to the United States after the failed 1956 revolution.[120] Decades later, the Obama and Trump administrations both intensified security vetting of prospective refugees.[121]

Media reports and political entrepreneurs stoke the public's fear of asylum-seekers and foreigners in general. Several prominent incidents involving asylum-seekers, their dependants, or terrorists who entered among people seeking asylum have shaped the public debate in North America and Europe.[122] Yet the chances of being killed by an asylum-seeker in a given year in the United States between 1975 and 2015 was 1 in 2.73 billion. The chances of being killed by a resettled refugee were even lower, at 1 in 3.6 billion. Of the 700,000 asylum-seekers who entered the United States during that period, four killed a total of four people on US soil in terror attacks. Of the 3.3 million refugees who entered, twenty of them committed acts of terror that killed a total of three people in the United States. The annual chance of being murdered by someone born in the United States was 252 times greater than being murdered by foreign-born terrorists who entered under all visa categories combined.[123] An analysis of 170 countries from 1990 to 2015 concluded: "We find no empirical evidence to suggest that increases in the share of immigrants from abroad is significantly correlated with higher rates of terrorism. These results hold for immigrants from both Muslim majority and conflict-torn countries of origin."[124] Despite the statistical evidence, security threats remain a master frame in the public debate about refugee and asylum policy.

Relationships with origin states

There are several historical examples of fears that refugees will create unwanted conflict between powerful host and origin states. President Woodrow Wilson vetoed the 1917 Immigration Act, which provided an exemption from the literacy requirement for people fleeing religious persecution, in part because he said that requiring US officials to make judgments about religious persecution by foreign governments was "a most invidious function" that could generate diplomatic problems. In the late 1930s, French Foreign Minister Georges-Étienne Bonnet, an advocate of appeasement with Nazi Germany, accused antifascist refugees of trying to drag France into a war with Germany. After Herschel Grynszpan, a Polish Jewish refugee, assassinated German diplomat Ernst vom Rath in Paris in 1938, even Radical French newspapers that had been sympathetic to refugees called for a halt to asylum and for restrictions on Jewish asylees.[125]

Offering asylum to nationals of a friendly country can impose diplomatic costs. The Canadian government was leery of granting asylum to Americans evading the draft or deserting the military during the Vietnam War, so it found a legal mechanism to allow them to enter as tourists and then adjust their status to landed immigrants. This legal device enabled the government to avoid granting asylum to the Americans, while at the same time protecting them from punishment back home.[126] By contrast, Sweden granted humanitarian asylum to around 800 US deserters and draft resisters during the war, which caused a major diplomatic rift with the United States. In order to avoid a further diplomatic breakdown, the Swedish government did not grant the Americans formal political refugee status.[127]

Racism, ethnocentrism, and xenophobia

Refugees are subject to many of the same formal and informal criteria for selection as other kinds of immigrants. Racism, the ideology that individuals can be sorted into hierarchically arranged categories based on their perceived ascriptive characteristics and moral capacities, has often been grounds for selecting refugees.[128] More broadly, ethnocentric preferences for and against certain cultural groups, and the perception that some cannot assimilate, is a basis for selection.[129] Xenophobia is a more general aversion to all things foreign. All these ideologies have spread around the world to powerfully shape refugee policy.

Nationalist reactions against refugees are a modern phenomenon. Indeed, one of the reasons that elite exiles from different countries often moved easily around Europe in the nineteenth century is that ruling elites did not consider their ethnic categorization or foreign birth to be particularly obnoxious. Many monarchies did not claim ethnic ties with the population they ruled, or even speak the local language. Aristocrats across the continent were intermarried in a giant kinship network. The rulers of Great Britain, Russia, and Germany during World War I were first cousins. In this context, the presence of elite foreign exiles was not considered a cultural threat, because a hegemonic national culture was not a strong ideal in the first place.[130] Nationalism, by contrast, promotes the fear of ethnic outsiders. Nation-states are based on the ideology that a national people deserves its own state that controls its sovereign territory, a principle that slides easily into other forms of exclusion. Racist, other ethnocentric, and xenophobic ideologies often overlap and are used to justify keeping out refugees.[131]

There is often a tension between the foreign policy goals of refugee programs, which point toward more generous admissions, and bigotry that motivates restrictive policies. Governments sometimes try to quietly accommodate small numbers of asylum-seekers to avoid a negative backlash from their own restrictionist publics, while maintaining their foreign policy goal of avoiding the reputational harm caused by open refoulement. As sketched above and in Chapter 3, foreign policy objectives in many English-speaking settler societies were met by opening a few refugee slots for Chinese who had fled the PRC for Hong Kong in the 1950s, yet immigration policies at the time banned or sharply restricted the immigration of Chinese and other Asians. The frequent solution was to resettle symbolic numbers of refugees, such as the fifty orphans resettled in New Zealand. The advantage of settling orphans was that children seemed less threatening, were more easily socialized into the new society, and generated less pressure for family reunification.[132]

Although US refugee policy by 1953 was on a firm anticommunist footing that lasted through the end of the Cold War, not everyone leaving communist countries was granted expansive admission in the United States. President Reagan cut the number of Indochinese resettled from communist countries in the 1980s and effectively tried to limit asylum grants for Nicaraguans, two acts that might suggest anti-Asian and anti-Latino animus. On the other hand, asylum rates at the same time were also low for Poles, who would be expected to enjoy anticommunist and white European privileges.[133] "Have we created a system of 'global apartheid' designed to exclude people simply because of their ethnicity?" asked Anthony Richmond in 2001 as he reassessed his 1994 argument that refugee and immigration restrictions created such a system.

The answer would seem to be yes and no. Europe and North America appear to be willing to accept "genuine" refugees from Africa and Asia, together with persons of color, or other religions, as long as the need is dire and the numbers are small enough not to be perceived as a threat to the livelihood, or to the traditional ways of life, of the members of the receiving country. At the same time, the fear of overwhelming numbers has led to draconian measures that have a differential impact on those in peril.[134]

Religious bigotry became a clear motivator of refugee and other migration policy during the presidency of Donald Trump. As a presidential candidate, Trump repeatedly called for a Muslim ban. Just a week after taking office in January 2017, he issued Executive Order 13769, which banned visitors, immigrants, and refugees from seven countries whose populations are mostly Muslim – Iran, Iraq, Libya, Somalia, Sudan, Syria, and Yemen. The order also suspended the US refugee resettlement program for 120 days, indefinitely suspended Syrian refugee admissions, and privileged resettlement of religious minorities, which in practice favored Christians over Muslims. After the ban was blocked by a federal court, the Trump administration issued Executive Order 13780, which kept the 120-day suspension of refugee admissions. The Supreme Court allowed the administration to continue its ban on nationals of six countries or refugees unless they had a "bona fide relationship" with a person or entity in the United States. The administration responded with Proclamation 9645, which the Supreme Court upheld in a 5–4 decision. In addition to the temporary restrictions on the US refugee resettlement program that were part of the first two bans, the Trump administration reduced refugee resettlements using several different techniques: reducing the ceiling from 85,000 in 2016 to 18,000 in 2020, ending a small in-country processing program in Central America, increased vetting for all refugee resettlements, and additional vetting for refugees from eleven countries. Under the Trump administration, these screenings were used to sharply reduce the number of refugees from primarily Muslim countries, which comprise nine of the eleven countries on the list of countries that it claims pose a "high risk" to national security.[135]

Islamophobia targeting refugees has also been prominent in many European countries. During the Syrian/European refugee crisis in 2015 and 2016, Slovakian Prime Minister Robert Fico declared that

"Islam has no place in Slovakia," and his interior ministry announced that any Syrian refugees accepted would have to be Christian.[136] Hungarian Prime Minister Viktor Orbán refused to accept its EU refugee resettlement quota because the Syrians in Europe were "Muslim invaders," not refugees.[137] Poland's ruling Law and Justice Party was resolutely opposed to the entrance of Muslims throughout the same period.[138] Many right-wing parties across the continent opposed the admission of Muslim refugees on similar grounds.[139] A conjoint survey experiment in fifteen European countries in 2016 found that "Muslim asylum seekers are about 11 percentage points less likely to be accepted than otherwise similar Christian asylum seekers." The only slight preference for Christian over agnostic asylum-seekers suggested more of an anti-Muslim than a pro-Christian bias.[140] A 2014/15 survey in twenty-one European countries found wide variation across countries in the public's willingness to admit Muslims from another country, ranging from 79 percent in Sweden to 10 percent in Hungary.[141] The percentage of the public preferring that those coming in "be white" ranged from 3 percent in Sweden and Germany to 45 percent in Lithuania, with a median score of 16 percent across the twenty-one countries, compared to 26 percent expressing a religious preference. In Poland, 43 percent of the public agreed the religious background of refugees was important and 22 percent agreed that being white was important.[142]

In the first two weeks of Russia's 2022 war in Ukraine, Poland received 1.7 million refugees, Hungary received 250,000, and Slovakia received 200,000.[143] The reasons for the generous initial reception of Ukrainian refugees by some of the same states that have been hostile to refugees from the Middle East, South Asia, and Africa are overdetermined, particularly in Poland. Ukrainian refugees were fleeing a war launched by a common historic enemy of Poland that continued to pose a military threat; they arrived from a neighboring country and shared a common Slavic pan-ethnicity, Christianity, and whiteness. Refugee policies cannot be reduced to any one factor, but perceptions of racial or religious difference and commonality clearly play a major role in many settings.

Remote control

Aristide Zolberg coined the term "remote border control" to describe the system of issuing visas at consulates abroad and screening passengers at European ports of embarkation.[144] These mechanisms devised in the late nineteenth and early twentieth centuries created for the first time a permanent means of selecting migrants from abroad before they could reach an intended destination overseas. Governments of potential destination countries have designed an increasingly sophisticated architecture of repulsion to keep out the unwanted. Many of these policies were developed before the advent of the international refugee regime. Other structures specifically target people seeking asylum to prevent them from reaching a territory where they can avail themselves of the principle of non-refoulement. Even states that generally observe the principle of non-refoulement try to prevent asylum-seekers from entering spaces where they will be able to enjoy effective legal representation and access to an independent appeals process if their case is first denied. Regardless of the intentions of government actors when particular policies were put into place, the cumulative effect of the architecture of repulsion is to systematically shut down most paths to asylum.[145]

Caging keeps refugees in their countries of origin or camps in other countries. Governments in the Global North work with the UNHCR and the IOM to fund refugee camps and centers for asylum-seekers, usually in countries neighboring conflict zones, and to repatriate refugees who are willing or can be made to return home. Refugee camps are core elements in the architecture of protection as well as repulsion. Caging involves techniques that fall along a continuum of coercion. The softest involves publicity campaigns to convince potential asylum-seekers to stay home. Designating a country of origin as "safe" is another method, which governments used to create a rebuttable presumption that asylum-seekers of particular nationalities are not refugees. The hardest approach to caging is military intervention.

A virtual *dome* over national territories has become a primary technique of mobility control that restricts access via airspace. The anchors of the dome are consulates across the planet where diplomats or their deputies decide whether to issue visas allowing travel to particular destinations. The global visa regime quietly keeps asylum-seekers away from the Global North. Visa requirements often have a "domino effect" as governments race to prevent the entrance of asylum-seekers barred from other countries. Sanctions against airlines that allow passengers to board without visas and provisions that make the airlines responsible for transporting rejected passengers back to the point of embarkation effectively deputize airline check-in agents to prevent asylum-seekers from ever getting on an aircraft. Liaison officers from rich countries are stationed abroad to advise the airlines whom to prohibit from boarding. The United States has even established pre-clearance operations in fifteen foreign airports where passengers must clear US passport control but are not allowed to ask for asylum. States use the international travel regime to control access to the international asylum regime.[146]

Governments of destination countries use their neighbors and transit countries further afield as *buffers* to repel unauthorized migrants, including asylum-seekers. Common techniques include running joint paramilitary patrols and funding and training to enhance control capacity. Legal tools include readmission agreements, in which the buffer states agree to take back rejected asylum-seekers who passed through their territory; "safe third country" designations that deny asylum to applicants who passed through a named buffer country where they will not be persecuted; and pressure on buffer states to criminalize irregular migration. Powerful states link controls on asylum-seekers and irregular migrants in transit countries to other forms of migration. For example, European "Mobility Partnerships" promise states that enact such controls greater ease for their nationals to obtain European member state visas for study or to engage in commerce.[147]

Transit countries are often caught between the competing demands of governments of countries of origin and destination. For example, during World War II, neutral Spain did not want to antagonize powerful countries of origin, namely Nazi Germany, by being too welcoming of refugees, but it acquiesced to the temporary presence of those in rapid transit. Spanish Foreign Minister Francisco Gómez-Jordana y Sousa described the goal of allowing foreigners to pass "through our country as light passes through a glass, leaving no trace." Neither did the Spanish government want to anger destination countries by acting too harshly. The Allies successfully pressured Spain not to return unauthorized refugees fleeing France.[148]

Countries with maritime borders use the sea as a *moat* to keep out the unwanted by intercepting boats carrying passengers without visas. The European, Australian, and US governments have all used the high seas as a zone in which to intercept asylum-seekers and keep them away from their coasts. When the US Coast Guard intercepts people on boats sailing from Caribbean islands, it engages in the most extreme form of externalization of borders. These interceptions control both entry to the United States and exit from Cuba or Haiti to any other country. Such policies turn an island into a cage.

This medieval landscape of domes, buffers, moats, and cages prevents the unwanted from finding refuge. A range of deterrence methods – first designed to keep out Jews fleeing the Nazis in the 1930s and 1940s – has now evolved into a pervasive global system. Remote controls have intensified and spread since the 1980s, with the basic set of techniques in place across North America, Europe, and Australia by the early 2000s. What is new about the system of contemporary remote control is that it involves governments reaching out beyond their territories in extensive, routine collaboration to track and deter millions of individuals and particular groups trying to cross borders. Governments of wealthy countries share with each other ideas about the most effective practices. They use funding, training, and information-sharing to build up the capacity of other states to control transit and exit. Each element in the system interlocks with others. For example, visa policies are only effective at keeping the unwanted away if transportation companies act on behalf of states to check documents. Maritime interceptions are only effective at deterrence if intercepted travelers are taken to spaces where they have fewer rights than if they had reached destination countries.

Conclusion

Refugee protection by powerful states is a tale of restriction, with exceptions carved out for particular groups and individuals who are wanted or at least tolerated. The sources of these policies span economics, demographics, foreign policy, and ideologies of nationalism, humanitarianism, and human rights. Foreign policy factors and the advocacy of domestic groups that have strong transnational ties – often the legacy of earlier forms of cross-border mobility and immigration – tend to be the strongest drivers when powerful states accept refugees. Internal factors tend to be more important for explaining restriction, though here again motivations span many domains.

Policies that favor refugees often treat them as immigrants desired for what they can accomplish for the host country, rather than as a response to their need for protection. Demographic and economic rationales fit into this umbrella category. Refugees have been used to boost the size of the national population, particularly after wartime losses, or as tools of settler colonialism. Nation-building projects are also more likely to bring in refugees who are coethnics, or at least groups thought to be assimilable to the dominant ethnicity.[149] Economic motivations for attracting refugees as immigrants include targeting groups based on their perceived characteristics to improve the human capital of the host economy or to increase the supply of the labor force willing to do jobs that native-born workers avoid. Economic rationales alone do not guide refugee resettlement policies in the main host countries, however, which have other immigration policies that are more efficient at maximizing strictly economic returns.

States have many foreign policy rationales for accepting refugees and promoting certain groups. Several rationales are driven by security. States attempt to stabilize the international system by avoiding large populations of stateless people who are not anchored in a state that owes them protection and takes responsibility for them. Particular kinds of refugees are accepted and often enticed with the goal of publicly shaming enemies, bleeding them of human capital, and gaining information from defectors. Accepting refugees is also a way to help friendly states by reducing their refugee populations and to help defeated allies. Refugee resettlement and asylum can serve softer goals as well, such as branding a country as humanitarian and a supporter of human rights. During the Cold War, Western countries typically preferred refugees fleeing communist countries for all these reasons, plus the fact that restrictions on exit by leading communist countries made it possible to enjoy these foreign policy goals at a minimal cost. Resettlement policy is intimately linked with policies of exit and hosting in communist states and in the Global South.

Asylum policy involves greater autonomy from the executive's foreign policy preferences, which are expressed in refugee resettlement programs, but the degree of autonomy is mediated by asylum institutions in each country. Demographic, economic, and foreign policy goals also interact with domestic interests. Even in the domestic arena, interest groups often reflect transnational ties that are inheritances of earlier paths of mobility such as descent from previous refugees and labor immigrants, or personal experiences of international mobility through military, missionary, or humanitarian organizations.

Views about refugees vary across time and place and by the particular kind of refugee, but nowhere does public opinion in support of hosting come anywhere near the number of refugees seeking sanctuary. Drivers of restriction are dominated by economic, security, and cultural concerns regardless of whether they are empirically accurate. On the economic side, restrictionists fear refugees for the same reasons they fear immigrants more generally – that people posing as refugees or even people who really are fleeing persecution and violence will take jobs from natives, accept lower wages, and impose fiscal costs in the form of integration and welfare services. Fiscal fears are nothing new, but they have increased with the rise of welfare states. On a security level, restrictionists are concerned that refugees may be terrorists or fifth columnists serving the interests of foreign enemies. More broadly, states are sometimes worried that hosting refugees will antagonize relations with the governments of their countries of origin, given that granting asylum is often understood as impugning the government of the asylee's country of origin. Security and economic issues are wrapped up tightly with racism, ethnocentrism, and xenophobia. Ethnocentrism became a greater factor with the rise of the nation-state, based on ideologies of national homogenization. Even in countries that sociologically are multicultural, or that have multiculturalist political programs to accommodate difference for citizens within the country, fears that refugees will create cultural change are rife.

Beyond refugee resettlement and asylum policy, one of the main ways that powerful states attempt to control the number and type of people seeking sanctuary is through remote control. States filter travelers and exclude the unwanted before they reach the state's territory. The metaphor of an architecture of repulsion renders visible a system of cages, domes, buffers, and moats patrolled by state agents and their proxies. By discussing these structures as a system of control, it is possible to observe how each of them is linked to another. When caging fails, visa policy and carrier sanctions make it difficult to board an aircraft and fly to the destination. Asylum-seekers then try to cross the moat, but maritime interceptions push them back into gulag spaces like Guantanamo, cages like Nauru, or coastal buffer states like Libya. When the system is viewed in its totality, it becomes clear why so many asylum-seekers do not simply get in line to wait their legal turn. For most, there is no line. States deploying their power beyond their territorial borders into countries of origin and transit and onto the high seas have deliberately blocked most paths for refugees so as only to allow in the trickle that they view as serving state interests.

8

Transnational Connections and Homeland Ties

"Every year I host a live video on my Facebook page. One video has a couple thousand views. People keep emailing me and asking me questions. And, I want to help as much as I can."

Wajih Asfour, discussing how he stays in touch with the diaspora

Wajih Asfour described being glued to the television early in 2013 as he and his family waited in Jordan's Za'atari camp for any indication that it would be safe to return home to Syria. Televised news reports conflicted with what Wajih's brother described was happening in their neighborhood over WhatsApp messages. The Asfours relied on their phones, but access to the internet was unreliable on both sides of the border. Wajih could usually get a stronger signal if he walked to the outskirts of the camp. He censored some of the sensitive topics he would have otherwise wanted to discuss with his family, especially regarding his brother's activities in the revolution and his father's experiences in ISIS-controlled territory. Any suggestion that Wajih was associated with violent actors – as defined by Jordanian authorities – could have put him at risk of refoulement. He began to speak freely about such issues in interviews after being resettled to Canada. Once established, he sent remittances to Jordan to support his sisters' education and began working with Canadians in his community to resettle one of his brothers. Displaced across borders and around the world, the Asfour family used communication technologies to maneuver around barriers in Syria, Jordan, and Canada.

Refugees stay in touch through electronic communication, send remittances, and engage in political action from abroad. The people who make up their networks extend far beyond those legally defined as refugees. As Jeff Crisp writes, "A Sudanese asylum-seeker in the UK ... may well be part of an extended social network that incorporates Sudanese migrant workers in Saudi Arabia, illegal Sudanese immigrants in the Netherlands, US citizens of Sudanese origin, other Sudanese who are present in the UK, as well as Sudanese in their own country."[1]

The ties linking the nodes across the diaspora belie the idea that different countries each have their own discrete refugee solutions.[2] Such dynamic cross-border connections are overlooked by siloed approaches that anchor displaced populations to bounded territories. For example, the law separates people who are displaced inside their home country from refugees who traverse state borders. By legal definition, refugees must be outside their country of nationality, or, if stateless, outside the country where they normally live.[3] Humanitarian organizations also maintain such separations. In the UNHCR's "durable solutions" framework, refugees make a permanent new life outside their country of origin through local integration or resettlement, or they voluntarily return home.[4] While durable solutions can work for some refugees, they are ultimately state-centric solutions to displacement. Researcher Katy Long explains that displacement is not a physical problem.[5] Physical dislocation can be fixed by moving, but the political barriers to entry and residence are far more burdensome. As anthropologist Nicholas Van Hear notes, cross-border ties are "arguably a 'solution' favored by the displaced, since it is the practice often pursued by them in everyday life."[6] An examination of the refugee system demonstrates how refugees employ transnational connections across the diaspora to try to circumvent restrictions imposed by states and global institutions.

This chapter shows that refugees are like many other international migrants in that their social networks can help them gain access to resources, learn new information, and navigate structural constraints on movement and societal inclusion. Yet unlike other migrants, the violent push factors that compelled refugees to leave shape their experiences and network connections in a distinctive way.[7] Violent conflict in the homeland shapes the needs and resources across refugees' networks, influences how refugees participate in long-distance political engagement, and raises the stakes for repatriation. For refugees who organize in the diaspora, the interests of their host governments can play a role in facilitating or impeding transborder action. Some refugees are caught up in the conflicts that catalyzed their displacement. Their cross-border connections are usually peaceful, but they can also involve violence. Refugees' networks are specifically influenced by return to conflict and post-conflict spaces. Their networks are marked by conflict even after the violence has subsided. Return is not always a one-way ticket. Refugees sometimes go home for short periods, or repatriation can be followed by subsequent moves, including circular mobility in which refugees split time between the homeland and one or more other countries. The term "homeland" denotes refugees' country of origin, yet some people – especially those born in exile – have never visited the place they consider to be their homeland, which further reflects the varied and dynamic connections that displaced people have across multiple territories.

The study of refugees' network ties can be situated within the broader literature on transnationalism, which has focused primarily on the cross-border connections of labor migrants. The term "transnationalism" denotes a broad, and sometimes conflicting, set of phenomena, which include the *singular* identification with a "nation" despite physical absence from the homeland and the *dual nationalism* of political identification with two distinct "nations."[8] Whether refugees or other migrants engage in cross-border nationalism, dual nationalism, have connections across multiple countries, and/ or are apathetic to any form of nationalism, varies widely. These distinctions matter because only some forms of political engagement attempt to act in different homes, and the ability of migrants to engage in multiple places at once is shaped by policies and politics in countries of origin and destination. Cross-border engagements also vary in the extent to which they are oriented toward national "imagined communities"[9] or smaller scales, such as families or particular hometowns. The forms of refugee organizing change along these scales, from national associations of exiles, to hometown associations, to kinship networks.[10]

Expanding the scope of analysis to include refugee migrations, humanitarian organizations and policies, and the impact of violence on political action promises to create a much better understanding of the conditions for, and consequences of, transborder ties. This chapter conceptualizes refugees' transborder connections, drawing from, and expanding beyond, the canonical works on immigrant transnationalism. We review the types of ties that refugees make and the conditions under which they rely on these kinds of engagements to circumvent restrictions placed on their movement and incorporation. We illustrate how networks shape refugees' return, as well as how connections to conflict and post-conflict societies affect the networks.

Types of ties

Refugees' lives and life chances are shaped by numerous types of ties. Electronic communication can typically find ways around state controls to allow refugees to stay in touch with their contacts back home. It is also possible to send remittances using multiple mechanisms outside a formal banking system subject to standard state controls, such as the *hawala* method. Political action across borders, particularly if it involves violence, is more contingent on conditions in both countries of origin and hosting.

Communication

Like other international migrants, refugees maintain contact across borders using many means of communication, including phone and video calls, text messages, and social media. Electronic communication has created qualitatively different experiences of transborder connectivity than was achieved by the early twentieth-century transatlantic exchange of letters tying peasants in Poland to their families in Chicago.[11] Mobile phone and internet technologies have increased the frequency of interactions, allowed them to become instantaneous, and have also lowered their cost, even if they are not universally accessible. According to a 2016 UNHCR report, "refugees are 50 per cent less likely than the general population to have an internet-enabled phone, and 29 per cent of refugee households have no phone at all."[12] Among refugee populations, those who live in urban areas are more likely to have high-speed mobile coverage when compared to refugees in rural areas. Despite these inequalities, scholars have found that "smartphones are lifelines [for refugees], as important as water and food."[13]

Refugees use smartphones for much more than calls. The ability to consult maps, translate foreign languages, transfer money, check weather conditions to determine whether passage is safe, share exact coordinates, and access legal, medical, and social services makes smartphones an entirely new instrument for connection. With the internet at their fingertips, refugees can draw on "weak ties" to reach a vast network.[14] Smartphones can make refugees less reliant on smugglers, especially when others in their networks share information about routes to follow. Asylum-seekers traveling to Europe in 2015 and 2016 turned to social media to fact-check rumors and track changing state policies.[15] "Facebook is our Homeland. It opens the sky they close in our faces at the frontiers," writes Syrian poet Maram Al-Masri.[16] When messaging applications like Facebook Messenger do not work, refugees turn to other applications like WhatsApp or Viber, making digital proficiency a potentially lifesaving skill.[17]

The practicalities of keeping smartphones usable creates new problems to be managed. Finding a place to charge a phone, purchasing SIM cards, keeping the device dry, searching for a public Wi-Fi connection, and strategically deleting applications when running out of memory are all considerations that refugees confront

Figure 8.1: Refugees charge their mobile phone batteries in a camp near the Greek–Macedonian border outside of Idomeni, Greece, in 2016. Photo by Kay Nietfeld/picture-alliance/dpa/AP Images.

because these wireless devices tether refugees to the people and resources they need.

Infinite possibilities for connection have also introduced new risks. Smartphones can place state surveillance in refugees' pockets. Public Wi-Fi and social media can be used to identify and track where refugees have been, which can make them especially vulnerable at border crossings.[18] Governments justify policies to search refugees' smartphones by claiming that social media reveals refugees' identities in the absence of official documents, allowing authorities to evaluate if they believe refugees to be a security threat.[19] There have been several reports of border guards coercing refugees into giving them access to the information on their smartphone. "When I got to the border in Turkey, the guard took my phone and asked me for my Facebook password. At first I wouldn't give it to him because I was so scared, but they threw me in prison for 15 days and they beat me, they stole my phone and I was stuck," one refugee explained.[20]

Monitoring can go both ways. While detained with other asylum-seekers on Manus Island in Papua New Guinea, Behrouz Boochani typed messages on a smuggled smartphone and shot video that became award-winning autobiographical accounts of Australia's offshore detention program and mistreatment of refugees.[21] Refugees have also used smartphones to provide evidence of the abuses they have suffered. A smartphone is a digital archive, simultaneously storing a family's photo album and photographic evidence of torture that can be used to substantiate asylum claims.

Remittances

Refugees send money back home, just like economic migrants. Remittances are used to support family members in need and the migration of family members left behind. Collectively, remittances can be used to fund conflict or post-conflict reconstruction. In some settings, refugees are more likely to remit than migrants from countries that are not in conflict, often contributing significantly to the home country's economy.[22] For example, more than 35 percent of Somalia's GDP in 2020 was the result of personal remittances.[23] In the context of forced displacement, "remittances are more likely to be a consequence rather than a driver of migration."[24] A remitter is likely to send money to multiple countries because refugee families are often scattered across several locations. Anthropologist Stephanie

Riak Akuei describes the experiences of a man who was resettled to
California and, within two years, became responsible for more than
twenty family members living in Egypt, Kenya, Libya, Uganda, and
Sudan.[25] Remittances may also flow from those who stay in the home
country to family members who were forced to flee to neighboring
states.[26]

The ability of refugees to remit is shaped by policies in countries
of origin and hosting. For example, Cubans in the United States have
often faced limits on remittances to Cuba because of US sanctions.[27]
Particularly since the 2001 Al-Qaeda terrorist attacks, many governments have introduced restrictions on remittances, such as strict
identification requirements for remitters, which are disproportionately difficult for refugees to meet when sending money to "high-risk"
countries that include major countries of refugee origin such as Syria,
Iraq, Sri Lanka, and Yemen. The shutdown of the *hawilaad* informal
transfer system around the world in November 2001 cut off a major
source of remittances for Somalis. "The refugees in the Dadaab
camps in Kenya are among those who will end up paying the highest
price of the measures taken against the *hawilaad* in the name of the
'war against terrorism',," warned one report.[28] There are ways of
dealing with money transfers despite these controls, but the ability to
remit easily reflects conditions at all points in a refugee system.

Family reunification

Once refugees are established, they often try to reunite with other
family members who stayed behind in the country of origin or in
other host countries. Family reunification policies renew ties between
countries of origin, hosting, and resettlement. When a conflict has
ended, what began as a refugee flow can transform into family chain
migration more typical of other types of international migration.
For example, while the vast majority of the first Vietnamese to move
to the United States, beginning in the 1970s, went as refugees, by
the 1990s, new arrivals were arriving through regular immigration
channels. People who arrived earlier had become US permanent
residents or citizens and were able to sponsor, depending on their
status, their spouses, children, siblings, and parents.

Canada's private sponsorship program has created a path toward
family reunification. As described in Chapter 4, a group of five
Canadian citizens or residents can sponsor a refugee for resettlement.

Refugees who have already been resettled to Canada can mobilize networks within their host community to sponsor members of their family. Refugee resettlement programs thus interact with other immigration programs over time to bring families together. Yet a resettled refugee cannot depend solely on formal programs to bring over family members. Resettlement programs include restrictions on which kinds of family members are eligible. National resettlement operations prioritize selection from some countries in the Global South over others. In its Projected Global Resettlement Needs report for 2021, the UNHCR identified a focus on the Central Mediterranean Priority Situation, expressing an interest in using resettlement to decrease "pull factors towards Libya and Niger."[29] Refugees' hopes of reconnecting with family are more likely to come to fruition if they reflect the priorities of resettlement operations.

Who counts as family? Refugees' notions of family can differ from those of humanitarian and state gatekeepers who make choices about who qualifies for resettlement as a family unit.[30] In 2008, the US government piloted a program in Kenya to test the DNA of almost 500 refugees, mainly from Ethiopia and Somalia, in order to assess the credibility of their claim of being a family unit. After more than 80 percent of these families "failed" the test, this family reunification program was suspended for four years. Families who failed the test included those with adopted children, including nephews and nieces who joined their extended families after losing their parents in the fighting in their home countries.[31]

Political agitation

People who have fled or been expelled from their home countries for their political opinions often continue their agitation from abroad. In cases where refugees have a path to political integration in the host society, they often play an important role in lobbying and advocating on behalf of others still trying to leave their countries of origin. For example, the activism of Vietnamese in the United States raised funds to rescue Vietnamese refugees at sea through Boat People SOS. Refugee organizations also lobbied for more visas.[32] Cubans in the United States have effectively used their concentration in the key electoral swing state of Florida to advocate on behalf of Cubans trying to reach Florida by sea and to create special visas for Cuban political refugees.[33]

Exiles have long organized for political changes in their countries of origin. Nineteenth-century examples include Karl Marx, who wrote his revolutionary treatises while in exile in London; Benito Juárez, who drafted the Plan de Ayutla while working in New Orleans in the 1850s before returning to Mexico to become president; and José Martí, who promoted Cuban independence from Spain while living in New York in the 1890s. Twentieth-century examples include Sun Yat-sen, the first president of the Chinese republic (1911–12), who learned that the revolution against the Qing dynasty had broken out while he was traveling through Denver on a US fundraising trip. Vladimir Lenin promoted revolution in Russia from his exile in Germany, the UK, and Switzerland. Sanctuary abroad allowed these and many other leaders the freedom to write, organize, raise money, and gain diplomatic support for their initiatives back home.

Refugees can also engage homeland politics through violence, often with the support of the host. Tiring of its public assistance to French exiles in the late nineteenth century, Britain called on refugees to join its ill-fated invasion of France in 1795 in support of France's counterrevolutionaries. French revolutionary forces at the battle of Quiberon captured, court-martialed, and executed 690 French exiles who accompanied British forces. The reaction in Britain was to become more accommodating toward French exiles and offer them protection rather than forcing them to fight or pay their own way. A failed policy of forcing them to return to fight promoted more generous conditions of asylum.[34]

In February 1850, in the wake of the failed Hungarian Revolution to gain independence from the Austrian Empire, the US Senate passed a resolution requesting that President Zachary Taylor ask the Ottoman government to release Hungarian leader Lajos Kossuth and his companions, who were in exile in the Ottoman Empire, and offer them "the United States as an asylum and home."[35] On March 11, 1850, the US ambassador requested that Sultan Abdulmejid allow "the Hungarian refugees" to leave for "a secure asylum in the United States."[36] The sultan agreed to their departure a year later, and on September 1, 1851, Kossuth and his companions in the port of Smyrna boarded a US Navy warship, the USS *Mississippi*, to steam for Britain and then on to the United States. Kossuth toured the United States for seven months, raising money to buy munitions, attempting to form an army to return with him to Europe, and meeting with the US president and Congress in a failed effort to obtain their support for Hungarian independence.[37] He returned to Europe in July 1852 after seven months of US asylum.

Powerful states have supported refugee fighters up to the present. The Soviet invasion of Afghanistan in 1979 created one of the world's largest refugee populations as more than 4 million people fled to Pakistan and 3 million to Iran.[38] Afghan *mujahidin* and volunteers from around the world operated from camps in Pakistan to eventually drive out the Soviet army in 1989. The *mujahidin* were part of a truly global system of conflict. The Pakistani government provided Afghan noncombatants and the *mujahedin* with sanctuary and support. The United States sent weapons, training, and funding to use the *mujahidin* as proxies in the US Cold War struggle against the Soviet Union. The Saudi government provided funding in an attempt to undermine the atheistic Soviet occupation, spread its own version of Islam, and curry favor with a US government that was Saudi Arabia's ultimate security guarantor in the Gulf region.[39] Among the many exiles to return to Afghanistan from Pakistan was Hamid Karzai, who became president of Afghanistan in 2001 following his collaboration with US forces to dislodge Al-Qaeda, led by Saudi national and former *mujahid* Osama bin Laden, and the Taliban following the September 11 terror attacks. While few refugees are armed fighters, historically they have included some leading actors in world politics. Treatments of refugees that exclusively represent them as victims ignore this phenomenon.

Conditions for transborder action

Refugees' connections to their communities and the larger diaspora are shaped by conditions in the homeland and across host countries. As this section shows, network ties tend to be stronger for those who have higher levels of human, financial, and social capital.[40] Violence influences how states facilitate or impede refugees' transborder connections. Legal precarity in host states affects refugees' residential security. That precarity then influences how refugees engage others in their network. Host governments may use refugees to pursue foreign policy interests or discourage transborder connections. The high diplomatic and security stakes imply that the host country context may be even more important in shaping room to maneuver for refugees than other international migrants.[41]

The diaspora is influenced by social pressure to remit or provide support for people back home. During Eritrea's successful war of independence from Ethiopia (1961–91), the Eritrean People's Liberation Front opened offices in the major host countries of the Eritrean diaspora to organize them politically and collect funds. The Front asked Eritreans to pay a 2 percent income tax to fund the struggle. Researchers found compliance to be high. While the tax was theoretically voluntary, social pressure to pay was strong and effective. At an Eritrean community center in Berlin, a list of those who had made extra contributions was publicly posted, which served as a positive incentive for donors to gain prestige, and as a negative incentive to shame those whose names were not on the list.[42]

The policies of the homeland state can depress or catalyze transborder engagement. Since independence, the Eritrean government has attempted to impose further levies on Eritreans abroad during periods of resumed conflict with Ethiopia.[43] However, it has enjoyed less fundraising success than it did during the independence struggle. Since 2002, hundreds of thousands of Eritreans have left their country, particularly men facing decades of forced conscription.[44] Homeland governments' ambivalence or hostility toward refugees can depress refugees' willingness to rebuild connections.[45]

The ability of refugees to organize cross-state activities is shaped by the integration policies of the host state as well. Integration in the host enables more intense homeland ties, at least in the short run, because refugees are secure enough in their own location to have the wherewithal to engage in transborder politics. On the other hand, a study of Bosnians in the UK, who had a precarious legal status compared to Bosnians in the Netherlands and Germany with more secure standing, found that, "as long as refugees are not certain about their legal status, that is, their right to reside permanently in the country of refuge, they will tend to avoid anything that might jeopardize this status."[46]

Host states sometimes grant asylum to nationals of a hostile state in order to promote their diasporic political activities, as Chapter 7 showed.[47] Sanctuary can also be provided without using asylum directly. Admitting refugees as workers achieves what political scientist Hélène Thiollet calls "asylum policy by proxy," in which political support for a refugee homeland movement is the primary goal. Saudi Arabia and other Gulf countries hosted Eritreans during the war of independence as part of their foreign policies of supporting the liberation movement.[48] On the other hand, host governments are often concerned that refugees will draw them into conflicts with refugees' states of origin. Some hosts promote outmigration to third countries to avoid this outcome. Other hosts resettle refugees in a dispersed way so they will be less likely to form nuclei of resistance, as Sweden did with Baltic refugees after World War II to discourage them from attacking the USSR, which had annexed their countries.[49] States may also move refugees away from border regions into the interior, where cross-border raids in either direction will be more difficult, as Mexico did with Guatemalan refugees encamped in the state of Chiapas in the 1980s.[50] In all these instances, the ability of refugees to engage in transborder politics is partly the product of the relationships between host and origin states.

Types of return

Voluntary return within the UNHCR's durable solutions framework signifies that it has become safe for refugees to repatriate. In practice, violence often continues to shape refugees' transborder connections, even after a conflict has apparently ended. There are many types of repatriation, ranging from permanent returns at the end of a conflict to temporary or circular returns. It is impossible to know in the moment where repatriation falls on this continuum. For refugees, knowing when it is safe to return can be a question of life or death. It is only with hindsight that the risks can be definitively determined. Of 53,000 Jews who left Germany in 1933 after Hitler took power, 16,000 returned after anti-Semitic persecutions appeared to ease.[51] Omniscient historical narrators want to shout a warning into the past for refugees to stay away. In the moment, refugees made the best decisions they could amid shifting circumstances, limited information, competing interests, and in the face of doors to sanctuary in other countries that clanged shut.

Refugees often experience cycles of displacement, return, and further displacement as conflicts wax and wane. Rohingya refugees, for example, fled from Myanmar to Bangladesh in the 1970s, 1990s, and 2010s when violence against them escalated. Return in these cases was not the final stop, but rather an intermediate stage. In general, the indeterminacy of return may have become more common since the early 1990s as civil wars have become more intractable. Of the conflicts in the early 2000s, 60 percent relapsed within five years. As civil wars have become more internationalized, fewer end quickly and definitively in political settlements. The spread of civil wars in the 2000s has been driven by the expansion of the Islamic State and affiliated groups, which often attract volunteers, ideological support, funding, and weapons from abroad. The millenarianism of their theology is not conducive toward negotiated settlements.[52] Foreign governments such as France and the United States then intervene in these conflicts in ways that can create further disruption and backlashes.

Sometimes refugees do not have a choice about their return. History is replete with instances of refoulement. Authorities in Hong Kong episodically pushed defeated Chinese nationalists back into the PRC after the communist victory in 1949.[53] The Thai military bused 42,000 Cambodian refugees to the border in 1979 and forced them to walk back to Cambodia, sometimes through minefields, at the cost of many lives.[54] Refoulement makes people doubly refugees, first from persecution in the country of origin, and then from persecution by the host government.[55]

Recognized refugees are repatriated with different degrees of coercion between forced and voluntary return. "We are adopting

Figure 8.2: A Congolese frontier guard opens the border to a bus transporting Congolese refugees returning to Congo from Gabon in 2011. Photo by Xavier Bourgois/AFP via Getty Images.

the term of 'dignified and secure' return," explained a representative of the Lebanese Ministry of State for Displaced Affairs in a 2017 conversation about encouraging Syrian refugees to leave Lebanon and return to Syria.[56] What qualities constituted "dignified and secure" remained unanswered. The most common incentives to return are dangled as carrots, such as promising returnees cash payments, land, infrastructure improvements in the areas to which they return, or loans for small businesses.

Structural conditions shaping return

Repatriation policies are not simply determined by an assessment of whether conditions are safe in the country of origin. The push factors for return extend to countries of origin, hosts, and international organizations funded by powerful patrons. Repatriation policies are also the product of policy diffusion from distant models. For example, strategies developed through the process to repatriate Central American refugees after the conclusion of civil wars in the early 1990s became a model for Sudanese repatriations of Eritreans several years later.[57]

Countries of origin

Some states refuse to accept returnees. This is clearest in instances of ethnic cleansing. The Israeli government has adamantly rejected the return of Palestinians who were forcibly deported by Zionist paramilitaries in 1948 or displaced by the wars in 1948 and 1967.[58] When in 1965 Israeli Prime Minister Levi Eshkol asked then-Chief of Staff Yitzhak Rabin what would happen if Palestinian refugees in Gaza tried to return to Israel, Rabin reassured Eshkol that the refugees would not try, and if they did, as soon as the Israel Defense Forces had killed the first hundred, the rest would flee back into Gaza.[59]

Totalitarian states often refuse to accept the return of "social undesirables" or dissidents who might form the nucleus of an opposition. For example, until there was a bilateral agreement with the United States in the 1990s, the Cuban government refused to accept the repatriation of Cubans who attempted to reach the United States but were declared inadmissible by US authorities because of criminal convictions or other factors. International law insists that

Figure 8.3: A mural in the Jenin refugee camp in the West Bank in 2020 depicts a house key – a symbol of the hope for return for Palestinians forced from their homes in 1948. Photo by Jaafar Ashtiyeh/AFP via Getty Images.

everyone has the right to return to their country of nationality, but this right is violated in contexts of ethnic cleansing and by totalitarian states trying to eliminate political enemies.

Origin states sometimes encourage return as a way of monitoring and repressing political opponents, or they screen returnees, accepting some while rejecting others. This form of securitized repatriation policy is practiced by Syrian officials from the ruling regime who check the political bona fides of potential returnees who have been living in Lebanon.[60] Governments sometimes accept returnees but then detain them or otherwise treat them harshly. Most South Vietnamese who left the country in 1975 wanted to flee as communist forces consolidated their victory, but 1,546 people who were held on the US territory of Guam were repatriated after agitating to be allowed to return home. Of these, 80 percent were low-ranking soldiers and airmen from the South Vietnamese military who had been on aircraft and vessels that escaped from Vietnam under the control of officers. The United States provided the repatriates with a boat to sail back to Vietnam, where, to their surprise, they were shipped to re-education camps by the communist government. A decade later, the communist government had become more established and was keen to improve its international relationships. The Vietnamese government accepted repatriates who had been held in detention centers in British-controlled Hong Kong and promised not to retaliate against them, in implicit exchange for improved relationships with the UK and United Nations.[61]

In another modality, origin states demand forced repatriation of their nationals. At the end of World War II, the Soviet Union insisted that the other Allied powers repatriate more than 5 million Soviet citizens under their control, using force if necessary. The USSR sought to rebuild a labor force that had been devastated by the war and prevent a nucleus of dissidents from forming abroad. Stalin's government persecuted more than a third of the returnees by means of sentences to hard labor, the gulag, internal relocation, or execution.[62] On a smaller scale, states routinely demand the extradition of opponents who may have committed political crimes. Chapter 3 detailed the importance of extradition treaties and law in the historical development of asylum policy. The efforts of the United States to extradite Edward Snowden after he leaked classified government documents and fled to Hong Kong and then Russia for asylum fall into this category.[63]

Refugees who are allowed to return can face extreme hostility. Polish Jews who had fled the Nazi advance in World War II for the relative safety of the Soviet Union returned to Poland after the war, where they were subject to pogroms and other forms of anti-Semitism. Many Polish Jews then fled to displaced persons camps in Germany or Palestine.[64] Historian Diana Dumitru describes the hostile reception that Jews faced on return to the territories of Bessarabia, Bucovina, and Transnistria. Jewish refugees discovered that their property had been stolen by neighbors. "When the Jewish survivors returned home, they had no difficulty recognizing their belongings in their neighbors' courtyards: barrels rolled out from cellars to be washed before the new harvest, laundry hanging to dry, pillows and carpets put out to be aired – all these had been stolen from them."[65] Such incidents demonstrate that there was no "home" to return to, only a place where they once lived.

Some states welcome repatriates and orchestrate their return. Returning refugees are sources of labor, entrepreneurialism, and trading ties with foreign countries. Returnees have also played major roles as brokers between international organizations or diasporic groups and the home country.[66] Where nation-state building has led to the fragmentation of multiethnic states, coethnic refugees are sometimes welcomed for their addition to a state's demographic strength, and resettled to vulnerable border regions. After the civil war in Yugoslavia, Bosniaks were resettled in Bosnia near the border of the Republika Srpska, and Serb refugees from Croatia were resettled in the Republika Srpska.[67] States of origin sometimes want refugees to return because their presence abroad is politically embarrassing and undermines the legitimacy of a government claiming to represent the entire nation.[68]

Returnees are often an important part of rebuilding a country at the conclusion of a peace process.[69] At the same time, repatriation can generate new forms of conflict in countries of origin, given that returnees from rich countries may have greater resources than those who never left, or are blamed for abandoning those who stayed.[70] Resentment is especially pronounced toward "diasporic leaders 'parachuting in' to tell those who have endured the suffering of war what to do from the safe confines of Western capitals."[71] Returnees are sometimes settled in areas of their home country far from their original hometowns, due to ongoing instability in parts of the country, shifted international borders, or greater economic opportunities outside their places of origin. These returns thus raise the prospect of tensions between local residents and repatriates, who might be co-nationals but otherwise share few social characteristics.[72]

Conditions in host countries

The word "repatriation" focuses attention on going back (re-) to the fatherland (patria), but conditions in the host country are at least as important as conditions in the patria for shaping returns. Understanding processes in both host and origin countries, not just an isolated assessment of whether conditions in the country of origin are safe, is necessary to explain the constraints within which refugees make decisions about return. Studies from Cyprus to Somalia to Syria have found that the least integrated into their host societies are the most likely to return.[73] Those who have made investments in their host societies, for instance by purchasing land or starting a business, are less likely to return.[74] In countries of refugee resettlement such as the United States, Australia, Canada, and New Zealand, and in Western Europe, there is an assumption that refugees will permanently stay rather than repatriate. By contrast, in most countries in the Global South, where the vast majority of refugees live, it is impossible or extremely difficult to naturalize, as described in Chapter 6. As a result, refugees living in countries in the Global South are more likely to repatriate once a conflict has subsided.[75]

Many people who have fled persecution or violence are reticent about returning to their home countries until they have verified that conditions are safe. Their decision-making is shaped by the policies of host states, which often strip people of refugee status if they have temporarily returned to their country of origin, under the logic that a refugee who was willing to return must be safe there and no longer requires international protection. Refugees thus have a disincentive to make a short trip home to assess the situation themselves. Syrian refugees who have been living in Turkey under a temporary protected status lose that status and their identification cards are confiscated if they return to Syria. They cannot reapply for protected status if they subsequently return to Turkey.[76] By contrast, in 2007, before the onset of the Syrian civil war, Syria hosted up to 1.5 million Iraqi refugees. The Syrian government generally allowed free circulation of refugees between Syria and Iraq.[77] Denmark, France, the Netherlands, and Sweden have created "look and see" schemes in which refugees can visit the homeland with an eye toward planning a definitive return, without risking the loss of their refugee legal status in the host country. Somali and Bosnian refugees availed themselves of these programs.[78]

Host and origin countries sometimes cooperate on return. The government of Tanzania signed a bilateral agreement with the government of Burundi in 2019 to coordinate Burundian refugees' return from Tanzania. Coerced return began with changes in host policies in Tanzania, which revoked Burundian refugee status based on prima facie criteria and required them to undergo individual refugee status determination. No Burundians were recognized as refugees between 2017 and 2019, despite nearly 25,000 asylum applications, and even though more than 200,000 had been recognized as refugees in the two years leading up to the new policy. The Burundian government used refugees' "choice to return" to signal to the international community that their human rights record was improving and the region had stabilized. Cooperation between host and origin states often serves the interests of those states more than refugees themselves.[79]

International organizations

International organizations have been critical actors in promoting repatriation. Recall from Chapter 3 that the League of Nations refugee system originated with the repatriation of Russian prisoners of war in the 1920s. After World War II, the focus of the United Nations Relief and Rehabilitation Administration was the repatriation of people who had been displaced by the war. The UNHCR became more active in promoting repatriations of various nationalities in the early 1990s. The IOM has since become the lead international actor in that role. It organizes small-scale repatriations of rejected asylum-seekers as well as large-scale repatriations of whole refugee communities living in neighboring countries. Both the IOM and the UNHCR have been periodically criticized for acting at the behest of host and donor states, rather than focusing on the best interests and wishes of refugees themselves, to push repatriation when conditions in countries of origin remain risky.[80]

Returns of refugees and IDPs in the 1990s after more than 3 million Guatemalans, Nicaraguans, and Salvadorans were displaced during the civil wars in Central America have been praised for the coordination between origin and host country governments, the UNHCR, NGOs, and networks of refugees and their advocates. Observers also lauded the CIREFCA process, known by the Spanish acronym for the International Conference on Central American Refugees, for the extent to which it consulted refugees. However, subsequent research found that fewer than 10 percent of displaced people received international assistance. Despite some successes, many Central Americans stayed abroad or migrated to the United States, notwithstanding their unauthorized or precarious legal status there. Many of those who did repatriate faced harsh economic adversity and physical insecurity, including government repression.[81]

To avoid home state retaliation against refugees, the UNHCR sometimes places monitors in the country of origin, as it did in Vietnam to encourage Vietnamese to return from camps in Hong Kong and Southeast Asia in the 1990s.[82] The largest repatriation campaign in UNHCR history involved the return of 3.5 million Afghans from Pakistan and Iran between 2002 and 2005.

Independent researchers noted that an undetermined number of them repatriated to receive international assistance packages and then rotated back to Pakistan or Iran.[83] While the UNHCR's formal policy is to only repatriate refugees who return voluntarily, there have been documented failings.[84]

Conclusion

Refugees, like other international migrants, often maintain cross-border ties. Except in the most extreme cases of genocidal ethnic cleansing, most still have family, friends, and other interests left behind. And except for those who have fled the most repressive countries with high state capacity, such as North Korea, refugees send remittances, maintain all kinds of communication, and sponsor family reunification where possible. The key difference between refugees and labor migrants is in some forms of long-distance political engagement. Advocacy, voting from abroad, returning to run for office, and other forms of peaceful engagement are common, at least after a conflict subsides, but to the extent that refugees are the product of political violence, only a small minority of them also engage in political tactics that include violence.

Refugees' ability to act across borders is shaped by conditions in both host and origin countries. Refugees who have a stable legal status and are allowed to integrate in the host country – conditions that do not apply in most cases – are more likely to be free to engage in sustained cross-border activities. Host governments concerned that refugees on their territory will draw them into conflict with origin states try to reduce cross-border activities, while other host states actively encourage refugees to work against states that are common enemies. Conditions in the homeland also shape engagement. Return is made difficult but not precluded by ongoing conflict. Some governments in places of origin insist on forced repatriation. Others do not allow the return of refugees and their descendants who wish to return. Still others selectively screen refugees to keep out political opponents, but otherwise welcome refugees and their resources.

Nonstate actors play important roles in homeland ties and return as well. Diasporic groups pressure refugees to provide support for their cause and are more successful when perceived existential crises continue at home and refugees are concentrated in destination hubs where compliance with demands can be more easily enforced. International organizations, from the alphabet soup of post-World War II organizations to the contemporary IOM, play a major role in negotiating, monitoring, and even forcing return.

9
Conclusion

The systems approach responds to siloed patterns of knowledge production in research about refugees that have six distinct limitations. The first three characteristics of siloed approaches include the tendency to be ahistorical (most policy studies), failure to explain or purposefully neglect the causes of displacement and treat refugees as though they have simply appeared in a host country (UNHCR *Global Trends* reports), and the use of an exclusively legal definition of refugees to define the scope conditions of the study (most legal and policy studies). These aspects of siloed approaches are manifested in the works of policymakers, lawyers, legal scholars, humanitarian professionals, and members of international organizations. Unlike academic scholars, practitioners have the responsibility to provide interventions for individuals or groups that depend on them. The knowledge they produce is influenced by that responsibility. Siloed approaches may be the right perspective for an asylum lawyer or refugee status determination officer, each of whom needs to support their client. Practitioners depend on categories of practice over categories of analysis to achieve their goals.

Knowledge production about refugees is further siloed in three additional ways: by only focusing on people who have moved and ignoring those who stay home despite the threat of violence (our previous essay);[1] a focus on so-called "durable solutions" of voluntary return, local settlement, and resettlement (humanitarian publications); and the study of a single isolated stage of displacement, such as resettlement, divorced from other stages (most social science studies). These six patterns of siloed knowledge production reproduce methodological nationalism rooted in assuming that the nation-state is the natural unit of analysis.[2] The goal of the UNHCR's "durable solutions," for example, is to put refugees back into single nation-state containers where they will remain.

Through a systems approach, we push against the above tendencies by considering how a displaced individual may see the world through interactive connections among places of origin, transit, and destination. Understanding forced immobility and displacement requires examining the nexus between immobility and mobility, policies of exit and reception, sequences of reception in the same host, sequences of migration among the same group, the effects of immobility in one migration circuit on movements and immobility in other circuits, and the iterative relationship between the actions of displaced people and policies in states of origin, transit, and hosting. All of these processes are shaped by the exercise of economic, political, military, and ideological power across borders.

A good way to establish whether a concept is useful is to ask whether it makes visible something important that was difficult to see with other concepts alone. What does an examination of the refugee system add that siloed approaches do not?

Movement must be explained, not assumed

Legal definitions of the refugee and sociological definitions derived from the study of international migration take as their starting point an individual's movement across an international border and/or fear of refoulement. By sampling on the dependent variable – those who have moved internationally – it is impossible to assess why some individuals move and others do not. Expanding the category of displaced persons to include IDPs only partly addresses this censoring because it does not account for why some individuals in similar circumstances do not move at all. The systems approach is attuned to a broader array of outcomes along the *continua of coercion and movement* discussed in Chapter 2 (see Figure 2.4). As we then show in Chapter 4 on decision-making and Chapter 5 on exit, individuals facing violence try to manage the structural constraints imposed on them by the policies of states of origin and potential destination, nonstate combatants, international organizations, and other members of their households and social networks. Rather than taking movement for granted, we show the conditions under which movement is possible, incentivized, and/or coerced.

Making the explanation of movement the analytical starting point illuminates several phenomena. It highlights why displaced people move, rather than placing a black box around why a "population of concern" ended up far from home. It is then possible to name the actors and processes responsible for displacement in nuanced ways. Refugees are not simply a generic result of war or persecution. Sometimes actors deliberately aim to produce refugees as a military strategy, an opportunity for extortion, or a project of ethnic or political cleansing. In ethnic cleansing, forced removal is but one grisly option that is part of several possible sequences involving genocide, expulsion, reciprocal population transfers, and autonomous flight from persecution. Other actors try to prevent refugees from leaving and demand the forced repatriation of those who left in an effort to radically transform captive societies. In still other situations, refugee displacement is an unintended consequence of conflict, but it is exacerbated by specific conditions, such as military strategies that create widespread collateral damage among civilian populations and the availability of affordable transportation to safety. Nation-state formation and internationalized civil wars are common sources of refugee flows.

We introduced the *new economics of displacement* in Chapter 4 to theorize refugees' decision-making processes by shifting the unit of analysis from the individual to the household and drawing on the new economics of labor migration to explain how households manage risks by sending family members to different locations.[3] A longitudinal case study of the Asfour family shows how the Asfours navigated challenges that restricted their movement, such as unexpected border closures and targeted persecution. We illustrated how serendipitous opportunities, such as resettlement for one member of the family, created pathways for other members of the Asfours to gain greater rights and protections. Networks bind together those who are mobile and immobile. Refugees who fled are connected to people who were unable to leave or who died before they could escape.

Policies of states of origin and reception are interlinked

Governments create their own exit and entrance policies, but one state's entrances and exits are connected to those in other states.

Attempts to expel populations can be stymied by closed entrances elsewhere, with the effect that strategies of forced removal turn to genocide. Conversely, restrictive exit policies in one state enable generous admissions policies in others. When exits open there, reception policies tighten here. Governments in countries of origin sometimes promote exit as a foreign policy tool against potential destination states, or rebel groups in countries of origin can encourage exit to invite foreign intervention by those same potential destination states.[4] There is nothing automatic about these dynamics. The refugee system is not a machine. But recurring patterns are evident.

In later phases of a "refugee cycle," policies and conditions in countries of origin and hosting become linked in new ways.[5] Chapter 8 shows that, all else being equal, refugees who enjoy secure statuses in host countries are more likely to engage their homelands than those in constant fear of expulsion from their hosts. Over time, however, refugees are more likely to return to their countries of origin if they have not been permitted to fully integrate in their host country. Their decisions are also shaped by the interventions of international organizations, states of return and hosting, and foreign powers.

Reception policies are interlinked across states

As Chapters 6 and 7 have shown, states and the actors within them have all manner of political, economic, demographic, and ideological interests that shape their policies around displacement. These policies almost always have a domestic component for which a systems approach may add modest analytical value. The advantage of the approach comes in recognizing how policies are also produced with other states. The refugee regime in its many origins and variants is the result of processes that unfolded over centuries, and which accelerated during periods of intensive interactions among groups of states attempting to manage slaves, political exiles, expelled and forcibly transferred migrants, and people autonomously fleeing persecution.

Ideas about human rights and humanitarian obligations did not spring up independently in one location. These ideas have spread across the world to the point that there is a widespread, albeit not universal, notion that people fleeing violence and persecution deserve protections in a way that people migrating exclusively for economic reasons do not. More specific principles have also spread, such as the idea that individuals whose only crimes are political should not be extradited, people should not be deported to countries where they will be tortured, and mass expulsion is illegitimate. Particular strategies have also diffused, including different tracks for individual and group refugee status determination, the adoption of military techniques of encampment, and public/private partnerships in refugee resettlement, to name but a few. There are multiple pathways for diffusion of these principles and strategies. Pathways include the negotiation of formal treaties, as well as informal modes of diffusion, such as emulation via epistemic communities of experts paying attention to what other states are doing.[6]

Southern and Northern host practices mutually constitute a global refugee system

Host states in the Global South and North share many goals in their refugee policies but with important distinctions derived from their differential power in the refugee system. These differences underpin the contemporary approach to refugee management that is fundamentally dependent upon Southern states, which house the vast majority of UN-recognized refugees, provide space for Northern refugee resettlement selection, and deter the movement of asylum-seekers to the North. Through the systems approach to displacement, we search for policy patterns among host states in the Global South and North, while also addressing variation within these categories as described in Chapters 6 and 7.

Table 9.1 compares major states of refugee resettlement in the Global North (primarily Canada, the United States, and Australia) with major refugee host states in the Global South (such as Pakistan, Lebanon, and Kenya).

Understanding state policies toward refugees begins with migration control mechanisms that shape the demographics of those permitted to enter. Northern states of refugee resettlement are able to exercise much stricter control over the types of refugees they will accept and whether an individual meets the statutory standard. They usually have time to plan their policies. Legally designated refugees who live in the Global North arrive as either resettled refugees or asylum-seekers. Northern states typically control the number of refugees they receive through resettlement programs that have designated quotas.

Table 9.1: Differences in Northern states of resettlement and Southern states of mass hosting

	Northern states of resettlement	Southern states of mass hosting
Borders	Strictly controlled.	Porous and sometimes open, or closed only after receiving large numbers of refugees.
Numbers	Predetermined resettlement quota, plus asylum-seekers whose numbers are kept low through remote control.	No predetermined number of refugees permitted to enter; autonomous refugee movements largely define how many people will cross the border.
Screening and selection	Rigorous individual security and selection process before they are allowed to enter state territory. Screening usually takes place on another state's territory.	Minimal screening at border; prima facie over individual screening; more rigorous screening may occur for select refugees once they have entered the territory.
International support	States depend on their own resources.	UNHCR or UNRWA are essential for refugee management and aid.
Rights	Refugees have secure legal status upon arrival, and most are offered a pathway to citizenship.	Refugees are rarely offered citizenship rights; instead, they depend on human rights and humanitarian support without political rights.
Freedom of movement	Refugees are free to travel within the state; they are not contained in camps.	Some refugees are confined in camps; those allowed to exit camps may be monitored and restricted.
Preparation time	States prepare for and control the rate of refugee reception, delaying reception if capacity is lacking.	States react to unexpected emergencies of arrivals and often receive fast inflows.
Protraction	Permanent integration in which naturalization ends the legal refugee status.	Hosting is expected to be temporary, even though refugee status often lasts for generations and is passed down to children. Local integration is often discouraged or made very difficult.

Twenty-seven countries resettled a total of only 63,726 individuals with UNHCR support in 2019.[7] Asylum-seekers ask for refugee protections after they have set foot on a state's territory. To control the number of asylum-seekers, Northern states deploy remote controls in the Global South to keep asylum-seekers away.[8] The strictest controls have not allowed asylum-seekers to present a claim, such as Australia's complete shutdown of asylum-seeking by unauthorized maritime arrivals under the "Pacific Solution," and pushbacks in Hungary, Greece, and the United States that arguably violated international law. Within Europe, since the establishment of the Iron Curtain shut down the largest outflows from communist countries, major spontaneous inflows of refugees were exceptional until the wars in the former Yugoslavia in the 1990s and in Ukraine in 2022.

By contrast, major host states in the Global South tend to have porous borders and are sometimes completely open to refugee inflows. Some Southern mass hosting states eventually develop controls and engage in ethnic selection, as described in Chapter 6, but, in general, they exercise weaker control over refugee admission than Northern states. Security and status screenings in the Global South are likely to take place after refugees enter their territory, while Northern states usually rely on strict border control mechanisms to screen future resettled refugees before they enter the state.

To host millions of refugees, Southern states depend on international support from donor states in the Global North. Foreign donors pay for much of the expense of hosting, either indirectly through the UNHCR, or directly through arrangements such as the EU–Turkey Deal. International organizations, namely the UNHCR, UNRWA, and the IOM, play a much stronger role in countries in the Global South. As legal scholar Michael Kagan elaborates, the UNHCR and UNRWA can become a kind of "surrogate state" that operates inside Southern host countries to provide refugees with humanitarian relief. As state officials navigate coordination with the "humanitarian complex," which includes many international NGOs, they relinquish some authority over internal affairs. Refugees depend on humanitarian organizations to secure access to nutritious food, housing, medical care, education, and cultural programs. The UNHCR also protects vulnerable refugees by providing them with identification and registration.

Northern states are wealthy, strictly control the number of resettled refugees, and therefore do not need to rely on international humanitarian agencies to support their national refugee response. They maintain greater autonomy over their affairs. With fewer refugees to care for, Northern states of resettlement provide them with greater rights. The treatment of refugees who have been resettled is much more favorable than for those who have moved independently to mass host states. Refugees in the North usually secure legal status upon arrival and are put on a pathway to citizenship. They often face many kinds of social discrimination, but they are on track to become permanent, legal members of the polity. They are able to travel freely inside the host country. By contrast, in Southern mass hosting states, refugees are rarely offered citizenship rights, particularly political rights. Even where citizenship is granted, it can easily be taken away. Refugees are dependent on the goodwill of national policies and humanitarian support. Some refugees in Southern states face limits on their freedom of movement or are monitored when they travel. Even though refugees in Southern states often end up in situations of protracted displacement that can stretch from one generation to the next, they are expected to be temporary guests who eventually return home. There is a classic "rights versus numbers" tradeoff in which small numbers of resettled refugees have high levels of rights, compared to large numbers of refugees in the Global South with low levels of rights.[9] Germany, with its high levels of refugees per capita as well as high levels of rights, is a major sustained exception to this general pattern.

While one may be tempted to read the two columns of Table 9.1 as separate – even opposite – approaches to refugee reception, it is important to recognize that approaches to refugee hosting are not separate entities. Southern and Northern host practices *mutually constitute* a global system. Southern hosting enables Northern immigration control. Resettlement states are able to strictly regulate refugee reception because they tend to have much higher capacities to control their borders, including by externalizing them to Southern states. This relationship is tied to pre-existing power differentials among states, particularly vestiges of colonialism, that fall along the axes of power described in Chapter 1.[10]

Early receptions shape later receptions

One of the basic insights of historical sociology is that policy options today are shaped by the policies of the past. Policymakers do not assess a situation objectively and then select the best possible response. They are often prisoners of path dependency, as certain policies and guiding principles have been reinforced, often over the course of long periods, such that the appropriate response to a policy question seems obvious.[11] Host states often frame refugees as a problem to be solved, and then draw on experiences in previous historical periods to solve their current problem.[12] Contemporary refugee resettlement programs vary in their details, but they follow a template consolidated around the end of World War II. On the other hand, states do not always mindlessly follow the path that came before them. Earlier experiences can be interpreted as cautionary tales. Recurring flows of refugees over decades shape the contemporary policies of hosts who are determined to prevent refugees from staying indefinitely, or, in the most extreme cases, forming a state within a state.

Early movements shape later movements

A core precept of theories of international migration is that migrations today tend to follow yesterday's flows. Migrants do not randomly pick destinations, and even those who are primarily seeking to improve their economic prospects do not simply select the most prosperous destinations. Migrants follow routes laid by pioneers and other members of their social networks who can provide the vision, information, funding, material assistance, and emotional support to make migration possible. As we elaborate in Chapter 4, similar dynamics guide refugees. Earlier labor and refugee migrations channel later refugee flows. Given cycles of persecution and the increasingly common pattern in which civil wars relapse, refugees may even follow their own footsteps. Once refugee migration is established to a particular place, family reunification and economically motivated migration is often channeled to the same place.

Initial migrations of pioneers are typically the result of processes that can be explained by world systems theory. Chapters 1 and 7 show how economic interventions, colonialism, imperialism, and military interventions by powerful core countries in the global periphery often boomerang back to the core. During decolonization, metropoles opened the gates to defeated colonial settlers and autochthonous collaborators. In the wake of military defeats abroad, powerful states have often resettled former allies.

Immobility in one circuit shapes movement in others

Changes in one part of a system affect outcomes in distant parts. When labor migrants are blocked from one traditional destination, they can be redirected thousands of kilometers away to other destinations and completely change historical patterns of settlement. For example, the closure of the United States to Japanese immigrants in the early twentieth century immediately redirected them to Brazil, which became the major country of immigration for Japanese outside East Asia.[13] A similar pattern holds true for refugees, as Chapter 5 illustrates, in its discussion of Jewish refugees from fascism. Even when exit from Nazi Germany was still possible, Jews were blocked by anti-Semitic immigration policies in other countries. These blockages before, during, and immediately after World War II redirected Jewish refugees to Palestine, where their establishment of the state of Israel in turn displaced Palestinians to neighboring Arab states. Even after refugees move to an initial country of safety, they are often immobilized in camps, or, increasingly, are permitted to live outside camps but with legal statuses that prevent full economic and social integration. One response to this form of immobility is secondary or tertiary migrations to host states with more favorable conditions.[14]

The actions of displaced people shape policies of exit, transit, hosting, and remote control

We have emphasized how states constrain the choices of people facing violence and persecution, but the relationship between displaced people and policies is interactive. When people move to find safety and meet their other goals, they create new realities on the ground. Much of the history of the refugee regime and policies of refugee management is a series of ad hoc reactions to perceived crises.[15] If individuals and groups were not moving across international borders, states would not respond with all their tools of surveillance, control, repulsion, protection, and assistance.

The systems approach offers explanatory power for understanding why, when, where, and how people respond to the threat of violence and displacement. Any analysis of a single type of refugee "stage" or "solution," or of policy at a particular time and place, would be fundamentally incomplete without taking into account the linkages described above. We now turn to some of the practical implications derived from our analysis of the refugee system.

Practical implications

We believe that ignoring the safety and dignity of displaced people and those persecuted in place is a moral failing on the part of the planet's bystanders. Governments and civil society should do a much better job of planning for new and ongoing refugee movements, preparing the public to understand the inevitability of refugee situations, and creating policies that maximize human dignity. Policy proposals face an inherent tradeoff. Proposals that stick close to the status quo can be feasible and pragmatic in the short run, but they will not create fundamental change. Interventions that support one group of refugees often neglect how others within the system will be affected by that change. Proposals that imagine a utopia open bold alternatives that are difficult to put into practice.[16] Yet even a borderless world that would facilitate movement in times of crisis would still leave catalysts of war, persecution, and poverty. Our normative recommendations draw from insights that a systems approach makes visible. By examining the power of states and their interconnected interests, we uncover how politics shapes humanitarian intervention, rights and legal protections, knowledge production, and possibilities for building public support. We also turn to lessons and policies from the past to imagine what is possible in the future.

Refugee-centered solutions

The 1951 Refugee Convention and other treaties set legal standards for the end of refugee status, due either to a change in circumstances in the home country or to the action of a refugee. In the former case, the circumstances in the country of origin on which refugee status was based must have fundamentally and enduringly ended. In the second set of cases, the individual refugee has availed herself of protection by the state of origin, reacquired home state nationality if previously stateless, naturalized in another state, or re-established herself in the state of origin.[17] From 2010 to 2019, only 128,600 refugees were categorized by the UNHCR as ending their status as a result of cessation.[18] The UNHCR's Executive Committee that interprets the Refugee Convention states that "cessation practices should be developed in a manner consistent with the goal of durable solutions."[19]

For whom are these durable solutions? Whose problem is solved by the cessation of refugee status? If the solutions are carried out according to the letter of the policy, solutions provide an individual protection from home state persecution. Yet repatriation in practice often means return under some duress, where the threat lurks of renewed persecution.[20] Local integration is often partial, allowing survival but without the full panoply of rights of citizenship. People who are resettled often face new challenges of racist hostility, family separation, and resettlement into poverty.[21] The point is not that repatriation, integration, and resettlement are bad policies. Rather, we wish to point out that they are *durable solutions for states* and for "the refugee administrator's view" that refugees stop being refugees when they are no longer a policy problem.[22] For people who have been displaced, repatriation, local integration, and resettlement are often *precarious solutions* that can even create new vulnerabilities.

The core logic of refugee policies is that people fleeing war and persecution deserve enhanced rights and are owed greater obligations than people moving across borders for other reasons. Yet as Chapter 8 makes clear, refugees have many different types of needs to live in dignity. Effective policies should take into account their multifaceted interests. Calls for states to allow greater mobility for recognized refugees are at least as old as the interwar refugee regime. In 1936, Jacques Rubinstein urged states to allow refugees greater movement and choice of residence, a call renewed in 2019 by Alex Aleinikoff and Leah Zamore.[23] Naturalization is the cleanest path toward travel documents that allow movement, but the Nansen passport system is another viable model, in which a consortium of states agrees to allow recognized refugees to move among them. Permitting refugees to move to areas where they are able to best work and open businesses and unite with family members encourages deep integration. The Economic Community of West African States (ECOWAS) formally allows refugees who are nationals of those states to enter other ECOWAS states to work and reside, although there are barriers in practice.[24] The Arab League's 1965 Casablanca Protocol for Palestinians gave Palestinians the same rights to work in signatory countries as their citizens, though major host states Kuwait and Lebanon signed with reservations, and Saudi Arabia never became party to the agreement.[25] In practice, in order to avoid the political backlash resulting from refugees disproportionately choosing a limited number of destinations, one option would be to establish limits on secondary movement during a transitional period, such as the temporary limitations on intra-EU mobility placed on nationals of new EU members in 2004, 2007, and 2013.

Refugee worker schemes in principle are a way for some refugees to enter a country with legal permission and protection, to support themselves, and to directly contribute to the host country's economy. As with temporary labor migration programs, there are known strategies that mitigate the most serious risks of exploitation.[26] These strategies include allowing the transportability of visas from one employer to another to avoid dynamics common to indentured servitude, maintaining local standards of wages and work conditions to avoid the fact or impression that employers are using refugees to undercut native workers, and providing a pathway to citizenship if temporary residence stretches past several years, so that temporary workers do not become a permanent underclass. Refugee workers who are afforded the opportunity to travel through legal channels and work should reduce some of the public backlash against refugee reception. Such programs are not a panacea for all refugees, particularly children, the elderly, and those unable to work. The experience of "the last million" in the displaced camps of Europe after World War II, discussed in Chapter 3, underscores the fact that no single strategy will equally meet the needs of all refugees and potential hosts, but the real-world alternatives to refugee worker policies may be much worse.[27]

Some refugees want to return to their country of origin, but they fear that if they leave their host country to determine whether conditions back home are safe and would allow them to sustain a livelihood, host states may not allow them back across the border. Many states strip asylum from anyone who has returned to their country of origin, based on the logic that if an asylee voluntarily returned to their country of origin, the threat of refoulement is over, and asylum can be terminated. The problem with such a policy is that it reduces refugees to one dimension and ignores the panoply of human needs. Such policies may even backfire by bottling up asylees in a host country who would prefer to repatriate if only they could ensure that conditions at home were adequate. The "look and see" programs discussed in Chapter 8, in which asylees can visit their country of origin to make an informed decision about a more definitive repatriation, comprise a model worthy of emulation.

Production of knowledge

Research by international organizations, think-tanks, and academics frames global discussions about refugees. Mass media reproduce this framing. The production and packaging of knowledge about refugees could be systematically improved to establish the accurate scale of displacement, pay less deference to state sovereignty and more attention to the experiences of refugees, and better explain why refugees leave their homes. Knowledge production is consequential because the social construction of a refugee problem creates parameters around what constitutes the array of possible solutions.

The claim that "we are now witnessing the highest levels of displacement on record,"[28] periodically made by the UNHCR, NGOs, experts, and journalists, is empirically wrong, as explained in Chapter 2. Neither the absolute number of displaced people nor the share of the world's population that is displaced is at an historic high. In fact, past emergencies have been much worse, and there is a large toolbox of public policies available to reduce human misery. Not every mention of the state of the world's refugees needs to include a comprehensive history lesson, but commentators should stop saying that the refugee crisis is unparalleled. In line with critiques wielded against the language of "crisis," an exaggeration of the numbers reinforces the larger narrative that refugee situations are unmanageable.

Even while exaggerating the scale of refugee displacement, standard accounts systematically exclude Palestinians from important assessments. In 2021, Palestinian refugees constituted the second largest refugee group in the world, making up more than one-fifth of the total number of UN-registered refugees. When Palestinians are excluded from documents like the UNHCR *Global Trends* report, or only mentioned as a side note, they are erased from the public's imagination of who refugees are and where attention is due. Because most experts rely on the UNHCR's database, they rate the scale of any given refugee crisis relative to a population that excludes Palestinians.[29] Assessments of major host countries ignore the hosting

of Palestinians, which then underestimates the extent to which
countries like Jordan and Lebanon have been affected by experiences of hosting Palestinian refugees when it comes to later policies
directed at other groups regarding admissions, encampment, signing
the Refugee Convention, and limitations on refugees' rights. Major
hosting areas like the West Bank and Gaza are absent in standard
UNHCR-based accounts, which contributes to the notion that
anything relating to the Israeli-Palestinian conflict is unique and
incomparable with other displacements. The artificial divide between
Palestinians and other refugees not only creates blinders about
who is counted, but also conceals the experiences of host states.
Generalizable evaluations of "solutions" to refugee displacement
are limited because Palestinians have been denied the right to return
by Israel and do not qualify for resettlement through UNRWA.
The publications of the Norwegian Refugee Council are a welcome
alternative that bring together all refugees into the same descriptive
statistics, data visualizations, and discussion.[30]

Public-facing work on refugees also needs to do a much better
job of explaining why refugees leave their homes in the first place.
International organizations such as the UNHCR are reluctant to
point out the obvious sources of refugee movements by stating their
causes and naming the actors responsible for them. Sometimes they
do not even state who the refugees are and rely on anodyne terms
such as "persons of concern." These organizations do not want to
jeopardize their access to refugees in countries in conflict or irritate
governments on whom they rely for funding. Independent researchers
and journalists do not have these constraints and should explicitly
explain the origins of conflict and persecution without shying from
identifying the persecutors. Autonomous production of knowledge
makes it possible to at least rhetorically hold accountable those
responsible for violence that induces forced migration. One good
example of this approach is the "Moving Targets" report published
by UC Berkeley's Othering and Belonging Institute.[31]

Interviews with more than 400 policymakers and experts on
migration across four world regions found that, when making sense
of migration, "accuracy is nice but not always necessary and what
matters is plausibility."[32] While that standard is little comfort for
scholars whose trade is accuracy and in-depth analysis, there are
recurring examples of research shaping policy responses. To give
just two examples, in the 1950s it was an open question whether

Chinese who had fled the PRC for Hong Kong were refugees under the UNHCR mandate. The Ford Foundation funded a project by Norwegian scholar and diplomat Edvard Hambro to study the question. He concluded that the Chinese refugees were "of international concern," a finding that had a major influence on the expansion of the international refugee regime.[33] Irving Abella and Harold Troper's damning 1983 book on Canada's response to Jewish refugees in the 1930s and 1940s, *None Is Too Many*, a title taken from the response of a Canadian official when asked how many Jews Canada should admit after the war, had a major impact on Canada's policy toward Vietnamese refugees. Unlike the United States, Australia, and France, Canada had not fought in the war in Indochina and did not have the same foreign policy motivations to admit refugees from South Vietnam. Canadian policymakers at the highest levels made *None Is Too Many* required reading, and told officials that "nothing akin to the voyage of the *St. Louis* was to occur" while they were in charge.[34]

Genocide museums, such as the US Holocaust Memorial Museum, offer a useful model for public-facing work on refugees. The establishment of a museum is a long-term process that lags conflicts, but these institutions play an important role in producing the kinds of knowledge that are consonant with a systems approach. They call out those who are responsible for killings and displacement and include in their histories people who were forcibly immobilized. These institutions also name those who were displaced, and specify why they were displaced, rather than using euphemisms that hide historical causes. The exhibits, publications, and programming in these museums include people who have been displaced across broad diasporas, defined not by whether they have necessarily been recognized as refugees by some legal authority, but by experiences of displacement that can take many legal and irregular pathways.

Refugees are rarely included in meaningful participation in the production of knowledge about their situation or in policy positions. The Global Compact on Refugees calls for "a strong partnership and participatory approach, involving refugees" as well as host communities.[35] The field of Critical Refugee Studies demands meaningful representation and self-representation of people who have been displaced.[36] History is a guide to serious participation of people who have lived the refugee experience. As Chapter 3 relates, the Nansen International Office charged with refugee affairs during the League of Nations period included two refugees on its advisory board. Jacques Rubinstein, a Russian refugee, co-drafted the 1933 Convention Relating to the International Status of Refugees. The first UN High Commissioner for Refugees, from 1951 to 1956, Gerrit Jan van Heuven Goedhart, was exiled from the Netherlands to Britain during World War II. Leading scholars of refugeedom include Hannah Arendt, who fled Nazi Germany after being briefly jailed for researching anti-Semitism, and Aristide Zolberg, whose Jewish family sent him to survive Nazi persecution in Belgium by living with a Catholic family. The author of the concept of "displaced person," Eugene Kulischer, had himself been displaced at least three times, having fled Russia in 1920, Germany in 1935, and France in 1941.[37] Efforts to "decolonize" refugee studies can learn from previous histories in which stateless refugees were central actors in policymaking and research.

Empirical research suggests lessons for how humanitarianism might be magnified. What is the effect of dramatic photographs of a single refugee suffering? In September 2015, after photographs spread around the world of the lifeless body of Syrian Kurdish child Alan Kurdi, washed ashore on a Turkish beach after he drowned trying to reach Greece, public interest in learning more information about Syrian refugees quickly increased. Google searches for "Alan" and "Syria" spiked immediately after publication of the photographs, and although the numbers had fallen a month later, they were still much higher than in the month preceding publication. Worldwide Google searches of the term "refugees" increased more than sixteen-fold from July 2015 to November 2015, after having been relatively low and steady since the start of the conflict in Syria.[38] Daily donations to the Swedish Red Cross were more than one hundred times higher in the week after publication compared to the week before, and the median size of daily donations increased fifty-five times, though both the number and size of donations reverted to their earlier levels in August within five to six weeks. Recurring monthly donations increased ten times in September compared to August, and remained at the new highs four months later.[39] As mass displacements continued to unfold in the years that followed, journalists compared other refugee children to Alan, hoping to garner attention for other plights. The body of Mohammed Shohayet, a Rohingya refugee boy, was photographed face-down in the muddy Naf River on the border between Myanmar and Bangladesh in 2017. He was called "The

Rohingya Alan Kurdi," but neither his name nor his image captured headlines in the same way.[40] The systems approach helps us explore the difference between the responses to Alan and to Mohammed. *Where* a child dies – at the gates of the Global North or in the South – skin color, dress, and other factors shape if and how that child's experience is represented and amplified.

Expanding protection

We explained how and why the refugee definition has changed over time in Chapters 2 and 3 and the distinction between a category of practice, such as a refugee status determination officer applying rules based on existing law, and categories of analysis, such as a sociological definition of refugees. What would a definition of refugees look like if it put the interests of vulnerable individuals, rather than the interests of states, at the center? From the perspective of a displaced person, the threat of violence is what is relevant, and it matters less whether one has crossed an international border. It also would not matter as much who is the source of threat. An invading state, despotic persecution, and targeted or ubiquitous street crime are all sources of violence. The populations that need protection include those who cannot leave because of barriers to exit or entrance, those who are threatened by violence but who stay in their place of origin to try to manage the many risks to a household, and those who repatriate but then become internally displaced. From states' perspectives, on the other hand, all these distinctions matter because of the particular problem created by movement across borders and the goal of using refugee policy as a tool of foreign policy.

The concept of "climate refugees" or "environmental refugees" has gained currency in the early twenty-first century. While the categories lie outside the 1951 Refugee Convention, jurists have developed rationales for legal protections of people displaced by climate change.[41] For example, the 2018 Sydney Declaration sets out principles of international protection for people displaced by rising sea levels.[42] Climate change contributes to droughts, reduces the arability of land in large swathes of the world, raises sea levels that threaten coastal communities, and worsens natural disasters such as storms, floods, and wildfires. These changes create stronger migration push factors. Estimates of the number of people who have been displaced, and are likely to be displaced in coming decades,

vary wildly.[43] Perhaps the most cited figure is 200 million environmental refugees by 2050, claimed by environmental scientist Norman
Myers in 2002, and later used by Christian Aid in 2007 as the main
basis for its estimate of 300 million by 2050. These figures are
based on "speculative common sense rather than actual figures and
estimates."[44] Such forecasts are usually published in research reports
that are not subject to peer review. While they generate intense
media interest, statisticians view them with skepticism. Manmade
climate change is a reality, but it is difficult to assess how large the
effect is likely to be on migration, given uncertainties over the precise
effects of climate change in different parts of the world, the extent
to which the changes will be mitigated by concerted action, the use
of technology to address the effects of climate change, and the interactions between climate change and the many other factors that drive
international migration.[45]

One certainty is that climate change disproportionately affects
people in the Global South, who did much less to contribute to global
warming via their consumption of fossil fuels than people in wealthy
countries who, along with their ancestors, have been pumping green-
house gases into the air since the industrial revolution. The ultimate
migration "system" is climate-induced migration, where conditions
in one place are affected by actions concentrated elsewhere, and
events in the distant past shape migration now.[46]

What are the political prospects for widespread adoption of
climate displacement protection protocols within a "refugee"
framework? There are several grounds for skepticism concerning
whether wealthy states will offer protection for large numbers of
people displaced by climate change. As Chapter 3 showed, the
refugee regime arose from several different bodies of law, but these
share the core principle that, to be protected, people escaping
violence typically must leave the source of violence. By contrast,
those facing other kinds of extreme deprivation, including starvation
due to famine, can in theory be offered relief in situ or at least in the
region.[47] Following this logic, the direct effects of climate change that
make a place truly uninhabitable, as rising seas wash over islands,
for example, provide a strong rationale for protection via relocation.
Changes that lead to increased stress on the environment and its
people lie in a grayer area.

It has always been difficult to unpack the origins of mixed
economic and violence-induced flows and make refugee protection in

these circumstances politically palatable. Those dynamics are likely to be at least as strong in the case of climate change. It may be easier to achieve protection for those fleeing acute natural disasters, for which there is a long precedent as outlined in Chapter 2, rather than the chronic problems created by climate change, such as drought. The "climate refugee" protection logic does not fit with many historic rationales for why states admit refugees, such as shaming enemies and calling out the cruelty of foreign governments who persecute their citizens. As Chapter 7 showed, protection policies rarely seek to minimize the distress of the most vulnerable individuals. Rather, the policies typically, or at least additionally, serve expressive functions of foreign policy. The implication is that states are likely to offer some kind of protection for persons displaced by climate change only in small-scale, symbolic ways. While there is arguably a moral obligation on states that have most benefited economically from their use of fossil fuels over the past many decades to help those who have been most negatively affected and who live in other countries, powerful states have historically only accepted refugees for whom they bear a special responsibility in targeted situations, such as the aftermaths of military and colonial interventions. The argument for a more diffuse responsibility around the globe is philosophi- cally credible but may be politically unconvincing. Finally, there is a tendency toward temporary humanitarian protection, rather than providing permanent asylum or resettlement, that would not meet the permanent protection needs of those displaced by climate change.

On the other hand, increased political will to address climate change at the international level may spill over into new protection programs for affected people. A 2016 conjoint experiment survey in Germany and the United States found publics were more supportive of settling people who migrated because of drought, flooding, and wildfires than economic migrants, but less supportive of settling migrants who moved for those environmental reasons than people who moved because of political, religious, or ethnic persecution.[48] The design of any climate migration program and elaboration of legal principles will benefit from a clear-eyed recognition of the factors that have encouraged and limited protection policies for people fleeing violence and persecution. For example, framing the issue to include the maintenance of political stability in areas severely affected by climate change may carry more weight with policymakers and publics than moral pleas alone.

Building public support

Public opinion about the merits of supporting refugees varies widely around the world. While there is significant support in most surveyed countries for the principle of asylum, there is far less support for the admission of large numbers of refugees who are not highly educated and who are perceived as difficult to assimilate.[49]

Citizens of host countries often believe that refugees enjoy better access to resources than citizens. That belief, which in some cases of impoverished countries of mass hosting may be true, engenders hostility toward refugees. One of the strategies for minimizing that hostility is co-development. Infrastructure projects such as building roads, clean water projects, and electrification, and communication systems in areas where large numbers of refugees are settled, such as camps, can be designed to benefit neighbors in the surrounding region as well.[50] Empirical studies have found that the sudden arrival of refugees can generate local economic growth and innovation as there are increased opportunities to work in the humanitarian sector and provide goods and services to it.[51]

Only a small minority of refugees live in camps, and the camp model has fallen out of favor to be anything but the most temporary solution to a large-scale influx. The UNHCR is increasingly providing refugees outside camps with cash benefits rather than delivering aid in kind. The economic benefits for the local economy are extensive, as refugees are not only making their own choices about what to buy, but they are also buying goods from local merchants rather than consuming goods imported from abroad directly to camps. A study of UNHCR cash transfers to Syrian refugees in Lebanon found that "families that received cash faced fewer verbal and physical conflicts with Lebanese host community residents."[52] The multiplier effect of these transfers in the local economy presumably lessens the political backlash.

The United States has long been the major country of reset-tlement in the world in terms of absolute numbers, with a total of more than 5 million refugees since World War II. Yet most major refugee admissions programs were opposed by the public, including proposals to increase admissions of European Jews after World War II, Hungarians after the 1956 revolution, and Indochinese in the 1970s. A conjoint survey experiment in the United States in 2011/12 found that a representative sample of US citizens viewed immigrants applying because they were escaping political or religious persecution slightly more favorably than others.[53] Americans have become generally more favorable to refugee resettlement over time, with a slight majority supporting refugee resettlement between 2017 and 2019, in an apparent backlash against the drastic cuts to refugee resettlement and other measures against immigrants and asylum-seekers during the Trump administration.[54]

It is not obvious how to increase public support for refugee protection. The ideology of humanitarianism has ancient roots in many traditions, but its modern incarnation dates to the nineteenth century and is characterized by a "disinterested concern for the suffering of distant strangers."[55] Given the "concentric circles of community" in which most individuals feel closer to those who share similar characteristics, convincing others to accept those across great social boundaries will always be an uphill slog. Many of the most successful instances of refugee protection include an element of self-interest on the part of host states, or are reserved for people suffering who are culturally and/or geographically proximate to their hosts.[56]

Refugee advocates use different frames to explain to the public why refugee protection is important and debate the merits of these frames, often with a paucity of clear evidence that points one way or the other. A survey experiment conducted with a nationally representative sample of American adults leading up to the 2016 US presidential election tested how two different treatments affected the likelihood of writing a letter to the new president supporting the admission of Syrian refugees. A prompt that encouraged taking the perspective of a Syrian refugee – by asking respondents to imagine themselves as a refugee and answer three questions about what they would do in that person's shoes – increased the likelihood of their writing a letter by two to five percentage points. By contrast, a prompt that provided information about low levels of resettlement of Syrian refugees in the United States relative to other industrialized democracies had no effect on the propensity to write a letter.[57] Much more systematic research is needed to establish the extent to which different frames motivate different audiences.

One way to encourage perspective-taking is to be reminded that positions in the refugee system can diametrically change. The annals record many instances of flows in one direction flipping 180 degrees. In the 1920s, many ethnic Greeks fleeing Turkey found safety in Syria. A century later, refugees from the Syrian civil war fled through

Figure 9.1: Yasser Hussein, a refugee from the Syrian city of Homs, carries his three-month-old son toward a registration center in southern Serbia in October 2015. Photo by Sam Tarling/Corbis via Getty Images.

Turkey to Greece. In 1944, refugees from Yugoslavia fled the Nazi occupation by taking to small boats and steering south for Allied-controlled North Africa. The British army organized the transfer of 30,000 Yugoslavs to camps in Egypt's Sinai Desert.[58] By the early twentieth century, the refugee route across the Mediterranean led north and west, rather than south and east.

On the border between France and Spain, the northbound flow of Republican refugees defeated in the Spanish Civil War in 1939 was replaced just a few years later by southbound flows across the Pyrenees of refugees fleeing fascism and the German invasion.[59] During the Japanese occupation of Hong Kong in World War II, a million Chinese fled the British colony for the Chinese mainland. Less than a decade later, 700,000 Chinese from the mainland fled to Hong Kong after the communist victory in the civil war.[60] Refugees from Sudan's first civil war from 1955 to 1972 fled to Uganda, where they depended on the hospitality of locals to procure food, shelter, and farmland. In 1979, tens of thousands of Ugandans fled their country for Sudan after the fall of President Idi Amin. "Having been well

Figure 9.2: The United Nations Relief and Rehabilitation Administration ran a desert camp for Yugoslav refugees in 1944 at El Shatt, Egypt. Photo by Otto Gilmore, Library of Congress.

received in their own time of trial earlier, many Sudanese felt a sense of obligation and debt to Ugandans when they came to Sudan in search of refuge," notes geographer Johnathan Bascom.[61] Similarly, during half a century of armed conflict involving guerrilla groups, drug gangs, paramilitaries, and the state, hundreds of thousands of Colombians fled to more stable neighboring countries, including Venezuela. In 2021, Colombian president Iván Duque announced his government would grant temporary legal status to more than 1.7 million Venezuelans who had fled their country's repression and economic collapse for safety in Colombia. "When Colombia faced difficult circumstances, many Colombians moved to Venezuela and found an opportunity," including his great uncle, President Duque explained.[62]

The refugee system is never static. Today's hosts can become tomorrow's refugees.

Notes

1 Menjívar 1993.
2 Bradley 2011, 21; García 2006; Terrazas 2010; Abrego 2017.
3 Wright 2014, 461–463.
4 Hickerson and Dunsmore 2016, 435. World Refugee Day is designated by the UN to bring attention to refugee issues every year on June 20.
5 Iraqi Refugee Crisis Explained. UNHCR, November 7, 2019: https://www.unrefugees.org/news/iraq-refugee-crisis-explained/.
6 Bali Process 2016, Review of region's response to Andaman Sea situation of May 2015: https://www.iom.int/fr/iscm/review-regions-response-andaman-sea-situation-may-2015; see also the discussion in Geddes 2021, 69.
7 Feller 2005; Betts and Collier 2017, 30.
8 Lim 2013, 1015.
9 Mabogunje 1970; Kritz and Zlotnik 1992; Massey et al. 1998; Fawcett 1989; Bakewell 2014.
10 Zolberg et al. 1989.
11 Tilly 1984; Aminzade 1992; Mahoney 2000.
12 White 2019; Betts and Collier 2017.
13 See Gatrell 2013 on refugeedom and Shacknove 1993 on refugeehood.
14 Kurdi 2018.
15 Brubaker 2004.
16 FitzGerald and Arar 2018.
17 UNHCR 2021.
18 FitzGerald and Arar 2018.
19 Mann 1993.
20 Wallerstein 1980.
21 Portes and Walton 1981.
22 Loescher 2001, 178.
23 Mayblin and Turner 2020.
24 Zolberg et al. 1989, 195.

25 Al-Ali et al. 2001.
26 Valenta and Strabac 2013.
27 Erdal and Oeppen 2018, 993.
28 Lubkemann 2008.
29 Chatty 2010.
30 García 2006.
31 Bruno 2021. Congressional Research Service, Iraqi and Afghan Special Immigrant Visa Programs: https://sgp.fas.org/crs/homesec/R43725.pdf.
32 Sims 2019.
33 FitzGerald 2019a.
34 Malkki 1995, 499.
35 Nasaw 2020.
36 Vang 2020, 32.
37 Betts 2009; FitzGerald 2019a.
38 Castles 2003, 17.
39 Weiner 1985, 448.
40 Cook-Martín and FitzGerald 2019.
41 Kritz and Zlotnik 1992, 15.
42 Mabogunje 1970, 16.
43 Wimmer and Glick Schiller 2003.
44 Gottwald 2014, 529.
45 Cited in Madokoro 2016, 92.
46 Lipman 2020, 55.
47 Huynh and Yiu 2015.
48 Cited in Madokoro 2016, 94.
49 Operation: Lebanon. 2021 Planning Summary. UNHCR, December 29, 2020: https://reporting.unhcr.org/sites/default/files/pdfsummaries/GA2021-Lebanon-eng.pdf.
50 Mencütek 2018.
51 Scalettaris 2007, 46–47.
52 Long 2014, 482; see also Monsutti 2008; Chatelard 2010; and Aleinikoff and Zamore 2019.
53 Rubinstein 1936, 722.
54 Mabogunje 1970; Richmond 1993.
55 Kritz and Zlotnik 1992; Massey et al. 1998; de Haas et al. 2020.
56 Cf. Richmond 1993; Mabogunje 1970, 10.
57 Cf. Etzold et al. 2019.
58 Bon Tempo 2008, 3; Neuman 2015; Dirks 1977.

Chapter 2: Who Is a Refugee?

1 Vallet 2021.
2 UNHCR 2020.

3 Hamlin 2021.
4 Hein 1993; FitzGerald and Arar 2018.
5 Akoka 2020.
6 Hardy 2003, 477. See also Malkki 1995, 496; Bascom 1999, 3; and Hamlin 2021.
7 Hardy 2003, 476.
8 Mountz 2010; Galli 2020.
9 Price 2009, 9.
10 Scalettaris 2007, 36.
11 Refugee statistics. UNHCR, n.d.: https://www.unrefugees.org/refugee-facts/statistics/.
12 Rotary works to alleviate refugee crisis. Rotary, 2019: https://www.rotary.org/en/rotary-helps-alleviate-refugee-crisis.
13 Editorial: Amidst the worst refugee crisis in history, Trump would be heartless to turn away the desperate. *Los Angeles Times*, September 16, 2017: https://www.latimes.com/opinion/editorials/la-ed-trump-refugee-resettlement-20170916-story.html.
14 World Refugee Day: What you should know. CNN, June 20, 2017: https://www.cnn.com/2017/06/20/world/world-refugee-day-worst-crisis-in-history/index.html.
15 Betts and Collier 2017; von Einsiedel et al. 2017, 1.
16 Gatrell 2013, 3, 151; UNHCR 2020.
17 Valk 2020, 77.
18 MacKinnon 2001, 120.
19 On counting refugees, see Crisp 1999.
20 Kunz 1973, 130.
21 Convention Relating to the Status of Refugees, July 28, 1951. UN Treaty Collection, vol. 189, p. 137, Art. 1(A)(2).
22 Costello and McAdam 2021.
23 UNHCR, *Handbook and Guidelines on Procedures and Criteria for Determining Refugee Status*. Geneva, December 2011: https://www.refworld.org/pdfid/4f33c8d92.pdf, p. 9.
24 Hsiung 1992.
25 Nasaw 2020.
26 Richmond 1993.
27 McAdam 2012.
28 Refugee Relief Act of 1953, Sec. 2(a).
29 Memorandum for the Operations Coordinating Board on Implementation of the Refugee Relief Act of 1953. Operations Coordinating Board, May 18, 1954: https://www.cia.gov/readingroom/docs/CIA-RDP80R01731R003000170004-1.pdf, p. 1.
30 Public Law 85-892.
31 Public Law 89-236, 203(a)(7).
32 Martin 1988, 9; see also Price 2009 and Hathaway 1997, 86.
33 Micinski 2021.

34 Zolberg et al. 1989.
35 Kunz 1973, 131–132.
36 Foster and Lambert 2019.
37 Zolberg et al. 1989, 7.
38 Rensink 2018, 64.
39 Lim 2013, 1032.
40 FitzGerald 2009.
41 Caestecker 2011, cited in Elie 2014, 30.
42 Marrus 2002, 39.
43 Castles 2003, 17.
44 Chimni 1998, 350.
45 Cf. Betts 2013, 12; Castles 2003, 17.
46 Caron 1999, 36.
47 Ther 2019, 191.
48 Central Intelligence Agency, Provisional Intelligence Report: Migration from West Germany to East Germany, 1952–54. CIA/RR PR-150 (ORR Project 41.995): https://www.cia.gov/readingroom/docs/DOC_0001109662.pdf, pp. 4–5.
49 Sheldon and Dutkowski 1952.
50 Marrus 2002, 358.
51 Zolberg et al. 1989, 187.
52 Arendt 1943, 264.
53 Pearlman 2018, 307.
54 Hein 1993.
55 See, respectively, Jászi 1939; Petersen 1958; Richmond 1988; and Betts and Collier 2017, 122.
56 Erdal and Oeppen 2018, 985.
57 Simpson 1939.
58 Act of June 30, 1834, 4 Stat. 743.
59 US Congressional Serial Set, vol. 258, doc. 353, p. 2, "Some notes concerning the situation of the Polish Exiles"; Hutchinson 1981, 24–25.
60 Zolberg et al. 1989, 32, 149.
61 Koser and Martin 2011; Crawley et al. 2016.
62 Feller 2005; Betts and Collier 2017, 30.
63 Hathaway 2007, 352.
64 Hathaway 2007, 350, 352.
65 Long 2013, 2, 19.
66 Bakewell 2008, 437, 449.
67 Brubaker 2004.
68 Binder 2000; Querton 2019, 379–397.
69 Hathaway 2007, 349.
70 Lubkemann 2008.
71 Shacknove 1993, 283.
72 On deportation as a form of forced migration, see Gibney 2013.
73 FitzGerald 2019a.

74 Galli 2020.
75 Saunders 2017; Ziegler 2017.
76 Haddad 2008, 35.
77 Convention Relating to the Status of Refugees, July 28, 1951. UN Treaty Collection, vol. 189, p. 137, Art. 1(F)(a).
78 Kunz 1973, 135.
79 Bowes 2014.
80 Ferrara and Pianciola 2019.
81 Zolberg et al. 1989, 227.
82 Orchard 2014, 65–66.
83 Bon Tempo 2008, 109.
84 Lischer 2001, 1.

Chapter 3: Making a Legal Refugee Regime

1   Ther 2019, 17.
2   Agamben 2013, 114.
3   Malkki 1995, 497, 500.
4   Gould 1973.
5   Bello 2018.
6   Arnaout 1987; Zaat 2007, 9.
7   Ther 2019, 17.
8   Kamen 1988, 39.
9   Barnett 2011a.
10 Arnaout 1987, 21.
11 Sinha 1971, 5–15, 36.
12 Art. V. §37, Peace Treaty of Osnabrück: http://www.pax-westphalica.de/ipmipo/pdf/o_1732en-treatys.pdf; Brought into Peace Treaty of Münster in §47: http://www.pax-westphalica.de/ipmipo/pdf/o_1732en-treatys.pdf.
13 Zolberg et al. 1989, 5.
14 Shaw 2015, 106–107.
15 Ther 2019, 34; Stanwood 2020, 21.
16 Bon Tempo 2008; Orchard 2014; García 2017.
17 Bretones Lane 2019.
18 Shaw 2015, 120.
19 FitzGerald and Cook-Martín 2014, 147.
20 Shaw 2015, 193, 202.
21 Price 2009, 35–44.
22 Orchard 2014: 97.
23 Immigration Act of 1903, 32 Stat. 1213, sec 2.
24 Peterson 2018, 277.
25 1889 Treaty on International Penal Law, Montevideo, Art. XVI.

26 Cf. Orchard 2014, 14, who dates the "attempt to provide protection through binding international law" to 1921.
27 Gilbert 1901; Arboleda 1991, 197.
28 Sinha 1971, 21, 207–245.
29 Instituto Matías Romero de Estudios Diplomáticos 1982.
30 Orchard 2014, 60–62.
31 Noiriel 1991.
32 Orchard 2014, 82–83.
33 Shaw 2015, 4–6.
34 Shaw 2015, 213.
35 Aliens Act 1905 (5 Ed. VII. c. 13), s. 1(3), our emphasis.
36 Bashford and Gilchrist 2012.
37 *Hansard*, February 10, 1911, vol. 21, cc661-2W.
38 FitzGerald and Cook-Martín 2014.
39 Goodwin-Gill 2014, 37; Karatani 2005, 518.
40 Ther 2019, 39; Chatty 2010, 61, 139.
41 Brubaker 1995.
42 Gatrell 2013, 3.
43 League of Nations, Arrangement with respect to the issue of certificates of identity to Russian Refugees, July 5, 1922. Treaty Series, vol. XIII, no. 35.
44 Hathaway 1984, 354–357 describes the debates over definition and inclusion of these groups.
45 Holborn 1939; Skran 1995, 285.
46 Marrus 2002, 88.
47 Marrus 2002, 46; Hirschon 2003, 17; Skran 1995, 286.
48 Skran 1995, 261–262.
49 Skran 1995, 267; Schaufuss 1939, 48.
50 Skran 1995, 278.
51 Marrus 2002, 110; Orchard 2014, 116.
52 Zolberg et al. 1989, 20; Orchard 2014, 127.
53 Caron 1999.
54 Zolberg 2006, 285; Neumann 2015, 40; Abella and Troper 1983, x; FitzGerald and Cook-Martín 2014, 66.
55 Gatrell 2013, 3.
56 Ther 2019, 178.
57 Baron 2009.
58 Ruthström-Ruin 1993, 16; Cohen 2011, 237, 23; UN General Assembly Resolution 8(I), February 12, 1946.
59 Constitution of the International Refugee Organization, 15 Dec. 1946, UN Treaty Collection, vol. 18, p. 3, Annex, Part 1, sec. C, Part 1(a).
60 Nasaw 2020.
61 Arendt 1968, 290.
62 Cohen 2012, 124; Marrus 2002, 365.
63 Loescher 2001, 54–57; Mayblin 2017, 135–137; Salomon 1991, 227.

64 Cuéllar 2006, 655–656.
65 White 2019, 108.
66 Mayblin 2017, 23.
67 Madokoro 2016, 78.
68 Convention Relating to the Status of Refugees, July 28, 1951. UN Treaty Collection, vol. 189, p. 137, Art. 1(D).
69 Akram 2014, 227; Zolberg et al. 1989, 23, 128.
70 Arar 2021.
71 Loescher 2001, 68–70; US Statutes at Large, Public Law 203, ch. 336, pp. 400–407.
72 Loescher 2001, 82–87.
73 Peterson 2018, 278–280.
74 Madokoro 2016; Zolberg et al. 1989, 156–157. Since its inception, the UNHCR assisted European refugees living in China, and from 1952 to 1969 it resettled 20,000 Europeans who had been living in China (Peterson 2012, 328–331).
75 UN General Assembly, Chinese Refugees in Hong Kong, November 26, 1957, A/RES/1167.
76 Ruthström-Ruin 1993, 23–24, 70; Loescher 2001, 92–95, 105–110.
77 White 2019, 109.
78 Ruthström-Ruin 1993, 42, 201.
79 Orchard 2014, ch. 7.
80 Loescher 2001, 128; see also Ruthström-Ruin 1993.
81 Peterson 2012, 338.
82 Hamlin and Wolgin 2012, 586–624; Loescher 2001, 124.
83 Vukašinović 2011, 157–158.
84 UNHCR, Note on the mandate of the High Commissioner for Refugees and his Office. October 2013: https://www.refworld.org/pdfid/5268c9474.pdf.
85 UNHCR, Report of the United Nations High Commissioner for Refugees, 73rd Session, supp. no 12, UN doc. A/73/12 (Part II). September 13, 2018.
86 FitzGerald 2019a; Chimni 2019; Arar 2017.
87 Goodwin-Gill 1983.
88 Jackson 1991, 191; Arboleda 1991.
89 Organization of African Unity (OAU) Convention, Governing the specific aspects of refugee problems in Africa. September 10, 1969. UN Treaty Series no. 14691, Art. 1(2): https://www.unhcr.org/en-us/about-us/background/45dc1a682/oau-convention-governing-specific-aspects-refugee-problems-africa-adopted.html.
90 Sharpe 2012.
91 White 2019, 109.
92 Asian-African Legal Consultative Organization, Bangkok Principles on the Status and Treatment of Refugees, December 31, 1966.
93 Davies 2006.

94 Loescher 2001.
95 Zolberg et al. 1989, 201.
96 Arboleda 1991, 201.
97 Cartagena Declaration on Refugees, Colloquium on the international protection of refugees in Central America, Mexico, and Panama. November 22, 1984. Art. III(3).
98 Freier and Parent 2019; Fischel de Andrade 2019.
99 Convention Relating to the Status of Refugees. July 28, 1951. UN Treaty Collection, vol. 189, p. 137, Art. 1.
100 Loescher 2001, 45.
101 Barnett 2011b, 141–142.
102 Loescher 2001, 147–150.
103 Barnett 2011b, 179; Loescher 2001, 293–295.
104 Crisp 2003, 79.
105 Orchard 2014, 232.
106 African Union, African Union Convention for the Protection and Assistance of Internally Displaced Persons in Africa ("Kampala Convention"), October 23, 2009, https://www.refworld.org/docid/4ae572d82.html.
107 Ruthström-Ruin 1993, 15.
108 Orchard 2014, 82–83.

Chapter 4: Should I Stay or Go?

1 Davenport et al. 2003, 31.
2 Zhukov 2015, 1157; Jose and Medie 2015; Lichtenheld 2020, 262.
3 Crawley and Skleparis 2018, 55.
4 Stark 1991; FitzGerald and Arar 2018; Poole 2021.
5 The name Asfour and all first names are pseudonyms that we chose to protect the identity of this family. In Arabic, the word *asfour* (عصفور) means "bird."
6 FitzGerald and Arar 2018.
7 Stark 1991.
8 Abdi 2015; Grace et al. 2018.
9 Belloni 2019.
10 Hyndman 2004.
11 Steele 2009.
12 Bergen 2016.
13 Berry 2018: 68.
14 Craig-Norton 2019; Qualls 2020.
15 Nobles and McKelvey 2015.
16 Sheldon and Dutkowski 1952.
17 Children on the move in Italy and Greece. UNICEF, June 2017: https://www.unicef.org/eca/sites/unicef.org.eca/files/2017-10/REACH_ITA_GRC_Report_Children_on_the_Move_in_Italy_and_Greece_June_2017.pdf.

18 Arar fieldnotes from Jordan.
19 Kvittingen et al. 2019, 116.
20 Adam Taylor, Refugee crisis: Denmark discourages asylum seekers with newspaper adverts in Lebanon. *Independent*, September 8, 2015: https://www.independent.co.uk/news/world/europe/refugee-crisis-denmark-discourages-asylum-seekers-with-newspaper-adverts-in-lebanon-10490666.html.
21 Cf. Burawoy 1976.
22 Weiner 1998, 3.
23 Arar fieldnotes from Jordan.
24 "I want a safe place": Refugee women from Syria uprooted and unprotected in Lebanon. Amnesty International, 2016: https://www.amnesty.org/en/wp-content/uploads/2021/05/MDE1835512016ENGLISH.pdf.
25 Hammond 2014, 508.
26 Bascom 1999, 157.
27 Holland and Peters 2020.
28 Kvittingen et al. 2019, 115.
29 Crawley and Skleparis 2018, 53; Kvittingen et al. 2019, 115. The same dynamic occurs in IDP situations, such as Colombia, where youths flee recruitment by guerrillas and paramilitary groups (Ibáñez and Vélez 2008, 662).
30 Cantor and Rodríguez Serna 2016; Arar 2016.
31 Tolnay and Beck 1992, 111.
32 Schultz 1971; Morrison and Pérez LaFaurie 1994, 123.
33 Rios Contreras 2014, 208; Massey et al. 2020; Fischbein et al. 2013.
34 Moore and Shellman 2007.
35 Zolberg et al. 1989, 136–137, 142.
36 Moore and Shellman 2007; Neumayer 2005.
37 Davenport et al. 2003.
38 Schmeidl 1997, 299.
39 Massey et al. 1998.
40 Zolberg et al. 1989, 260.
41 Al-Khalidi et al. 2007, 10; Zolberg et al. 1989, 165, 194.
42 Pedraza-Bailey 1985.
43 Marrus 2002, 28.
44 Boustan 2007.
45 Morrison and May 1994, 124.
46 Crawley and Skleparis 2018, 53.
47 Stanley 1987, 147.
48 Lundquist and Massey 2005, 47.
49 Adhikari 2013, 87.
50 Engel and Ibáñez 2007, 361.
51 Ibáñez and Vélez 2008, 669.
52 Engel and Ibáñez 2007, 356.
53 Gibney 2004, 126. Statement by Mr. Poul Hartling, United Nations

High Commissioner for Refugees, to the Third Committee of the United Nations General Assembly, November 12, 1984: https://www.unhcr.org/uk/admin/hcspeeches/3ae68fb38/statement-mr-poul-hartling-united-nations-high-commissioner-refugees-third.html.
54 Martin 1988, 8–9.
55 Koslowski 2011, 68–69.
56 By contrast, non-refugee migrants traveled much greater distances, an average of 3,657 km in 2000; see Fransen and de Haas 2019, 20–21.
57 Hatton and Williamson 2005, 37–41, 131.
58 Barnett 2011a, 113.
59 Gao 2013.
60 FitzGerald 2019a.
61 Iqbal 2007, 114.
62 Hatton 2017, 460.
63 Thomas and Znaniecki 1927.
64 Belloni 2019.
65 Edict of Fontainebleau. October 22, 1685. Arts. IV, X: http://huguenotsweb.free.fr/english/edict_1685.htm.
66 Stanwood 2020, 16–17.
67 Garland 2014, 92.
68 Ther 2019, 159.
69 Garland 2014, 105.
70 Letter of January 30, 1940 from Sd. N. S. Ronald to V. Jabotinsky, reproduced in Yahil 1974, 264.
71 Erbelding 2018, 267.
72 Dowty 1989; Sheldon and Dutkowski 1952, 590.
73 Fransen and de Haas 2019, 22.
74 Devictor et al. 2020, 7.
75 FitzGerald and Cook-Martín 2014.
76 Moore and Shellman 2007, 828.
77 FitzGerald 2019a.
78 Zolberg et al. 1989, 153.
79 Böcker and Havinga 1998, 256–257; Moore and Shellman 2007, 830; Neumayer 2005.
80 Belloni 2019.
81 Stanwood 2020, 20.
82 Zolberg et al. 1989, 140.
83 Dekker et al. 2018.
84 Belloni 2019.
85 Crawley and Skleparis 2018, 55–56.
86 Collyer 2010, 275.
87 Van Selm 2014, 512.
88 UNHCR, Sixth regional survey on Syrian refugees' perceptions and intentions on return to Syria. March 26, 2021: https://data2.unhcr.org/en/documents/details/85739, p. 5.

89 Müller-Funk and Fransen 2020, 8–15.
90 Chatelard 2010, 61.
91 Schwartz 2022.
92 Iraq: Humanitarian Bulletin. UN Office for the Coordination of Humanitarian Affairs, October 2020: https://reliefweb.int/report/iraq/iraq-humanitarian-bulletin-october-2020.
93 Cf. Fiddian-Qasmiyeh 2016.
94 Bradley 2011, 19; Al-Ali et al. 2001, 592.
95 Kvittingen et al. 2019, 117.
96 Abdi 2015.
97 Mark MacKinnon, How I found the teenager who inadvertently sparked the Syrian War. *The Globe and Mail*, December 2, 2016: https://www.theglobeandmail.com/news/world/graffiti-kids-of-syria-the-backstory/article33120311/.
98 Calculated from UNHCR Resettlement Data Finder 2020: https://rsq.unhcr.org/.
99 Pearlman 2017.
100 Jordan allows one-off aid drop to Rukban border camp. Al Jazeera, January 8, 2018: https://www.aljazeera.com/news/2018/1/8/jordan-allows-one-off-aid-drop-to-rukban-border-camp.
101 Daher 2019.
102 Canada's response to the conflict in Syria. Government of Canada, January 2020: https://www.international.gc.ca/world-monde/issues_development-enjeux_developpement/response_conflict-reponse_conflits/crisis-crises/conflict_syria-syrie.aspx?lang=eng.
103 In nine years, the Syrian regime has dropped nearly 82,000 barrel bombs, killing 11,087 civilians, including 1,821 children. Syrian Network for Human Rights, April 15, 2021: https://sn4hr.org/wp-content/pdf/english/In_Nine_Years_the_Syrian_Regime_Has_Dropped_Nearly_82,000_Barrel_Bombs_Killing_11087_Civilians_Including_1821_Children_en.pdf, p.21.
104 Kritz and Zlotnik 1992, 1.

Chapter 5: Exit

1 Zolberg 1997.
2 Universal Declaration of Human Rights, 1948, Art. 13.
3 Mitchell 1989, 700.
4 E.g. Lubkemann 2010; Orchard 2018.
5 Ther 2019, 60.
6 Gatrell 2005.
7 Ibáñez and Vélez 2008, 662.
8 Loescher and Scanlan 1986, 90; Zolberg et al. 1989, 157–159.

9 Zolberg et al. 1989, 238; Dubnov and Robson 2019; Bessel and Haake 2009.
10 Ther 2019, 8.
11 Marrus 2002, 8.
12 Pilkington 1998.
13 Years after Crimea's annexation, integration of Ukraine's internally displaced population remains uneven. Migration Policy Institute, September 19, 2019: https://www.migrationpolicy.org/article/fyears-after-crimea-annexation-integration-ukraine-internally-displaced-population; "Operational data portal: Ukraine refugee situation," UNHCR, March 13, 2022: https://data2.unhcr.org/en/situations/ukraine#_ga=2.168113121.1352064381.1647299624-25151545.1644451322.
14 Bessel and Haake 2009.
15 Kamen 1988, 39; Temimi 1993.
16 FitzGerald 2017.
17 Chatty 2010, 61, 94.
18 Manasek 2017, 304–305.
19 Chatty 2010, 77–78, 83, 145.
20 Ferrara and Pianciola 2019, 625, 631; Blumi 2013, 150.
21 Ther 2019, 46–47.
22 Hirschon 2003. Around 125,000 Greeks in what had become Istanbul eventually fled the Septembrianá pogrom for Greece in 1955; see Ther 2019, 67.
23 Ther 2019: 66, 75–77; Schechtman 1946.
24 Ther 2019: 81.
25 Potsdam Agreement (1945), Art XII: https://www.nato.int/ebookshop/video/declassified/doc_files/Potsdam%20Agreement.pdf.
26 Chatty 2010, 61, 139.
27 Ther 2019, 62.
28 Caestecker and Moore 2010.
29 Marrus 2002, 219, 231–233.
30 Pappé 2007.
31 Schmeidl 1997.
32 Haddad 2008, 1, 4.
33 Bowes 2014, 68–73.
34 Sturgis 2007, 2.
35 UNHCR, Sitting Bull (Tatanka Yotanka). August 2, 2017: https://www.unhcr.org/ceu/9507-sitting-bull-tatanka-yotanka.html. We thank Giuseppe Sciortino for bringing this case to our attention.
36 Rensink 2018, 71–113; HR 8820, An Act making provision for the deportation of refugee Canadian Cree Indians from the state of Montana and their delivery to Canadian authorities. May 13, 1896.
37 Herbst 1989, 679.
38 Allott 1974, cited in Herbst 1989, 680.

39 Gould 1974, 350.
40 Swindell 1995, 197; Fresia 2014, 542.
41 For differing interpretations of the role of colonialism and slavery in the *Mfecane*, see Cobbing 1988 and Omer-Cooper 1993.
42 Fraenkel and Murray 1985.
43 Crush and Chikanda 2014, 556; Christopher 2001; UN Economic Commission for Africa 1981, 52.
44 UN Economic Commission for Africa 1981, 23.
45 Cited in Glasman 2019, fn 22.
46 Lubkemann 2008, 458; Lubkemann 2010, 51–52.
47 Herbst 1989, 682–684.
48 Nault 2020, ch. 2.
49 Marrus 2002, 234.
50 Zolberg et al. 1989; Schmeidl 1997.
51 Annals of Congress, House of Representatives, 3rd Congress, 1st Session, January 1794, pp. 169–172, 1418.
52 Report of the Committee on Revolutionary Claims, 19th Congress. 1st Session, January 3, 1826, p. 2.
53 Ramasubramanyam 2021.
54 Elkind 2014.
55 Zolberg et al. 1989, 233.
56 Zolberg et al. 1989; Crush and Chikanda 2014, 557.
57 Herbst 1989, 674–675.
58 Ballinger 2020.
59 Gatrell 2019; Ther 2019.
60 Watt 2009, 1.
61 Cf. Orchard 2014, 203.
62 von Einsiedel et al. 2017, 2.
63 Weiner 1996, 29.
64 von Einsiedel et al. 2017, 5–6.
65 Schmeidl 1997, 284, 301.
66 Zolberg et al. 1989.
67 von Einsiedel et al. 2017, 4–5.
68 Neumayer 2005; Rotberg 2004; Betts and Collier 2017.
69 Adepoju 1995, 94.
70 Marrus 2002, 236.
71 Nasaw 2020; Milton 1991.
72 Zolberg et al. 1989, 236.
73 Hintjens 1999; Newbury 1998.
74 Jamal 1976.
75 Kumin 2008, 50.
76 Pedraza-Bailey 1985.
77 García 2017, 18.
78 Erbelding 2018, 131–133.
79 Weitz 1994.

80 Horster 2004, 403.
81 Russian soup for the soul. *The Age*, September 20, 2005: https://www.theage.com.au/entertainment/art-and-design/russian-soup-for-the-soul-20050920-ge0wea.html.
82 Loescher and Scanlan 1986, 136.
83 Greenhill 2010, 2–4.
84 Greenhill 2010, 2–4, ch. 2; see also FitzGerald 2019a, ch. 6.
85 FitzGerald 2019a.
86 Cited in Arendt 1968, 269.
87 Loescher and Scanlan 1986, 90.
88 Why Belarus is using migrants as a political weapon. *Vox*, November 14, 2021: https://www.vox.com/2021/11/14/22781335/belarus-hybrid-attack-immigrants-border-eu-poland-crisis.
89 Zolberg 1997.
90 Stanwood 2020, 17.
91 Torpey 2000.
92 Wolman 2019.
93 Marrus 2002, 59, 139.
94 García 2017, 21.
95 Axt 1997, 6.
96 Cuba relaxes travel restrictions for citizens. *Guardian*, January 15, 2013: https://www.theguardian.com/world/2013/jan/15/cuba-relaxes-travel-restrictions.
97 Chan and Schloenhardt 2007, 221.
98 Dowty 1989.
99 Stepick 1982.
100 Zolberg et al. 1989, 16–17.
101 Kibreab 2013.
102 Zhukov 2015, 1155.
103 Zhukov 2015, 1156. On Algeria, see Bourdieu and Sayad 2020 [1964].
104 Valentino 2004, 82.
105 Lichtenheld 2020, 290.
106 See also Steele 2018.
107 FitzGerald 2019a.
108 Wolman 2019, 46.
109 Crisp 2003, 76.

Chapter 6: Hosting in the Many Global Souths

1 Strictly speaking, there are different ways of becoming a party to the Convention, of which signing is only one. We use "non-signatory states" as a shorthand for states that are not party to the Convention and/or Protocol.
2 Balsari et al. 2015.

3 UNHCR, Minister of Interior achieve milestone in refugee rights in Iraq with new memorandum signing. October 31, 2016: https://reliefweb.int/report/iraq/unhcr-ministry-interior-achieve-milestone-refugee-rights-iraq-new-memorandum-signing.

4 Hathaway 1984; Davies 2006.

5 Methodology. UN Statistics Division, n.d.: https://unstats.un.org/unsd/methodology/m49/.

6 FitzGerald 2019b discusses the merits and challenges of different global categorization schemes. See Palomino 2019 for a critical historiography of the Global South.

7 For a review of South–South studies, see Fiddian-Qasmiyeh and Daley 2019.

8 Fransen and de Haas 2019, 19, 22.

9 This assessment includes Turkey as part of the Middle East. Note that Turkey is included in European regional refugee population assessments in the 2020 Global Trends report.

10 Antwi-Boateng and Braimah 2021.

11 UNHCR 2021, 10.

12 Syrian Emergency. UNHCR: https://www.unhcr.org/en-us/syria-emergency.html.

13 This percentage decreases to 41.5 percent when 3.6 million Venezuelans displaced across state borders are included in the overall count.

14 Freier et al. 2020.

15 Venezuela. UNHCR n.d.: https://data2.unhcr.org/en/situations/vensit.

16 Freier et al. 2020.

17 UNHCR 2020.

18 Gaza: Internally displaced people 20 May 2021. OCHA, May 22, 2021: https://www.ochaopt.org/content/gaza-internally-displaced-people-20-may-2021.

19 Quoted in Olivia Goldhill, Palestine's head of mental health services says PTSD is a western concept. *Quartz*, January 13, 2019: https://qz.com/1521806/palestines-head-of-mental-health-services-says-ptsd-is-a-western-concept/.

20 Jacobsen 1996, 656.

21 Chan and Schloenhardt 2007, 222.

22 On the concept of legibility, see Scott 1998.

23 Crisp 1999.

24 This estimate excludes Jordan, which hosts large numbers of UNRWA-registered Palestinian refugees who also have Jordanian citizenship, and the West Bank and Gaza, which host more refugees, but where the Palestinian entity is a "non-member observer state" in the UN.

25 Turkey Fact Sheet. UNHCR, July 2019: https://reliefweb.int/sites/reliefweb.int/files/resources/71061.pdf; Carlotta Gall, Turkey's radical plan: send a million refugees back to Syria. *New York Times*, September 10, 2019: https://www.nytimes.com/2019/09/10/world/middleeast/turkey-syria-refugees-erdogan.html; Stephen Burgen, How a small Turkish city

successfully absorbed half a million migrants. *Guardian*, June 19, 2019: https://www.theguardian.com/cities/2019/jun/19/gaziantep-turkish-city-successfully-absorbed-half-a-million-migrants-from-syria.

26 Arar 2017, 14.
27 Kristin Dalen and Jon Pedersen, Iraqis in Jordan: their number and characteristics, 2007. Government of Jordan/Fafo/UNFPA: https://www.fafo.no/en/publications/other-publications/item/iraqis-in-jordan-their-number-and-characteristics.
28 Crisp 2017.
29 Arar 2017.
30 Aid groups: 8,500 Syrians still held in Jordanian no-go camp. Associated Press, January 30, 2018: https://apnews.com/article/5782dcbf32af4fb1 9f78de317717bd1b.
31 Berry 2018, 63.
32 Rohingya Refugee crisis majorly underfunded in all areas of need. International Rescue Committee, October 23, 2017: https://www. rescue.org/press-release/rohingya-refugee-crisis-majorly-underfunded-all-areas-need.
33 UNHCR, Rohingya Emergency, 2019: https://www.unhcr.org/uk/rohingya-emergency.html.
34 Whitaker 2003.
35 McConnachie 2014, 53.
36 Operations, https://reporting.unhcr.org/operations; Non-governmental Organizations, 2021: https://www.unhcr.org/en-us/non-governmental-organizations.html; UNHCR, Implementing Partners. August 15, 1997: https://www.unhcr.org/en-us/excom/standcom/3ae68d0628/implementing-partners.html.
37 Government partners: https://www.unhcr.org/en-us/donors.html.
38 UNHCR Funding update 2020: https://reporting.unhcr.org/sites/default/files/Global%20Funding%20Overview%2031%20December %202020.pdf#_ga=2.176478370.601111763.1623177811-1111210481.1622106449.
39 How does UNHCR use unearmarked funds? UNHCR, March 20, 2019: https://www.unhcr.org/en-us/news/videos/2019/3/5c9202124/how-does-unhcr-use-unearmarked-funds.html.
40 Harrell-Bond 2002, 53.
41 Barnett 2018, 293.
42 Slaughter and Crisp 2009.
43 Kagan 2011; Hanafi 2014b.
44 Lipman 2020.
45 Norman 2020.
46 Turner 2015.
47 UNHCR 2020, 44.
48 Fiddian-Qasmiyeh and Daley 2019.
49 Chatty 2010.

50 Cf. Czaika 2005.
51 Refugee Camps. UNHCR, n.d.: https://www.unrefugees.org/refugee-facts/camps/.
52 Loescher and Milner 2005, 159.
53 Jacobsen 2002, 591.
54 Holzer 2015.
55 Crisp 2003, 78; Baylouny 2020.
56 Jacobsen 1996, 581.
57 Zetter 2021.
58 Loschmann 2020.
59 Taylor et al. 2016.
60 Whitaker 2002.
61 Lipman 2020, 70.
62 Ward 2020.
63 Kagan 2011, 6.
64 Zetter 2012.
65 Loschmann 2020, 5; Betts 2021.
66 Stephanie Nebehay, Europe must share refugee burden with Turkey: UNHCR chief. Reuters, March 7, 2016: https://www.reuters.com/article/us-europe-migrants-un/europe-must-share-refugee-burden-with-turkey-unhcr-chief-idUSKCN0W9276.
67 Terry 2021.
68 Arar 2017, 308.
69 Greenhill 2010, 30–31.
70 FitzGerald 2019a.
71 Cuéllar 2006. In rare instances, Northern resettlement states have chosen refugees directly from their countries of origin through "in-country processing," such as US programs in Vietnam, Haiti, the Soviet Union, Romania, and Cuba (Frelick 2003).
72 UNHCR n.d., Information on UNHCR resettlement: https://www.unhcr.org/en-us/information-on-unhcr-resettlement.html.
73 Lipman 2020.
74 Bon Tempo 2008, 193.
75 FitzGerald and Cook-Martín 2014.
76 FitzGerald et al. 2018.
77 Lipman 2020.
78 Adhikari 2021.
79 Fee 2021, 4.
80 Fee 2021; Fee and Arar 2019.
81 Lipman 2020; Biehl 2015, 67.
82 FitzGerald 2019a.
83 Ronzitti 2009, 132; FitzGerald 2019a.
84 Bar-Tuvia 2018.
85 Ziegler 2015, 176.
86 Bar-Tuvia 2018, 486.

87 Memorandum of Understanding between The Ministry of Foreign Affairs and The Ministry of Immigration and Integration of the Kingdom of Denmark and the Ministry of Foreign Affairs and International Cooperation of The Republic of Rwanda Regarding Cooperation on Asylum and Migration Issues. April 27, 2021: https://www.minaffet.gov.rw/fileadmin/user_upload/Minaffet/Publications/MoU_on_Asylum_and_Migration_between_Rwanda_and_Denmark.pdf.
88 Ziegler 2015.
89 How Israel tried to dump African refugees in blood-drenched dictatorships. *Haaretz*, December 25, 2020: https://www.haaretz.com/israel-news/.premium.MAGAZINE-how-israel-tried-to-dump-african-refugees-in-blood-drenched-dictatorships-1.9398948.
90 Birger et al. 2018.
91 Eugene Sibomana and Linda Muriuki, Grandi praises Rwanda for offering life-saving haven for refugees. UNHCR, April 26, 2021: http.
92 Libya. Global Detention Project 2020: https://www.globaldetentionproject.org/wp-content/uploads/2019/10/GDP-Submission-to-the-UPR-Libya-1910-e-version.pdf, p.3.
93 Third group of refugees evacuated to Rwanda from Libya with UNHCR support. UNHCR, November 25, 2019: https://www.unhcr.org/en-us/news/press/2019/11/5ddbd69b4/third-group-refugees-evacuated-rwanda-libya-unhcr-support.html.
94 Cook-Martín and FitzGerald 2019.
95 Revised Uganda country refugee response plan. UNHCR, July 2020–December 2021: https://data2.unhcr.org/en/documents/details/84715.
96 Betts 2021.
97 Hanafi and Long 2010.
98 Mourad 2017.
99 Janmyr 2017.
100 Cf. Janmyr and Stevens 2021.
101 Peru. UNHCR n.d.: https://reporting.unhcr.org/peru.
102 Ble et al. 2020.
103 Freier and Pérez 2021.
104 Bahrain, Kuwait, Oman, Qatar, Saudi Arabia, and the United Arab Emirates
105 Betts 2010b.
106 UNHCR 2019.
107 Cf. Chatty 2018.
108 Regional strategic overview, 2021–2022. Regional Refugee & Resilience Plan, 2020: http://www.3rpsyriacrisis.org/wp-content/uploads/2021/03/rso_up.pdf.
109 Abdelaaty 2021.
110 Janmyr 2017.
111 Abdelaaty 2021.

112 See Ruhs 2013 on the empirical trade-off between labor migrant rights and their share of the host population.

Chapter 7: Powerful Hosts

1 Haddad 2008, 56, 92.
2 Teitelbaum 1984.
3 See generally, Weiner 1985, 444.
4 Hansen 2014, 261; see also Gibney 2003, 29.
5 Thielemann 2003, 254–258; Orchard 2014; Mountz 2010.
6 On organizational migrants generally, see Lucassen and Smit 2015.
7 Marrus 2002, 6, 113–114.
8 Shaw 2015, 100.
9 Stanwood 2020, 4–6.
10 Shaw 2015, 109.
11 Zolberg et al. 1989, 10.
12 Shaw 2015, 109.
13 Robson 2017, 630.
14 Friedman 2021, ch. 10.
15 Hirschon 2003.
16 Cohen 2012, 108; Nasaw 2020.
17 Ther 2019.
18 Zolberg et al. 1989, 7.
19 Cited in Long 2013, 14.
20 Salomon 1991, 197.
21 Nasaw 2020.
22 Neuwirth 1988.
23 Shaffer et al. 2020, 31725.
24 Bansak et al. 2016.
25 Cohen 2012, 105.
26 Quoted in Gatrell 2013, 110.
27 Cohen 2012, 106.
28 Nasaw 2020.
29 UNHCR Resettlement Submission Categories, 2018: https://www.unhcr.org/3d464e842.pdf, p. 257.
30 Capps and Newland 2015.
31 Van Selm 2014, 521.
32 A significant contribution: the economic, social and civic contributions of first- and second-generation humanitarian entrants. Summary of findings. Commonwealth of Australia, 2011: https://immi.homeaffairs.gov.au/settlement-services-subsite/files/economic-social-civic-contributions-booklet.pdf, p. 25.
33 Kaida et al. 2020.
34 Joshua Cooper Ramo, Andrew Grove: A survivor's tale. *Time*,

December 29, 1997: http://content.time.com/time/subscriber/article/0,33009,987588-1,00.html.
35 Bevelander 2020.
36 Price 2009.
37 Bon Tempo 2008.
38 Bon Tempo 2008, 2; Sana 2020. Migration Policy Institute tabulation of WRAPS data from the Department of State's Bureau of Population, Refugees, and Migration: www.wrapsnet.org/admissions-and-arrivals/.
39 Migration and Refugee Assistance Act of 1962, P.L. 87-510 June 28, 1962. Sec. 2(b) 2.
40 Van Selm 2014, 512.
41 Watson 2009; Salehyan and Gleditsch 2006.
42 Shacknove 1993, 529–530.
43 Betts 2003.
44 Zolberg et al. 1989, 166; Espiritu 2014.
45 Bon Tempo 2008, 157.
46 Jen Kirby, Why thousands of Afghans are still on US military bases. *Vox*, October 28, 2021: https://www.vox.com/22728486/afghanistan-evacuation-us-military-bases-refugee-resettlement-fort-bliss-fort-pickett.
47 García 2017, 138–153.
48 Loescher 2001, 56, 57.
49 Micinski 2018, 274.
50 Zolberg et al. 1989, 152.
51 Price 2009.
52 Zolberg et al. 1989, 128, 162–163.
53 Loescher 2001, 55.
54 Loescher and Scanlan 1986.
55 Dowty 1989, 122.
56 Carter 1995, 213.
57 8 U.S.C. § 1157(a)(5).
58 Central Intelligence Agency, Provisional Intelligence Report: Migration from West Germany to East Germany, 1952–54. CIA/RR PR-150 (ORR Project 41.995): https://www.cia.gov/readingroom/docs/DOC_0001109662.pdf, pp. 4–5.
59 Ther 2019, 172–173.
60 FitzGerald and Cook-Martín 2014.
61 Madokoro 2016, 14, 67.
62 Higgins 2017, 14–16.
63 Higgins 2017, 12.
64 Madokoro 2016, 153, 167.
65 Lipman 2020, 54.
66 Bon Tempo 2008.
67 Rosenblum and Salehyan 2004, 692–693.
68 Zolberg et al. 1989, 7.
69 Ther 2019, 263.

70 Loescher and Scanlan 1986, 44, 91; Nasaw 2000.
71 Lautenberg Amendment of the 1990 Foreign Operations Appropriations Act.
72 Orchard 2014, 215.
73 HIAS Welcome Campaign Congregations, n.d.: https://www.hias.org/welcome-campaign-congregations.
74 Hollinger 2017; Zolberg et al. 1989, 191.
75 Betts 2010a.
76 FitzGerald 2019a.
77 Toshkov and de Haan 2013.
78 Burmann and Valeyatheepillay 2017.
79 Basic Law for the Federal Republic of Germany, May 23, 1949, Art. 16.
80 Gibney 2004, 86–102; Guiraudon 2000.
81 Hamlin 2014.
82 Price 2009, 91–92.
83 Rosenblum and Salehyan 2004, 690.
84 Rottman et al. 2009, 29.
85 UNHCR, Position paper on the strategic use of resettlement, July 6–8, 2010: https://www.unhcr.org/4fbcfd739.pdf, p. 2.
86 UNHCR, Position paper, p. 5.
87 Van Selm 2014, 513.
88 Nasaw 2020, 533–534.
89 Panama: Resettlement of Cuban migrants protected on Guantanamo. Wikileaks, June 24, 2008: https://wikileaks.org/plusd/cables/08PANAMA520_a.html.
90 FitzGerald 2019a, 118, 242.
91 US Statutes at Large, Public Law 203, ch. 336, pp. 400–407.
92 Emergency migration of escapees, expellees, and refugees. Hearings before the Subcommittee of the Committee on the Judiciary, United States Senate, 83rd Congress, 1st Session. May 26, 27, 28, and July 1, 1953, p. 86; see FitzGerald and Cook-Martín 2014.
93 Emergency Immigration Program, Hearings before Subcommittee No. 1 of the Committee of the Judiciary, House of Representatives, 83rd Congress, 1st Session. May 21–July 9, 1953, pp. 232, 235.
94 Report of the Subcommittee on the Near East and Africa, Foreign Relations Committee on the Problem of Arab Refugees from Palestine. US Government Printing Office. July 24, 1953, pp. 3, 193–194.
95 Report of the Administrator of the Refugee Relief Act of 1953. US Government Printing Office. State Department, November 15, 1957, p. 81.
96 Bon Tempo 2008, 193.
97 Yuen 2014.
98 Quoted in Lipman 2020, 146.
99 Lipman 2020, 194, 195.
100 Mayblin 2017, 157.
101 Zucker and Zucker 1987.

102 Tsartas et al. 2020.
103 Shaw 2015, 103.
104 Bean et al. 2012; National Academies of Sciences, Engineering, and Medicine 2017.
105 Benton and Diegert 2018; Capps and Newland 2015.
106 Shaw 2015, 103; Stanwood 2020.
107 Marrus 2002, 20–23.
108 Caestecker and Moore 2010; FitzGerald and Cook-Martín 2014.
109 Marrus 2002, 8.
110 Calculated from UNHCR Refugee Data Finder 2020: https://www.unhcr.org/refugee-statistics/download/?url=nJ4R and ILO 2017, Table B-16.
111 Switzerland seizing assets from refugees to cover costs. *Guardian*, January 15, 2016: https://www.theguardian.com/world/2016/jan/15/switzerland-joins-denmark-in-seizing-assets-from-refugees-to-cover-costs; Danish parliament approves plan to seize assets from refugees. *Guardian*, January 26, 2016: https://www.theguardian.com/world/2016/jan/26/danish-parliament-approves-plan-to-seize-assets-from-refugees.
112 Global attitudes towards refugees. Ipsos, June 2019: https://www.ipsos.com/sites/default/files/ct/news/documents/2019-06/World-Refugee-Day-2019-Ipsos.pdf.
113 Castles 2003, 16.
114 Shaw 2015, 30.
115 Gatrell 2013, 34.
116 Jenkinson 2016, 102–105.
117 Caron 1999, 20–21; Wyman 2019.
118 Loescher and Scanlan 1986, 27.
119 Security screening of refugees. Hearing before the Subcommittee to investigate the administration of the Internal Security Act and other internal security laws of the Committee on the Judiciary, United States Senate, 84th Congress, 1st session. June 9, 1955, pp. 15–16.
120 Bon Tempo 2008, 72, 83–84.
121 Refugee resettlement: security screening information. Human Rights First, April 2016: https://www.humanrightsfirst.org/sites/default/files/SyrianRefugeesVettingFacts.pdf.
122 FitzGerald 2019, 42–43.
123 Alex Nowrasteh, Terrorism and immigration: a risk analysis. Cato Institute, September 13, 2016: https:// object.cato.org/ sites/ cato.org/ files/ pubs/ pdf/ pa798_ 1_1.pdf.
124 Forrester et al. 2019.
125 Caron 1999, 356–360.
126 Hawkins 1988, 182, 248.
127 Scott 2001.
128 FitzGerald and Cook-Martín 2014, 15.
129 Blitz 2017, 394; FitzGerald et al. 2018.

130 Hobsbawm and Ranger 1992.
131 Caestecker and Moore 2010; FitzGerald and Cook-Martín 2014.
132 Madokoro 2016, 17.
133 Bon Tempo 2008, 4, 190.
134 Richmond 2001, 12.
135 This section draws on FitzGerald and Hirsch 2021.
136 Slovakia's leader said Islam has "no place" in his country. *Washington Post*, June 21, 2016: https://www.washingtonpost.com/news/worldviews/wp/2016/06/21/the-next-e-u-president-says-islam-has-no-place-in-his-country/.
137 Hungary's Orbán tells Germany: "You wanted the migrants, we didn't," *Deutsche Welle*, January 8, 2018: https://www.dw.com/en/hungarys-orban-tells-germany-you-wanted-the-migrants-we-didnt/a-42065012.
138 Dudzińska and Kotnarowski 2019.
139 Kallis 2018.
140 Bansak et al. 2016.
141 Heath and Richards 2020, Table 4.
142 Heath and Richards 2020, Table 3.
143 "Operational data portal: Ukraine refugee situation," UNHCR, March 13, 2022: https://data2.unhcr.org/en/situations/ukraine#_ga=2.168113121.1352064381.1647299624-25151545.1644451322.
144 Zolberg 1997.
145 This section draws from FitzGerald 2019a.
146 Betts 2010b.
147 Brocza and Paulhart 2015.
148 Marrus 2002, 260–262.
149 Ther 2019.

Chapter 8: Transnational Connections and Homeland Ties

1 Crisp 1999, 4.
2 Belloni 2019.
3 UN Refugee Convention 1951, Art. 1(A)2.
4 UNHCR, Solutions. 2021: https://www.unhcr.org/en-us/solutions.html.
5 Long 2014.
6 Van Hear 2006, 13.
7 Arar 2016.
8 Smith and Guarnizo 1998.
9 Anderson 1983.
10 FitzGerald 2004, 230; Van Hear 2006.
11 Cf. Waldinger and FitzGerald 2004; Vertovec 2004.
12 Connecting Refugees. UNHCR, September 2016: https://www.unhcr.org/5770d43c4.pdf.

13 Gillespie et al. 2018.
14 Granovetter 1973.
15 Dekker et al. 2018.
16 Cited in Gillespie et al. 2018, 1.
17 Gillespie et al. 2018.
18 Jumbert et al. 2018.
19 Jumbert et al. 2018; Balakian 2020.
20 Gillespie et al. 2018, 6.
21 Boochani 2018.
22 Carling et al. 2012.
23 World Bank Data: https://data.worldbank.org/country/somalia.
24 Vargas-Silva 2017, 1838.
25 Riak Akuei 2005, 6.
26 Jacobsen et al. 2014; Dalen and Pedersen 2007.
27 Díaz-Briquets and Pérez-López 1997.
28 Horst and Van Hear 2002.
29 UNHCR Projected Global Resettlement Needs 2021: https://www.unhcr.org/en-us/protection/resettlement/5ef34bfb7/projected-global-resettlement-needs-2021-pdf.html, p. 14.
30 Holland 2011.
31 Balakian 2017.
32 Lipman 2020, 85.
33 Zolberg et al. 1989, 190; FitzGerald 2019a.
34 Shaw 2015, 38–39.
35 US Senate, 31st Congress, 1st Session, Misc. No. 13, "Resolution," February 5, 1850.
36 US Congressional Serial Set, vol. 607, Session vol. 1, 32nd Congress, Special Senate Session, S. Exec. Doc. 2, March 11, 1851.
37 Wilson 1989: 39.
38 Turton and Marsden 2002, 1.
39 Rubin 2002.
40 Al-Ali et al. 2001, 596; Belloni 2019.
41 Waldinger and FitzGerald 2004.
42 Al-Ali et al. 2001, 593–596.
43 Al-Ali et al. 2001, 587–593.
44 Kibreab 2013.
45 Al-Ali et al. 2001, 589.
46 Al-Ali et al. 2001, 582–583.
47 Price 2009, 79.
48 Thiollet 2011, 113.
49 Ther 2019, 171.
50 FitzGerald 2019a.
51 Marrus 2002, 134.
52 von Einsiedel 2017, 1.
53 Madokoro 2016, 45.

54 Vickery 1984, 31.
55 Zolberg et al. 1989, 68; UNHCR condemns forced return of 1,700 Rwandans from Uganda. UNHCR, July 16, 2010: https://www.unhcr.org/en-us/news/latest/2010/7/4c406edb6/unhcr-condemns-forced-return-1700-rwandans-uganda.html.
56 Kelsey Norman, Concerns over a coercive return of Syrian refugees from Lebanon. *Political Violence at a Glance*, February 20, 2018: https://politicalviolenceataglance.org/2018/02/20/concerns-over-a-coercive-return-of-syrian-refugees-from-lebanon/.
57 McSpadden 1999.
58 Pappé 2007.
59 Segev 2007, 524.
60 Müller-Funk and Fransen 2020, 7.
61 Lipman 2020, ch. 1, 182.
62 Baron 2009.
63 Kendall 2014.
64 Nasaw 2020.
65 Dumitru 2016, 315.
66 Galipo 2018; Eastmond 2006, 156.
67 Koser and Black 1999, 8.
68 Crisp 1984.
69 Smith 2007.
70 Schwartz 2019.
71 Smith 2007: 13.
72 Koser and Black 1999: 8.
73 Zetter 1994; Hammond 2014, 502; Müller-Funk and Fransen 2020, 11.
74 Lubkemann 2008, 261.
75 Kibreab 2003.
76 Müller-Funk and Fransen 2020, 7.
77 Chatelard 2010, 61.
78 Van Hear 2006, 13.
79 Boeyink and Falisse 2021.
80 Harrell-Bond 1989; Geiger and Pécoud 2020.
81 Bradley 2011.
82 Lipman 2020, 152.
83 Monsutti and Balci 2014, 601–604.
84 Koch 2014; Crisp and Long 2016.

Chapter 9: Conclusion

1 FitzGerald and Arar 2018.
2 Wimmer and Schiller 2003.
3 Stark 1991.
4 Weiner 1985; Greenhill 2010; Zolberg et al. 1989.

5 Koser and Black 1999.
6 Cook-Martín and FitzGerald 2019.
7 Information on UNHCR Resettlement: https://www.unhcr.org/en-us/information-on-unhcr-resettlement.html.
8 FitzGerald 2019a.
9 See Ruhs 2013.
10 Mann 1993.
11 Pierson 2004.
12 See Haydu 1998.
13 FitzGerald and Cook-Martín 2014.
14 White 2019; Belloni 2019.
15 Mountz 2010; Orchard 2014; FitzGerald 2019a.
16 Carens 2013.
17 FitzPatrick and Bonoan 2003.
18 UNHCR 2020, 4.
19 Guidelines on international protection. Cessation of refugee status under Article 1C(5) and (6) of the 1951 Convention relating to the Status of Refugees (the "Ceased Circumstances" Clauses). UNHCR, February 10, 2003: https://www.unhcr.org/publications/legal/3e637a202/guidelines-international-protection-3-cessation-refugee-status-under-article.html.
20 Scalettaris and Gubert 2019.
21 Abdi 2015; Ludwig 2016.
22 Kunz 1973, 128.
23 Rubinstein 1936, 722; Aleinikoff and Zamore 2019.
24 Adepoju et al. 2007.
25 Hanafi 2014a, 588.
26 Ruhs and Chang 2004.
27 Nasaw 2020.
28 Refugee statistics. UNHCR, 2020: https://www.unrefugees.org/refugee-facts/statistics/.
29 For examples of the general erasure of Palestinian refugees when making comparisons or assessing the global refugee situation by state, international organization, think-tank, and academic researchers, see UNHCR Global Report 2019: https://reporting.unhcr.org/sites/default/files/gr2019/pdf/GR2019_English_Full_lowres.pdf#_ga=2.185019433.1468355965.1614379561-1322392530.1600106218.See also the Regional Refugee and Resilience Plan (3RP) reports reflecting the perspectives of Middle Eastern host states and the comparisons in Understanding the Venezuelan refugee crisis, Wilson Center, September 13, 2019: https://www.wilsoncenter.org/article/understanding-the-venezuelan-refugee-crisis.
30 Norwegian Refugee Council, Global Displacement Figures: https://www.nrc.no/global-figures.
31 Elsheikh and Ayazi 2017.
32 Geddes 2021, 5.

33 Madokoro 2016, 77.
34 Madokoro 2016, 200–201.
35 Global Compact on Refugees, III(13), 2018: https://www.unhcr. org/5c658aed4.pdf.
36 Malkki 1996; Espiritu 2006.
37 Jaffe 1962, 187–190.
38 Google Trends is a search engine provided by Google that shows the relative popularity of a search term. According to the Google Trends Help Center, "Each data point is divided by the total searches of the geography and time range it represents, to compare relative popularity": https://support.google.com/trends/answer/4365533?hl=en.
39 Slovic et al. 2017.
40 Rebecca Wright, "The Rohingya Alan Kurdi": Will the world take notice now? *CNN.com*, September 13, 2017: https://www.cnn. com/2017/01/03/asia/myanmar-alan-kurdi/index.html.
41 McAdam 2012; Martin et al. 2018; Scott 2020.
42 Sydney Declaration of Principles on the Protection of Persons Displaced in the Context of Sea Level Rise. International Law Association, 2018: https://environmentalmigration.iom.int/sites/default/files/ILA Resolution_6_2018_SeaLevelRise_SydneyDeclaration.pdf.
43 IOM, World Migration Report 2020: https://www.un.org/sites/un2. un.org/files/wmr_2020.pdf.
44 Gemenne 2011, S44–S45.
45 Martin 2010.
46 Bascom 1999, 106.
47 Zolberg et al. 1989, 271.
48 Arias and Blair 2021.
49 Blitz 2017.
50 Jacobsen 2002.
51 Loschmann 2020.
52 Masterson 2016.
53 Hainmueller and Hopkins 2015, 539.
54 For a nuanced analysis, see Sana 2020.
55 Barnett 2011b, 122, 229–230.
56 Ther 2019, 263; Abdelaaty 2021.
57 Adida et al. 2018.
58 Erbelding 2018, 145.
59 Soo 2016; Linhard 2019.
60 Gatrell 2013, 186.
61 Bascom 1999, 20.
62 A discussion with President Iván Duque on granting temporary legal protection to Venezuelan migrants in Colombia. Center for Strategic and International Studies, February 26, 2021: https://www.csis.org/analysis/ discussion-president-iv%C3%A1n-duque-granting-temporary-legal-protection-venezuelan-migrants.

References

Abdelaaty, L. E. 2021. *Discrimination and Delegation: Explaining State Responses to Refugees.* Oxford University Press.

Abdi, C. M. 2015. *Elusive Jannah: The Somali Diaspora and a Borderless Muslim Identity.* University of Minnesota Press.

Abella, I., and Troper, H. M. 2012 [1983]. *None Is Too Many: Canada and the Jews of Europe, 1933–1948.* University of Toronto Press.

Abrego, L. J. 2017. On silences: Salvadoran refugees then and now. *Latino Studies*, 15(1), 73–85.

Adepoju, A. 1995. Migration in Africa: An overview. In Baker, J., and Aina, T. A., eds., *The Migration Experience in Africa.* Nordic Africa Institute, 87–108.

Adepoju, A., Boulton, A., and Levin, M. 2007. Promoting integration through mobility: free movement and the ECOWAS Protocol. UNHCR: https://www.unhcr.org/476650ae2.pdf.

Adhikari, P. 2013. Conflict-induced displacement, understanding the causes of flight. *American Journal of Political Science*, 57(1), 82–89.

Adhikari, R. 2021. Temporalities of resettlement: date-waiting for an American future in a Bhutanese refugee camp in Nepal. *American Anthropologist*, 123(2), 237–249.

Adida, C. L., Lo, A., and Platas, M. R. 2018. Perspective taking can promote short-term inclusionary behavior toward Syrian refugees. *Proceedings of the National Academy of Sciences*, 115(38), 9521–9526.

Agamben, G. 2013. We refugees. *Symposium: A Quarterly Journal in Modern Literatures*, 49(2), 114–119.

Akoka, K. 2020. *L'asile et l'exil: une histoire de la distinction réfugiés/migrants.* La Découverte.

Akram, S. 2014. UNRWA and Palestinian refugees. In Fiddian-Qasmiyeh, E., et al., eds., *The Oxford Handbook of Refugee and Forced Migration Studies.* Oxford University Press, 227–240.

Al-Ali, N., Black, R., and Koser, K. 2001. Refugees and transnationalism: The experience of Bosnians and Eritreans in Europe. *Journal of Ethnic and Migration Studies*, 27(4), 615–634.

Aleinikoff, T. A., and Zamore, L. 2019. *The Arc of Protection: Reforming the International Refugee Regime*. Stanford University Press.

Al-Khalidi, A., Hoffmann, S., and Tanner, V. 2007. Iraqi refugees in the Syrian Arab Republic: A field-based snapshot. Brookings Institution–University of Bern Project on Internal Displacement. https://www.brookings.edu/research/iraqi–refugees–in–the–syrian–arab–republic–a–field–based–snapshot/.

Allott, A. 1974. The changing legal status of boundaries in Africa: A diachronic view. In Ingham, K., ed., *Foreign Relations of African States*. Butterworth.

Aminzade, R. 1992. Historical sociology and time. *Sociological Methods & Research*, 20(4), 456–480.

Anderson, B. 1983. *Imagined Communities: Reflections on the Origin and Spread of Nationalism*. Verso Books.

Antwi-Boateng, O., and Braimah, M. K. 2021. The dilemma of Ghana-based Liberian refugees and the challenges of repatriation and integration. *Journal of Refugee Studies*, 34(1), 1185–1201.

Arar, R. 2021. Understanding refugees. In Yom, S., ed., *Societies of the Middle East and North Africa: Structures, Vulnerabilities, and Forces*. 2nd ed. Routledge.

Arar, R. 2017. The new grand compromise: How Syrian refugees changed the stakes in the global refugee assistance regime. *Middle East Law and Governance*, 9(3), 298–312.

Arar, R. M. 2016. How political migrants' networks differ from those of economic migrants: "Strategic anonymity" among Iraqi refugees in Jordan. *Journal of Ethnic and Migration Studies*, 42(3), 519–535.

Arboleda, E. 1991. Refugee definition in Africa and Latin America: The lessons of pragmatism. *International Journal of Refugee Law*, 3(2), 185–207.

Arendt, H. 1943. We refugees. *Menorah Journal*, 31(1), 69–77.

Arendt, H. 1968. *The Origins of Totalitarianism*. Harcourt, Brace & World.

Arias, S. B., and Blair, C. 2021. Changing tides: Public attitudes on climate migration. *The Journal of Politics*.

Arnaout, G. M. 1987. *Asylum in the Arab-Islamic Tradition*. UNHCR.

Axt, H.-J. 1997. The impact of German policy on refugee flows from former Yugoslavia. In Münz, R., and Weiner, M., eds., *Migrants, Refugees and Foreign Policy: US and German Policies toward Countries of Origin*. Berghahn Books, 1–34.

Bakewell, O. 2008. Research beyond the categories: The importance of policy irrelevant research into forced migration. *Journal of Refugee Studies*, 21(4), 432–453.

Bakewell, O. 2014. Relaunching migration systems. *Migration Studies*, 2(3), 300–318.

Balakian, S. 2020. Navigating patchwork governance: Somalis in Kenya, national security, and refugee resettlement. *African Studies Review*, 63(1), 43–64.

Balakian, S. A. 2017. The fraudulent family: Humanitarianism, security, and kinship in refugee resettlement from Kenya. PhD dissertation, University of Illinois at Urbana-Champaign. https://www.ideals.illinois.edu/handle/2142/97747.

Ballinger, P. 2020. *The World Refugees Made: Decolonization and the Foundation of Postwar Italy*. Cornell University Press.

Balsari, S., et al. 2015. Syrian refugee crisis: When aid is not enough. *The Lancet*, 385(9972), 942–943.

Bansak, K., Hainmueller, J., and Hangartner, D. 2016. How economic, humanitarian, and religious concerns shape European attitudes toward asylum seekers. *Science*, 354(6309), 217–222.

Barnett, M. 2011a. *Empire of Humanity: A History of Humanitarianism*. Cornell University Press.

Barnett, M. 2011b. Humanitarianism, paternalism, and the UNHCR. In Betts, A., and Loescher, G., eds., *Refugees in International Relations*. Oxford University Press, 105–132.

Barnett, M. 2018. Humanitarianism and human rights. In Brown, C., and Eckersley, R., eds., *The Oxford Handbook of International Political Theory*. Oxford University Press, 289–303.

Baron, N. 2009. Remaking Soviet society: The filtration of returnees from Nazi Germany, 1944–49. In Gatrell, P., and Baron, N., eds., *Warlands: Population Resettlement and State Reconstruction in the Soviet–East European Borderlands, 1945–1950*. Palgrave Macmillan, 89–116.

Bar-Tuvia, S. 2018. Australian and Israeli agreements for the permanent transfer of refugees: Stretching further the (Il)legality and (Im)morality of Western externalization policies. *International Journal of Refugee Law*, 30(3), 474–511.

Bascom, J. 1999. *Losing Place: Refugee Populations and Rural Transformations in East Africa*. Berghahn Books.

Bashford, A., and Gilchrist, C. 2012. The colonial history of the 1905 Aliens Act. *The Journal of Imperial and Commonwealth History*, 40(3), 409–437.

Baylouny, A. M. 2020. *When Blame Backfires*. Cornell University Press.

Bean, F. D., et al. 2012. The dimensions and degree of second-generation incorporation in US and European cities: A comparative study of inclusion and exclusion. *International Journal of Comparative Sociology*, 53(3), 181–209.

Bello, D. A. 2018. Cultivating Torghut Mongols in a semi-arid steppe. *Journal of Chinese History*, 2, 355–372.

Belloni, M. 2019. *The Big Gamble: The Migration of Eritreans to Europe*. University of California Press.

Benton, M., and Diegert, P. 2018. *A Needed Evidence Revolution: Using*

Cost-Benefit Analysis to Improve Refugee Integration Programming. Bertelsmann Stiftung.

Bergen, D. 2016. *War and Genocide: A Concise History of the Holocaust.* Rowman & Littlefield.

Berry, M. E. 2018. *War, Women, and Power: From Violence to Mobilization in Rwanda and Bosnia-Herzegovina.* Cambridge University Press.

Bessel, R., and Haake, C. 2009. Introduction: Forced removal in the modern world. In Bessel, R., and Haake, C., eds., *Removing Peoples: Forced Removal in the Modern World.* Oxford University Press, 3–11.

Betts, A. 2003. Public goods theory and the provision of refugee protection: The role of the joint-product model in burden-sharing theory. *Journal of Refugee Studies,* 16(3), 274–296.

Betts, A. 2009. *Forced Migration and Global Politics.* Wiley–Blackwell.

Betts, A. 2010a. *Protection by Persuasion: International Cooperation in the Refugee Regime.* Cornell University Press.

Betts, A. 2010b. The refugee regime complex. *Refugee Survey Quarterly,* 29(1), 12–37.

Betts, A. 2013. *Survival Migration: Failed Governance and the Crisis of Displacement.* Cornell University Press.

Betts, A. 2021. *The Wealth of Refugees: How Displaced People Can Build Economies.* Oxford University Press.

Betts, A., and Collier, P. 2017. *Refuge: Transforming a Broken Refugee System.* Penguin UK.

Bevelander, P. 2020. Integrating refugees into labor markets. *IZA World of Labor,* 269, 1–9.

Biehl, K. S. 2015. Governing through uncertainty: Experiences of being a refugee in Turkey as a country for temporary asylum. *Social Analysis,* 59(1), 57–75.

Binder, A. 2000. Gender and the membership in a particular social group category of the 1951 Refugee Convention. *Columbia Journal of Gender and Law,* 10, 167.

Birger, L., Shoham, S., and Bolzman, L. 2018. "Better a prison in Israel than dying on the way." Humboldt-Universität. https://edoc.hu–berlin.de/handle/18452/21030.

Ble, M. G., Leghtas, I., and Graham, J. 2020. From displacement to development: How Peru can transform Venezuelan displacement into shared growth. Center for Global Development. https://www.cgdev.org/sites/default/files/from–displacement–to–development–peru.pdf.

Blitz, B. 2017. Another story: What public opinion data tell us about refugee and humanitarian policy. *Journal on Migration and Human Security,* 5(2), 379–400.

Blumi, I. 2013. *Ottoman Refugees, 1878–1939: Migration in a Post-Imperial World.* Bloomsbury.

Böcker, A., and Havinga, T. 1998. Asylum applications in the European

Union: Patterns and trends and the effects of policy measures. *Journal of Refugee Studies*, 11(3), 245–266.

Boeyink, C., and Falisse, J.-B. 2021. Kicking refugees out makes everyone less safe. *Foreign Policy*. https://foreignpolicy.com/2021/02/18/tanzania–burundi–kicking–refugees–out–makes–everyone–less–safe/.

Bon Tempo, C. J. 2008. *Americans at the Gate: The United States and Refugees during the Cold War.* Princeton University Press.

Boochani, B. 2018. *No Friend but the Mountains: Writing from Manus Prison.* Picador.

Bourdieu, P., and Sayad, A. 2020 [1964]. *Uprooting: The Crisis of Traditional Agriculture in Algeria.* Polity.

Boustan, L. P. 2007. Were Jews political refugees or economic migrants? Assessing the persecution theory of Jewish emigration, 1881–1914. In Hatton, T. J., O'Rourke, K. H., and Alan M. Taylor, eds., *The New Comparative Economic History: Essays in Honor of Jeffrey G. Williamson.* MIT Press, 267–290.

Bowes, J. P. 2014. American Indian removal beyond the Removal Act. *Journal of the Native American and Indigenous Studies Association*, 1(1), 65–87.

Bradley, M. 2011. Unlocking protracted displacement: Central America's "success story" reconsidered. *Refugee Survey Quarterly*, 30(4), 84–121.

Bretones Lane, F. 2019. Spain, the Caribbean, and the making of religious sanctuary. Unpublished PhD dissertation. Vanderbilt University.

Brocza, S., and Paulhart, K. 2015. EU mobility partnerships: A smart instrument for the externalization of migration control. *European Journal of Futures Research*, 3(1), 1–7.

Brubaker, R. 1995. Aftermaths of empire and the unmixing of peoples: Historical and comparative perspectives. *Ethnic and Racial Studies*, 18(2), 189–218.

Brubaker, R. 2004. *Ethnicity Without Groups.* Harvard University Press.

Bruno, A., 2021. Iraqi and Afghan Special Immigrant Visa Programs. Washington, DC: Congressional Research Service. https://sgp.fas.org/crs/homesec/R43725.pdf.

Burawoy, B. 1976. The functions and reproduction of migrant labor: Comparative material from Southern Africa and the United States. *American Journal of Sociology*, 81(5), 1050–1087.

Burmann, M., and Valeyatheepillay, M. 2017. Asylum recognition rates in the top 5 EU countries. *ifo DICE Report*, 15(2), 48–50.

Caestecker, F. 2011. Refugees in the European historiography: Beyond the administrative category. Conference on *Historiographies sans frontières. Les migrations internationales saisies par les histoires nationales (XIXe–XXe siècles).* Paris, October 4.

Caestecker, F., and Moore, B. 2010. *Refugees from Nazi Germany and the Liberal European States.* Berghahn Books.

Cantor, D., and Rodríguez Serna, N., eds. 2016. *The New Refugees: Crime and Forced Displacement in Latin America.* University of London.

Capps, R., and Newland, K. 2015. The integration outcomes of US refugees: Successes and challenges. Migration Policy Institute. https://www.migrationpolicy.org/research/integration–outcomes–us–refugees–successes–and–challenges.

Carens, J. 2013. *The Ethics of Immigration*. Oxford University Press.

Carling, J., Erdal, M. B., and Horst, C. 2012. How does conflict in migrants' country of origin affect remittance-sending? Financial priorities and transnational obligations among Somalis and Pakistanis in Norway. *International Migration Review*, 46(2), 283–309.

Caron, V. 1999. *Uneasy Asylum: France and the Jewish Refugee Crisis, 1933–1942*. Stanford University Press.

Carter, J. 1995. *Keeping Faith: Memoirs of a President*. University of Arkansas Press.

Castles, S. 2003. Towards a sociology of forced migration and social transformation. *Sociology*, 37(1), 13–34.

Chan, E., and Schloenhardt, A. 2007. North Korean refugees and international refugee law. *International Journal of Refugee Law*, 19(2), 215–245.

Chatelard, G. 2010. Cross-border mobility of Iraqi refugees. *Forced Migration Review*, (34), 60.

Chatty, D. 2010. *Displacement and Dispossession in the Modern Middle East*. Cambridge University Press.

Chatty, D. 2018. *Syria: The Making and Unmaking of a Refuge State*. Oxford University Press.

Chimni, B. S. 1998. The geopolitics of refugee studies: A view from the South. *Journal of Refugee Studies*, 11(4), 350–374.

Chimni, B. S. 2019. Global compact on refugees: One step forward, two steps back. *International Journal of Refugee Law*, 30(4), 630–634.

Christopher, A. J. 2001. *The Atlas of Changing South Africa*. Psychology Press.

Cobbing, J. 1988. The Mfecane as alibi: Thoughts on Dithakong and Mbolompo. *The Journal of African History*, 29(3), 487–519.

Cohen, G. D. 2012. *In War's Wake: Europe's Displaced Persons in the Postwar Order*. Oxford University Press.

Collyer, M. 2010. Stranded migrants and the fragmented journey. *Journal of Refugee Studies*, 23(3), 273–293.

Cook-Martín, D., and FitzGerald, D. S. 2019. How their laws affect our laws: Mechanisms of immigration policy diffusion in the Americas, 1790–2010. *Law & Society Review*, 53(1), 41–76.

Costello, C., Foster, M., and McAdam, J., eds. 2021. *The Oxford Handbook of International Refugee Law*. Oxford University Press.

Craig-Norton, J. 2019. *The Kindertransport: Contesting Memory*. Indiana University Press.

Crawley, H., et al. 2016. Unpacking a rapidly changing scenario: Migration flows, routes and trajectories across the Mediterranean. Unravelling the Mediterranean Migration Crisis (MEDMIG). http://www.medmig.

info/wp–content/uploads/2016/03/MEDMIG–Briefing–01–March–2016–FINAL–1.pdf.

Crawley, H., and Skleparis, D. 2018. Refugees, migrants, neither, both: Categorical fetishism and the politics of bounding in Europe's "migration crisis." *Journal of Ethnic and Migration Studies*, 44(1), 48–64.

Crisp, J. 1984. Voluntary repatriation programmes for African refugees: A critical examination. Refugees Studies Programme, Queen Elizabeth House, University of Oxford.

Crisp, J. 1999. Who has counted the refugees? UNHCR and the politics of numbers. https://www.unhcr.org/en–us/research/working/3ae6a0c22/counted–refugees–unhcr–politics–numbers–jeff–crisp.html.

Crisp, J. 2003. Refugees and the global politics of asylum. *The Political Quarterly*, 74(s1), 75–87.

Crisp, J. 2017. Finding space for protection: An inside account of the evolution of UNHCR's Urban Refugee Policy. *Refuge: Canada's Journal on Refugees*, 33(1), 87–96.

Crisp, J., and Long, K. 2016. Safe and voluntary refugee repatriation: From principle to practice. *Journal on Migration and Human Security*, 4(3), 141–147.

Crush, J., and Chikanda, A. 2014. Forced migration in Southern Africa. In Fiddian-Qasmiyeh, E., et al., eds., *The Oxford Handbook of Refugee and Forced Migration Studies*. Oxford University Press, 554–570.

Cuéllar, M.-F. 2006. Refugee security and the organizational logic of legal mandates. *Georgetown Journal of International Law*, 37, 583–723.

Czaika, M. 2005. A Refugee Burden Index: Methodology and its application. *Migration Letters*, 2(2), 101–125.

Daher, J. 2019. The deep roots of the depreciation of the Syrian pound. European University Institute. https://cadmus.eui.eu/bitstream/handle/1814/65585/MED_WPCS_2019_18.pdf?sequence=1&isAllowed=y.

Dalen, K., and Pedersen, J. 2007. Iraqis in Jordan: Their number and characteristics. Oslo: Fafo. https://www.fafo.no/en/publications/other-publications/item/iraqis-in-jordan-their-number-and-characteristics.

Davenport, C., Moore, W., and Poe, S. 2003. Sometimes you just have to leave: Domestic threats and forced migration, 1964–1989. *International Interactions*, 29(1), 27–55.

Davies, S. E. 2006. The Asian rejection? International refugee law in Asia. *Australian Journal of Politics & History*, 52(4), 562–575.

de Haas, H., Miller, M. J., and Castles, S. 2020. *The Age of Migration: International Population Movements in the Modern World*. Guilford Press.

Dekker, R., et al. 2018. Smart refugees: How Syrian asylum migrants use social media information in migration decision–making. *Social Media + Society*, 4(1).

Devictor, X., Do, Q.-T., and Levchenko, A. A. 2020. The globalization of refugee flows. The World Bank. https://openknowledge.worldbank.org/handle/10986/33580.

Díaz-Briquets, S., and Pérez-López, J. 1997. Refugee remittances: conceptual issues and the Cuban and Nicaraguan experiences. *International Migration Review*, 31(2), 411–437.

Dirks, G. E. 1977. *Canada's Refugee Policy: Indifference or Opportunism?* McGill-Queen's University Press.

Dowty, A. 1989. *Closed Borders: The Contemporary Assault on Freedom of Movement.* Yale University Press.

Dubnov, A. M., and Robson, L. 2019. *Partitions: A Transnational History of Twentieth-Century Territorial Separatism.* Stanford University Press.

Dudzińska, A., and Kotnarowski, M. 2019. Imaginary Muslims: How the Polish right frames Islam. Washington, DC: Brookings Institution. https://www.brookings.edu/research/imaginary–muslims–how–polands–populists–frame–islam/.

Dumitru, D. 2016. Returning home after the Holocaust. Jewish–Gentile encounters in the Soviet borderland. In Bajohr, F., and Löw, A., eds., *The Holocaust and European Societies: Social Processes and Social Dynamics.* Palgrave Macmillan, 307–320.

Eastmond, M. 2006. Transnational returns and reconstruction in post-war Bosnia and Herzegovina. *International Migration*, 44(3), 141–166.

Elie, J. 2014. Histories of refugee and forced migration studies. In Fiddian-Qasmiyeh, E., et al., eds., *The Oxford Handbook of Refugee and Forced Migration Studies.* Oxford University Press, 23–35.

Elkind, J. 2014. "The Virgin Mary is going south": Refugee resettlement in South Vietnam, 1954–1956. *Diplomatic History*, 38(5), 987–1016.

Elsheikh, E., and Ayazi, H. 2017. Moving targets: An analysis of global forced migration. Haas Institute, University of California, Berkeley. https://belonging.berkeley.edu/moving–targets–analysis–global–forced–migration.

Engel, S., and Ibáñez, A. M. 2007. Displacement due to violence in Colombia: A household-level analysis. *Economic Development and Cultural Change*, 55(2), 335–365.

Erbelding, R. 2018. *Rescue Board: The Untold Story of America's Efforts to Save the Jews of Europe.* Knopf Doubleday.

Erdal, M. B., and Oeppen, C. 2018. Forced to leave? The discursive and analytical significance of describing migration as forced and voluntary. *Journal of Ethnic and Migration Studies*, 44(6), 981–998.

Espiritu, Y. L. 2014. *Body Counts: The Vietnam War and Militarized Refugees.* University of California Press.

Espiritu, Y. L. 2006. Toward a critical refugee study: The Vietnamese refugee subject in US scholarship. *Journal of Vietnamese Studies*, 1(1–2), 410–433.

Etzold, B., et al. 2019. Transnational figurations of displacement: Conceptualising protracted displacement and translocal connectivity through a process-oriented perspective. Bonn International Centre for Conflict Studies. https://trafig.eu/output/working–papers/2019–01.

Fawcett, J. T. 1989. Networks, linkages, and migration systems. *International Migration Review*, 23(3), 671–680.

Fee, M. 2021. Lives stalled: The costs of waiting for refugee resettlement. *Journal of Ethnic and Migration Studies*, 1–19.

Fee, M., and Arar, R. 2019. What happens when the United States stops taking in refugees? *Contexts*, 18(2), 18–23.

Feller, E. 2005. Refugees are not migrants. *Refugee Survey Quarterly*, 24(4), 27–35.

Ferrara, A., and Pianciola, N. 2019. The dark side of connectedness: Forced migrations and mass violence between the late Tsarist and Ottoman empires (1853–1920). *Historical Research*, 92(257), 608–631.

Fiddian-Qasmiyeh, E. 2016. Refugees hosting refugees. *Forced Migration Review*, (53), 25–27.

Fiddian-Qasmiyeh, E., and Daley, P., eds. 2019. *Routledge Handbook of South–South Relations*. Routledge.

Fischbein, J., et al. 2013. US border enforcement in an era of economic uncertainty. In FitzGerald, D. S., Díaz, J. H., and Keyes, D., eds., *The Wall Between Us: A Mixteco Migrant Community in Mexico and the United States*. Center for Comparative Immigration Studies, 19–37.

Fischel de Andrade, J. H. 2019. The 1984 Cartagena Declaration: A critical review of some aspects of its emergence and relevance. *Refugee Survey Quarterly*, 38(4), 341–362.

FitzGerald, D. S. 2004. Beyond "transnationalism": Mexican hometown politics at an American labour union. *Ethnic and Racial Studies*, 27(2), 228–247.

FitzGerald, D. S. 2009. *A Nation of Emigrants: How Mexico Manages Its Migration*. University of California Press.

FitzGerald, D. S. 2017. The history of racialized citizenship. In Shachar, A., et al., eds., *The Oxford Handbook of Citizenship*. Oxford University Press, 129–152.

FitzGerald, D. S. 2019a. *Refuge beyond Reach: How Rich Democracies Repel Asylum Seekers*. Oxford University Press.

FitzGerald, D. S. 2019b. Rethinking units of analysis in comparative studies of international migration. *Renewing the Migration Debate*. Amsterdam: KNAW Academy Colloquium, 108–114. https://www.migrationinstitute.org/publications/renewing–the–migration–debate–building–disciplinary–and–geographical–bridges–to–explain–global–migration–1/@@download/file.

FitzGerald, D. S., and Arar, R. 2018. The sociology of refugee migration. *Annual Review of Sociology*, 44, 387–406.

FitzGerald, D. S., and Cook-Martín, D. 2014. *Culling the Masses: The Democratic Origins of Racist Immigration Policy in the Americas*. Harvard University Press.

FitzGerald, D. S., et al. 2018. Can you become one of us? A historical comparison of legal selection of "assimilable" immigrants in Europe and the Americas. *Journal of Ethnic and Migration Studies*, 44, 27–47.

FitzGerald, D. S., and Hirsch, A. 2021. Norm-busting: Rightist challenges in US and Australian immigration and refugee policies. *Third World Quarterly*.

Fitzpatrick, J., and Bonoan, R. 2003. Cessation of refugee protection. In Feller, E., Türk, V., and Nicholson, F., eds., *Refugee Protection in International Law: UNHCR's Global Consultations on International Protection*. Cambridge University Press, 491–544.

Forrester, A. C., et al. 2019. Do immigrants import terrorism? CATO Institute. https://www.cato.org/publications/working-paper/do-immigrants-import-terrorism.

Foster, M., and Lambert, H. 2019. *International Refugee Law and the Protection of Stateless Persons*. Oxford University Press.

Fraenkel, P. L., and Murray, R. 1985. *The Namibians*. Minority Rights Group.

Fransen, S., and de Haas, H. 2019. The volume and geography of forced migration. International Migration Institute. https://www.migrationinstitute.org/publications/the-volume-and-geography-of-forced-migration.

Freier, L., and Parent, N. 2019. The regional response to the Venezuelan exodus. *Current History*, 118(805), 56–61.

Freier, L. F., Berganza, I., and Blouin, C. 2020. The Cartagena refugee definition and Venezuelan displacement in Latin America. *International Migration*.

Freier, L. F., and Pérez, L. M. 2021. Nationality-based criminalisation of South–South migration: The experience of Venezuelan forced migrants in Peru. *European Journal on Criminal Policy and Research*, 1–21.

Frelick, B. 2003. In-country refugee processing of Haitians: The case against. *Refuge: Canada's Journal on Refugees*, 66–72.

Fresia, M. 2014. Forced migration in West Africa. In Fiddian-Qasmiyeh, E., et al., eds., *The Oxford Handbook of Refugee and Forced Migration Studies*. Oxford University Press, 541–553.

Friedman, M. 2021. Uganda and the Sixth Congress. *Theodor Herzl's Zionist Journey: Exodus and Return*. De Gruyter, 236–284.

Galipo, A. 2018. *Return Migration and Nation Building in Africa: Reframing the Somali Diaspora*. Routledge.

Galli, C. 2020. Humanitarian capital: how lawyers help immigrants use suffering to claim membership in the nation-state. *Journal of Ethnic and Migration Studies*, 46(11), 2181–2198.

Gao, B. 2013. *Shanghai Sanctuary: Chinese and Japanese Policy toward European Jewish Refugees during World War II*. Oxford University Press.

García, M. C. 2006. *Seeking Refuge: Central American Migration to Mexico, the United States, and Canada*. University of California Press.

García, M. C. 2017. *The Refugee Challenge in Post-Cold War America*. Oxford University Press.

Garland, L. 2014. *After They Closed the Gates: Jewish Illegal Immigration to the United States, 1921–1965*. University of Chicago Press.

Gatrell, P. 2005. *A Whole Empire Walking: Refugees in Russia during World War I.* Indiana University Press.

Gatrell, P. 2013. *The Making of the Modern Refugee.* Oxford University Press.

Gatrell, P. 2019. *The Unsettling of Europe: How Migration Reshaped a Continent.* Basic Books.

Geddes, A. 2021. *Governing Migration beyond the State: Europe, North America, South America, and Southeast Asia in a Global Context.* Oxford University Press.

Geiger, M., and Pécoud, A., eds. 2020. *The International Organization for Migration: The New "UN Migration Agency" in Critical Perspective.* Palgrave Macmillan.

Gemenne, F. 2011. Why the numbers don't add up: A review of estimates and predictions of people displaced by environmental changes. *Global Environmental Change*, 21, S41–S49.

Gibney, M. J. 2003. *Globalizing Rights: The Oxford Amnesty Lectures 1999.* Oxford University Press.

Gibney, M. J. 2004. *The Ethics and Politics of Asylum: Liberal Democracy and the Response to Refugees.* Cambridge University Press.

Gibney, M. J. 2013. Is deportation a form of forced migration? *Refugee Survey Quarterly*, 32(2), 116–129.

Gilbert, B. 1901. The right of asylum in the legations of the United States in Central and South America. *Harvard Law Review*, 15(2), 118–139.

Gillespie, M., Osseiran, S., and Cheesman, M. 2018. Syrian refugees and the digital passage to Europe: Smartphone infrastructures and affordances. *Social Media + Society*, 4(1), 1–12.

Glasman, J. 2019. *Humanitarianism and the Quantification of Human Needs: Minimal Humanity.* Routledge.

Goodwin-Gill, G. S. 1983. *The Refugee in International Law.* Clarendon Press.

Goodwin-Gill, G. S. 2014. The international law of refugee protection. In Fiddian-Qasmiyeh, E., et al., eds., *The Oxford Handbook of Refugee and Forced Migration Studies.* Oxford University Press, 36–47.

Gottwald, M. 2014. Burden sharing and refugee protection. In Fiddian-Qasmiyeh, E., et al., eds., *The Oxford Handbook of Refugee and Forced Migration Studies.* Oxford University Press, 525–537.

Gould, J. 1973. Hiketeia. *The Journal of Hellenic Studies*, 93, 74–103.

Gould, W. 1974. Refugees in tropical Africa. *International Migration Review*, 8(3), 413–430.

Grace, B. L., Nawyn, S. J., and Okwako, B. 2018. The right to belong (if you can afford it): Market-based restrictions on social citizenship in refugee resettlement. *Journal of Refugee Studies*, 31(1), 42–62.

Granovetter, M. S. 1973. The strength of weak ties. *American Journal of Sociology*, 78(6), 1360–1380.

Greenhill, K. M. 2010. *Weapons of Mass Migration: Forced Displacement, Coercion, and Foreign Policy.* Cornell University Press.

Guiraudon, V. 2000. European integration and migration policy: Vertical policy-making as venue shopping. *Journal of Common Market Studies*, 38(2), 251–271.

Haddad, E. 2008. *The Refugee in International Society: Between Sovereigns*. Cambridge University Press.

Hainmueller, J., and Hopkins, D. J. 2015. The hidden American immigration consensus: A conjoint analysis of attitudes toward immigrants. *American Journal of Political Science*, 59(3), 529–548.

Hamlin, R. 2014. *Let Me Be a Refugee: Administrative Justice and the Politics of Asylum in the United States, Canada, and Australia*. Oxford University Press.

Hamlin, R. 2021. *Crossing: How We Label and React to People on the Move*. Stanford University Press.

Hamlin, R., and Wolgin, P. E. 2012. Symbolic politics and policy feedback: The United Nations Protocol relating to the status of refugees and American refugee policy in the Cold War. *International Migration Review*, 46(3), 586–624.

Hammond, L. 2014. "Voluntary" repatriation and reintegration. In Fiddian-Qasmiyeh, E., et al., eds., *The Oxford Handbook of Refugee and Forced Migration Studies*. Oxford University Press, 499–511.

Hanafi, S. 2014a. Forced migration in the Middle East and North Africa. In Fiddian-Qasmiyeh, E., et al., eds., *The Oxford Handbook of Refugee and Forced Migration Studies*. Oxford University Press, 585–598.

Hanafi, S. 2014b. UNRWA as a "phantom sovereign": Governance practices in Lebanon. In Hanafi, S., Hilal, L., and Takkenberg, L., eds., *UNRWA and Palestinian Refugees*. Routledge, 129–142.

Hanafi, S., and Long, T. 2010. Governance, governmentalities, and the state of exception in the Palestinian refugee camps of Lebanon. *Journal of Refugee Studies*, 23(2), 134–159.

Hansen, R. 2014. State controls: Borders, refugees, and citizenship. In Fiddian-Qasmiyeh, E., et al., eds., *The Oxford Handbook of Refugee and Forced Migration Studies*. Oxford University Press, 253–264.

Hardy, C. 2003. Refugee determination: Power and resistance in systems of Foucauldian power. *Administration & Society*, 35(4), 462–488.

Harrell-Bond, B. 2002. Can humanitarian work with refugees be humane? *Human Rights Quarterly*, 24(1), 51–85.

Harrell-Bond, B. E. 1989. Repatriation: Under what conditions is it the most desirable solution for refugees? An agenda for research. *African Studies Review*, 32(1), 41–70.

Hathaway, J. C. 1984. The evolution of refugee status in international law: 1920–1950. *International & Comparative Law Quarterly*, 33(2), 348–380.

Hathaway, J. C. 1997. *Reconceiving International Refugee Law*. Martinus Nijhoff.

Hathaway, J. C. 2007. Forced migration studies: Could we agree just to "date"? *Journal of Refugee Studies*, 20(3), 349–369.

Hatton, T. J. 2017. Refugees and asylum seekers, the crisis in Europe and the future of policy. *Economic Policy*, 32(91), 447–496.

Hatton, T. J., and Williamson, J. G. 2005. *Global Migration and the World Economy: Two Centuries of Policy and Performance.* MIT Press.

Hawkins, F. 1988. *Canada and Immigration: Public Policy and Public Concern.* McGill-Queen's University Press.

Haydu, J. 1998. Making use of the past: Time periods as cases to compare and as sequences of problem solving. *American Journal of Sociology*, 104(2), 339–371.

Heath, A. F., and Richards, L. 2020. Contested boundaries: consensus and dissensus in European attitudes to immigration. *Journal of Ethnic and Migration Studies*, 46(3), 489–511.

Hein, J. 1993. Refugees, immigrants, and the state. *Annual Review of Sociology*, 19, 43–59.

Herbst, J. 1989. The creation and maintenance of national boundaries in Africa. *International Organization*, 43(4), 673–692.

Hickerson, A., and Dunsmore, K. 2016. Locating refugees. *Journalism Practice*, 10(3), 424–438.

Higgins, C. M. 2017. *Asylum by Boat: Origins of Australia's Refugee Policy.* NewSouth Publishing.

Hintjens, H. M. 1999. Explaining the 1994 genocide in Rwanda. *Journal of Modern African Studies*, 241–286.

Hirschon, R. 2003. *Crossing the Aegean: An Appraisal of the 1923 Compulsory Population Exchange between Greece and Turkey.* Berghahn Books.

Hobsbawm, E., and Ranger, T. 1992. *The Invention of Tradition.* Cambridge University Press.

Holborn, L. W. 1939. The League of Nations and the refugee problem. *The Annals of the American Academy of Political and Social Science*, 203, 124–135.

Holland, A. C., and Peters, M. E. 2020. Explaining migration timing: Political information and opportunities. *International Organization*, 74(3), 560–583.

Holland, E. 2011. Moving the virtual border to the cellular level: Mandatory DNA testing and the US refugee family reunification program. *California Law Review*, 99(6), 1635–1682.

Hollinger, D. 2017. *Protestants Abroad: How Missionaries Tried to Change the World but Changed America.* Princeton University Press.

Holzer, E. 2015. *The Concerned Women of Buduburam: Refugee Activists and Humanitarian Dilemmas.* Cornell University Press.

Horst, C., and Van Hear, N. 2002. Counting the cost: Refugees, remittances and the "war against terrorism." *Forced Migration Review*, 14, 32–34.

Horster, M. 2004. The trade in political prisoners between the two German states, 1962–89. *Journal of Contemporary History*, 39(3), 403–424.

Hsiung, J. C. 1992. The military dimension, 1942–1945. In Hsiung, J. C., and Levine, S. I., eds., *China's Bitter Victory: The War with Japan*. M.E. Sharpe, 157–184.

Hutchinson, E. P. 1981. *Legislative History of American Immigration Policy, 1798–1965*. University of Pennsylvania Press.

Hyndman, J. 2004. Mind the gap: Bridging feminist and political geography through geopolitics. *Political Geography*, 23(3), 307–322.

Ibáñez, A. M., and Vélez, C. E. 2008. Civil conflict and forced migration: The micro determinants and welfare losses of displacement in Colombia. *World Development*, 36(4), 659–676.

Instituto Matías Romero de Estudios Diplomáticos, 1982. *Asilo y protección internacional de refugiados en América Latina*. Universidad Nacional Autónoma de México, Instituto de Investigaciones Jurídicas.

Iqbal, Z. 2007. The geo-politics of forced migration in Africa, 1992–2001. *Conflict Management and Peace Science*, 24(2), 105–119.

Jackson, I. C. 1991. The 1951 Convention Relating to the Status of Refugees: A universal basis for protection. *International Journal of Refugee Law*, 3, 403–413.

Jacobsen, K. 1996. Factors influencing the policy responses of host governments to mass refugee influxes. *International Migration Review*, 30(3), 655–678.

Jacobsen, K. 2002. Can refugees benefit the state? Refugee resources and African statebuilding. *The Journal of Modern African Studies*, 40(4), 577–596.

Jacobsen, K., Ayoub, M., and Johnson, A. 2014. Sudanese refugees in Cairo: Remittances and livelihoods. *Journal of Refugee Studies*, 27(1), 145–159.

Jaffe, A. J. 1962. Notes on the population theory of Eugene M. Kulischer. *The Milbank Memorial Fund Quarterly*, 40(2), 187–206.

Jamal, V. 1976. Asians in Uganda, 1880–1972: Inequality and expulsion. *The Economic History Review*, 29(4), 602–616.

Janmyr, M. 2017. No country of asylum: "Legitimizing" Lebanon's rejection of the 1951 Refugee Convention. *International Journal of Refugee Law*, 29(3), 438–465.

Janmyr, M., and Stevens, D. 2021. Regional refugee regimes: Middle East. In Costello, C., Foster, M., and McAdam, J., eds., *The Oxford Handbook of International Refugee Law*. Oxford University Press, 334–351.

Jászi, O. 1939. Political refugees. *The Annals of the American Academy of Political and Social Science*, 203(1), 83–93.

Jenkinson, J. 2016. Soon gone, long forgotten: Uncovering British responses to Belgian refugees during the First World War. *Immigrants and Minorities*, 34(2), 101–112.

Jose, B., and Medie, P. A. 2015. Understanding why and how civilians resort to self-protection in armed conflict. *International Studies Review*, 17(4), 515–535.

Jumbert, M. G., Bellanova, R., and Gellert, R. M. 2018. Smart phones for refugees. Tools for survival, or surveillance? Peace Research Institute. https://www.prio.org/publications/11022.

Kagan, M. 2011. "We live in a country of UNHCR": The UN surrogate state and refugee policy in the Middle East. UNHCR. https://www.unhcr.org/en-us/research/working/4d5a8cde9/live-country-unhcr-un-surrogate-state-refugee-policy-middle-east-michael.html.

Kaida, L., Hou, F., and Stick, M. 2020. The long-term economic integration of resettled refugees in Canada: A comparison of privately sponsored refugees and government-assisted refugees. *Journal of Ethnic and Migration Studies*, 46(9), 1687–1708.

Kallis, A. 2018. The Radical Right and Islamophobia. In Rydgren, J., ed., *The Oxford Handbook of the Radical Right*, Oxford University Press, 42–60.

Kamen, H. 1988. The Mediterranean and the expulsion of Spanish Jews in 1492. *Past & Present*, 119, 30–55.

Karatani, R. 2005. How history separated refugee and migrant regimes: in search of their institutional origins. *International Journal of Refugee Law*, 17(3), 517–541.

Kendall, E. C. 2014. Sanctuary in the 21st century: The unique asylum exception to the extradition rule. *Michigan State International Law Review*, 23, 153–176.

Kibreab, G. 2003. Citizenship rights and repatriation of refugees. *International Migration Review*, 37(1), 24–73.

Kibreab, G. 2013. The national service/Warsai-Yikealo Development Campaign and forced migration in post-independence Eritrea. *Journal of Eastern African Studies*, 7(4), 630–649.

Koch, A. 2014. The politics and discourse of migrant return: The role of UNHCR and IOM in the governance of return. *Journal of Ethnic and Migration Studies*, 40(6), 905.

Koser, K., and Black, R., eds. 1999. *The End of the Refugee Cycle? Refugee Repatriation and Reconstruction*. Berghahn Books.

Koser, K., and Martin, S., eds. 2011. *The Migration-Displacement Nexus: Patterns, Processes, and Policies*. Berghahn Books.

Koslowski, R. 2011. Global mobility regimes: A conceptual framework. In Koslowski, R., ed., *Global Mobility Regimes*. Palgrave Macmillan, 1–25.

Kritz, M. M., and Zlotnik, H. 1992. Global interactions: Migration systems, processes, and policies. *International Migration Systems: A Global Approach*. Clarendon Press, 1–16.

Kumin, J. 2008. Orderly departure from Vietnam: Cold War anomaly or humanitarian innovation? *Refugee Survey Quarterly*, 27(1), 104–117.

Kunz, E. F. 1973. The refugee in flight: Kinetic models and forms of displacement. *International Migration Review*, 7(2), 125–146.

Kurdi, T. 2018. *The Boy on the Beach: My Family's Escape from Syria and Our Hope for a New Home*. Simon & Schuster.

Kvittingen, A., et al. 2019. The conditions and migratory aspirations of Syrian and Iraqi refugees in Jordan. *Journal of Refugee Studies*, 32(1), 106–124.

Lichtenheld, A. G. 2020. Explaining population displacement strategies in civil wars: A cross-national analysis. *International Organization*, 74(2), 253–294.

Lim, J. 2013. Immigration, asylum, and citizenship: A more holistic approach. *California Law Review*, 101, 1013–1078.

Linhard, T. 2019. Moving barbed wire: Geographies of border crossing during World War II. In Linhard, T., and Parsons, T. H., eds., *Mapping Migration, Identity, and Space*. Palgrave Macmillan, 117–136.

Lipman, J. K. 2020. *In Camps: Vietnamese Refugees, Asylum Seekers, and Repatriates*. University of California Press.

Lischer, S. K. 2001. Refugee-related political violence: When? Where? How much? Inter-University Committee on International Migration. http://hdl.handle.net/1721.1/97620.

Loescher, G. 2001. *The UNHCR and World Politics: A Perilous Path*. Oxford University Press.

Loescher, G., and Scanlan, J. A. 1986. *Calculated Kindness: Refugees and America's Half-Open Door, 1945 to the Present*. Simon and Schuster.

Loescher, G. D., and Milner, J. H. S. 2005. *Protracted Refugee Situations: Domestic and International Security Implications*. Routledge.

Long, K. 2013. When refugees stopped being migrants: Movement, labour and humanitarian protection. *Migration Studies*, 1(1), 4–26.

Long, K. 2014. Rethinking "durable" solutions. In Fiddian-Qasmiyeh, E., et al., eds., *The Oxford Handbook of Refugee and Forced Migration Studies*. Oxford University Press, 475–487.

Loschmann, C. 2020. Taking stock of the evidence on the consequences of hosting refugees in the Global South. In Rayp, G., Ruyssen, I., and Marchand, K., eds., *Regional Integration and Migration Governance in the Global South*. Springer, 117–130.

Lubkemann, S. C. 2008. Involuntary immobility: On a theoretical invisibility in forced migration studies. *Journal of Refugee Studies*, 21(4), 454–475.

Lubkemann, S. C. 2010. *Culture in Chaos: An Anthropology of the Social Condition in War*. University of Chicago Press.

Lucassen, L., and Smit, A. X. 2015. The repugnant other: Soldiers, missionaries, and aid workers as organizational migrants. *Journal of World History*, 26(1), 1–39.

Ludwig, B. 2016. "Wiping the refugee dust from my feet": Advantages and burdens of refugee status and the refugee label. *International Migration*, 54(1), 5–18.

Lundquist, J. H., and Massey, D. S. 2005. Politics or economics? International migration during the Nicaraguan Contra War. *Journal of Latin American Studies*, 37(1), 29–53.

Mabogunje, A. L. 1970. Systems approach to a theory of rural-urban migration. *Geographical Analysis*, 2(1), 1–18.

MacKinnon, S. 2001. Refugee flight at the outset of the Anti-Japanese War. In Lary, D., and MacKinnon, S., eds., *Scars of War: Impact of Warfare on Modern China*. University of British Columbia Press, 118–134.

Madokoro, L. 2016. *Elusive Refuge: Chinese Migrants in the Cold War.* Harvard University Press.

Mahoney, J. 2000. Path dependence in historical sociology. *Theory and Society*, 29(4), 507–548.

Malkki, L. H. 1995. Refugees and exile: From "refugee studies" to the national order of things. *Annual Review of Anthropology*, 24, 495–523.

Malkki, L. H. 1996. Speechless emissaries: Refugees, humanitarianism, and dehistoricization. *Cultural Anthropology*, 11(3), 377–404.

Manasek, J. 2017. Protection, repatriation and categorization: Refugees and empire at the end of the nineteenth century. *Journal of Refugee Studies*, 30(2), 301–317.

Mann, M. 1993. *The Sources of Social Power.* Cambridge University Press.

Marrus, M. R. 2002. *The Unwanted: European Refugees from the First World War through the Cold War.* Temple University Press.

Martin, D. A. 1988. *The New Asylum Seekers: Refugee Law in the 1980s: The Ninth Sokol Colloquium on International Law.* Martinus Nijhoff.

Martin, P. 2010. *Climate change, agricultural development, and migration.* German Marshall Fund.

Martin, S., et al. 2018. The Global Compacts and environmental drivers of migration. Global Knowledge Partnership on Migration and Development. https://www.knomad.org/publication/global–compacts–and–environmental–drivers–migration.

Massey, D. S., et al. 1998. *Worlds in Motion: Understanding International Migration at the End of the Millennium.* Clarendon Press.

Massey, D. S., Durand, J., and Pren, K. A. 2020. Lethal violence and migration in Mexico: An analysis of internal and international moves. *Migraciones Internacionales*, 11.

Masterson, D. 2016. Giving better: Lessons from cash grants for Syrian refugees in Lebanon. American University of Beirut Policy Institute. http://ubi.earth/studies/lebanon.pdf.

Mayblin, L. 2017. *Asylum after Empire: Colonial Legacies in the Politics of Asylum Seeking.* Roman & Littlefield.

Mayblin, L., and Turner, J. 2020. *Migration Studies and Colonialism.* John Wiley & Sons.

McAdam, J. 2012. *Climate Change, Forced Migration, and International Law.* Oxford University Press.

McConnachie, K. 2014. *Governing Refugees: Justice, Order and Legal Pluralism.* Routledge.

McSpadden, L. A. 1999. Contradictions and control in repatriation: Negotiations for the return of 500,000 Eritrean refugees. In Koser, K., and Black, R., eds., *The End of the Refugee Cycle.* Berghahn, 69–84.

Mencütek, Z. Ş. 2018. *Refugee Governance, State and Politics in the Middle East.* Routledge.

Menjívar, C. 1993. History, economy, and politics: Macro and micro-level factors in recent Salvadorean migration to the US. *Journal of Refugee Studies*, 6(4), 350–371.

Micinski, N. R. 2018. Refugee policy as foreign policy: Iraqi and Afghan refugee resettlements to the United States. *Refugee Survey Quarterly*, 37(3), 253–278.

Micinski, N. R. 2021. *UN Global Compacts: Governing Migrants and Refugees*. Routledge.

Milton, S. 1991. Gypsies and the Holocaust. *The History Teacher*, 24(4), 375–387.

Mitchell, C. 1989. International migration, international relations, and foreign policy. *International Migration Review*, 23(3), 681–708.

Monsutti, A. 2008. Afghan migratory strategies and the three solutions to the refugee problem. *Refugee Survey Quarterly*, 27(1), 58–73.

Monsutti, A., and Balci, B. 2014. Forced migration in broader Central Asia. In Fiddian-Qasmiyeh, E., et al., eds., *The Oxford Handbook of Refugee and Forced Migration Studies*. Oxford University Press, 613–625.

Moore, W. H., and Shellman, S. M. 2007. Whither will they go? A global study of refugees' destinations, 1965–1995. *International Studies Quarterly*, 51(4), 811–834.

Morrison, A. R., and May, R. A. 1994. Escape from terror: Violence and migration in post-revolutionary Guatemala. *Latin American Research Review*, 29(2), 111–132.

Morrison, A. R., and Pérez Lafaurie, M. 1994. Elites, guerrillas and narcotraficantes: Violence and internal migration in Colombia. *Canadian Journal of Latin American and Caribbean Studies*, 19(37–38), 123–154.

Mountz, A. 2010. *Seeking Asylum: Human Smuggling and Bureaucracy at the Border*. University of Minnesota Press.

Mourad, L. 2017. "Standoffish" policy-making: Inaction and change in the Lebanese response to the Syrian displacement crisis. *Middle East Law and Governance*, 9(3), 249–266.

Müller-Funk, L., and Fransen, S. 2020. Return aspirations and coerced return. International Migration Institute. https://www.merit.unu.edu/publications/uploads/1585643872.pdf.

Nasaw, D. 2020. *The Last Million: Europe's Displaced Persons from World War to Cold War*. Penguin Press.

National Academies of Sciences, Engineering. and Medicine. 2017. *The Economic and Fiscal Consequences of Immigration*. The National Academies Press.

Nault, D. M. 2020. *Africa and the Shaping of International Human Rights*. Oxford University Press.

Neumann, K. 2015. *Across the Seas: Australia's Response to Refugees*. Black Inc.

Neumayer, E. 2005. Bogus refugees? The determinants of asylum migration to Western Europe. *International Studies Quarterly*, 49(3), 389–410.

Neuwirth, G. 1988. Refugee resettlement. *Current Sociology*, 36(2), 27–41.

Newbury, C. 1998. Ethnicity and the politics of history in Rwanda. *Africa Today*, 45(1), 7–24.

Nobles, J., and McKelvey, C. 2015. Gender, power, and emigration from Mexico. *Demography*, 52(5), 1573–1600.

Noiriel, G. 1991. *La tyrannie du national: le droit d'asile en Europe (1793–1993)*. Calmann-Lévy.

Norman, K. P. 2020. *Reluctant Reception: Refugees, Migration and Governance in the Middle East and North Africa*. Cambridge University Press.

Omer-Cooper, J. D. 1993. Has the Mfecane a future? A response to the Cobbing critique. *Journal of Southern African Studies*, 19(2), 273–294.

Orchard, P. 2014. *A Right to Flee: Refugees, States, and the Construction of International Cooperation*. Cambridge University Press.

Orchard, P., 2018. *Protecting the Internally Displaced: Rhetoric and Reality*. Routledge.

Palomino, P. 2019. On the disadvantages of "Global South" for Latin American Studies. *Journal of World Philosophies*, 4(2), 22–39.

Pappé, I. 2007. *The Ethnic Cleansing of Palestine*. Simon and Schuster.

Pearlman, W. 2018. Becoming a refugee: Reflections on self-understandings of displacement from the Syrian case. *Review of Middle East Studies*, 52(2), 299–309.

Pearlman, W. R. 2017. *We Crossed a Bridge and It Trembled: Voices from Syria*. HarperCollins.

Pedraza-Bailey, S. 1985. Cuba's exiles: Portrait of a refugee migration. *International Migration Review*, 19(1), 4–34.

Petersen, W. 1958. A general typology of migration. *American Sociological Review*, 256–266.

Peterson, G. 2012. The uneven development of the international refugee regime in postwar Asia: Evidence from China, Hong Kong and Indonesia. *Journal of Refugee Studies*, 25(3), 326–343.

Peterson, G. 2018. Forced migration, refugees and China's entry into the "Family of Nations," 1861–1949. *Journal of Refugee Studies*, 31(3), 274–291.

Pierson, P. 2004. *Politics in Time: History, Institutions, and Social Analysis*. Princeton University Press.

Pilkington, H. 1998. Going home? The implications of forced migration for national identity formation in post-Soviet Russia. In Koser, K., and Lutz, H., eds., *The New Migration in Europe*. Palgrave, 85–106.

Poole, A. 2021. Migration as conflict risk-management: testing the new economics of labour migration as a framework for understanding refugee decision-making. *Journal of Ethnic and Migration Studies*, 1–18.

Portes, A., and Walton, J., eds. 1981. *Unequal Exchange and the Urban Informal Sector*. Academic Press.

Price, M. E. 2009. *Rethinking Asylum: History, Purpose, and Limits*. Cambridge University Press.

Qualls, K. D. 2020. *Stalin's Niños: Educating Spanish Civil War Refugee Children in the Soviet Union, 1937–1951.* University of Toronto Press.

Querton, C. 2019. Gender and the boundaries of international refugee law: Beyond the category of "gender-related asylum claims." *Netherlands Quarterly of Human Rights,* 37(4), 379–397.

Ramasubramanyam, J. 2021. Regional Refugee Regimes: South Asia. In Costello, C., Foster, M., and McAdam, J., eds., *The Oxford Handbook of International Refugee Law.* Oxford University Press, 407–422.

Rensink, B. W. 2018. *Native but Foreign: Indigenous Immigrants and Refugees in the North American Borderlands.* Texas A&M University Press.

Riak Akuei, S. 2005. Remittances as unforeseen burdens: The livelihoods and social obligations of Sudanese refugees. Global Commission on International Migration. https://www.refworld.org/docid/42ce4d354.htm.

Richmond, A. H. 1988. Sociological theories of international migration: The case of refugees. *Current Sociology,* 36(2), 7–25.

Richmond, A. H. 1993. Reactive migration: Sociological perspectives on refugee movements. *Journal of Refugee Studies,* 6(1), 7–24.

Richmond, A. H. 2001. Global apartheid: A postscript. *Refuge: Canada's Journal on Refugees,* 19(4), 8–13.

Rios Contreras, V. 2014. The role of drug-related violence and extortion in promoting Mexican migration: Unexpected consequences of a drug war. *Latin American Research Review,* 49(3), 199–217.

Robson, L. 2017. *States of Separation: Transfer, Partition, and the Making of the Modern Middle East.* University of California Press.

Ronzitti, N. 2009. The treaty on friendship, partnership and cooperation between Italy and Libya: New prospects for cooperation in the Mediterranean? *Bulletin of Italian Politics,* (1), 125–133.

Rosenblum, M. R., and Salehyan, I. 2004. Norms and interests in US asylum enforcement. *Journal of Peace Research,* 41(6), 677–697.

Rotberg, R. I. 2004. *State Failure and State Weakness in a Time of Terror.* Brookings Institution Press.

Rottman, A. J., Fariss, C. J., and Poe, S. C. 2009. The path to asylum in the US and the determinants for who gets in and why. *International Migration Review,* 43(1), 3–34.

Rubin, B. R., 2002. *The Fragmentation of Afghanistan: State Formation and Collapse in the International System.* Yale University Press.

Rubinstein, J. L. 1936. The refugee problem. *International Affairs,* 15(5), 716–734.

Ruhs, M. 2013. *The Price of Rights: Regulating International Labor Migration.* Princeton University Press.

Ruhs, M., and Chang, H.-J. 2004. The ethics of labor immigration policy. *International Organization,* (1), 69–102.

Ruthström-Ruin, C. 1993. *Beyond Europe: The Globalization of Refugee Aid.* Lund University Press.

Salehyan, I., and Gleditsch, K. S. 2006. Refugees and the spread of civil war. *International Organization*, 60(2), 335–366.

Salomon, K. 1991. *Refugees in the Cold War. Toward a New International Refugee Regime in the Early Postwar Era*. Lund University Press.

Sana, M. 2020. Public opinion on refugee policy in the United States, 1938–2019: Increasing support for refugees and the sympathy effect. *International Migration Review*, 55(2), 574–604.

Saunders, N. 2017. *International Political Theory and the Refugee Problem*. Routledge.

Scalettaris, G. 2007. Refugee studies and the international refugee regime: A reflection on a desirable separation. *Refugee Survey Quarterly*, 26(3), 36–50.

Scalettaris, G., and Gubert, F. 2019. Return schemes from European countries: Assessing the challenges. *International Migration*, 57(4), 91–104.

Schaufuss, T. 1939. The White Russian refugees. *The Annals of the American Academy of Political and Social Science*, 203(1), 45–54.

Schechtman, J. B. 1946. *European Population Transfers*. Oxford University Press.

Schmeidl, S. 1997. Exploring the causes of forced migration: A pooled time-series analysis, 1971–1990. *Social Science Quarterly*, 78(2), 284–308.

Schultz, T. P. 1971. Rural-urban migration in Colombia. *The Review of Economics and Statistics*, 53(2), 157–163.

Schwartz, S. 2019. Home, again: Refugee return and post-conflict violence in Burundi. *International Security*, 44(2), 110–145.

Schwartz, S. 2022. Return without refoulement: How states avoid hosting refugees in the Global South. https://www.stephanierachelschwartz.com/uploads/1/0/6/2/106215427/schwartz_return_without_refoulement_032022.pdf.

Scott, C.-G. 2001. Swedish sanctuary of American deserters during the Vietnam War: A facet of Social Democratic domestic politics. *Scandinavian Journal of History*, 26(2), 123–142.

Scott, J. C. 1998. *Seeing Like a State: How Certain Schemes to Improve the Human Condition have Failed*. Yale University Press.

Scott, M. 2020. *Climate Change, Disasters, and the Refugee Convention*. Cambridge University Press.

Segev, T. 2007. *1967: Israel, The War, and the Year that Transformed the Middle East*. Metropolitan Books.

Shacknove, A. 1993. From asylum to containment. *International Journal of Refugee Law*, 5(4), 516–533.

Shaffer, R., et al. 2020. Local elected officials' receptivity to refugee resettlement in the United States. *Proceedings of the National Academy of Sciences*, 117(50), 31722–31728.

Sharpe, M. 2012. The 1969 African Refugee Convention: Innovations, misconceptions, and omissions. *McGill Law Journal*, 58(1), 95–147.

Shaw, C. 2015. *Britannia's Embrace: Modern Humanitarianism and the Imperial Origins of Refugee Relief*. Oxford University Press.

Sheldon, R. C., and Dutkowski, J. 1952. Are Soviet satellite refugee interviews projectable? *Public Opinion Quarterly*, 16(4), 579–594.

Simpson, J. H. 1939. *The Refugee Problem: Report of a Survey*. Oxford University Press.

Sims, L. J. 2019. Memories of a French migration crisis. In Menjívar, C., Ruiz, M., and Ness, I., eds., *The Oxford Handbook of Migration Crises*. Oxford University Press, 57–72.

Sinha, S. P. 1971. *Asylum and International Law*. Martinus Nijhoff.

Skran, C. M. 1995. *Refugees in Inter-war Europe: The Emergence of a Regime*. Oxford University Press.

Slaughter, A., and Crisp, J. 2009. A surrogate state? The role of UNHCR in protracted refugee situations. UNHCR. https://www.unhcr.org/en–us/research/working/4981cb432/surrogate–state–role–unhcr–protracted–refugee–situations–amy–slaughter.html.

Slovic, P., et al. 2017. Iconic photographs and the ebb and flow of empathic response to humanitarian disasters. *Proceedings of the National Academy of Sciences*, 114(4), 640–644.

Smith, H. 2007. Diasporas in international conflict. In Smith, H., and Stares, P., eds., *Diasporas in Conflict: Peace-makers or Peace-wreckers*. United Nations University Press, 3–16.

Smith, M. P., and Guarnizo, L. E. 1998. *Transnationalism from Below*. Transaction Publishers.

Soo, S. 2016. *The Routes to Exile: France and the Spanish Civil War Refugees, 1939–2009*. Manchester University Press.

Stanley, W. D. 1987. Economic migrants or refugees from violence? A time-series analysis of Salvadoran migration to the United States. *Latin American Research Review*, 22(1), 132–154.

Stanwood, O. 2020. *The Global Refuge: Huguenots in an Age of Empire*. Oxford University Press.

Stark, O. 1991. *The Migration of Labor*. Basil Blackwell.

Steele, A. 2009. Seeking safety: Avoiding displacement and choosing destinations in civil wars. *Journal of Peace Research*, 46(3), 419–429.

Steele, A. 2018. IDP resettlement and collective targeting during civil wars: Evidence from Colombia. *Journal of Peace Research*, 55(6), 810–824.

Stepick, A. 1982. Haitian boat people: A study in the conflicting forces shaping US immigration policy. *Law and Contemporary Problems*, 45(2), 163–196.

Sturgis, A. H. 2007. *The Trail of Tears and Indian Removal*. Greenwood Publishing.

Swindell, K. 1995. People on the move in West Africa: From pre-colonial polities to post-independence states. In Cohen, R., ed., *The Cambridge Survey of World Migration*. 196–202.

Taylor, J. E., et al. 2016. Economic impact of refugees. *Proceedings of the National Academy of Sciences*, 113(27), 7449–7453.

Teitelbaum, M. S. 1984. Immigration, refugees, and foreign policy. *International Organization*, 38(3), 429–450.

Temimi, A., ed. 1993. *Actes du Ve Symposium international d'études morisques sur: Le Ve centenaire de la chute de Grenade, 1492–1992.* Ceromdi.

Terrazas, A. 2010. Salvadoran immigrants in the United States in 2008. Migration Policy Institute. https://www.migrationpolicy.org/article/salvadoran–immigrants–united–states–2008.

Terry, K. 2021. The EU–Turkey deal, five years on: A frayed and controversial but enduring blueprint. Migration Policy Institute. https://www.migrationpolicy.org/article/eu–turkey–deal–five–years–on.

Ther, P. 2019. *The Outsiders: Refugees in Europe Since 1492.* Princeton University Press.

Thielemann, E. R. 2003. Between interests and norms: Explaining burden-sharing in the European Union. *Journal of Refugee Studies*, 16(3), 253–273.

Thiollet, H. 2011. Migration as diplomacy: Labor migrants, refugees, and Arab regional politics in the oil-rich countries. *International Labor and Working-Class History*, 79(1), 103–121.

Thomas, W. I., and Znaniecki, F. 1927. *The Polish Peasant in Europe and America.* Knopf.

Tilly, C. 1984. *Big Structures, Large Processes, Huge Comparisons.* Russell Sage.

Tolnay, S. E., and Beck, E. M. 1992. Racial violence and black migration in the American South, 1910 to 1930. *American Sociological Review*, 57(1), 103–116.

Torpey, J. 2000. *The Invention of the Passport: Surveillance, Citizenship and the State.* Cambridge University Press.

Toshkov, D., and de Haan, L. 2013. The Europeanization of asylum policy: an assessment of the EU impact on asylum applications and recognitions rates. *Journal of European Public Policy*, 20(5), 661–683.

Tsartas, P., et al. 2020. Refugees and tourism: A case study from the islands of Chios and Lesvos, Greece. *Current Issues in Tourism*, 23(11), 1311–1327.

Turner, L. 2015. Explaining the (non-) encampment of Syrian refugees: Security, class and the labour market in Lebanon and Jordan. *Mediterranean Politics*, 20(3), 386–404.

Turton, D., and Marsden, P. R. V. 2002. Taking refugees for a ride? The politics of refugee return to Afghanistan. Afghanistan Research and Evaluation Unit. https://www.refworld.org/pdfid/47c3f3cb1a.pdf.

UN Economic Commission for Africa. 1981. *International Migration, Population Trends and their Implications for Africa.* UN Economic Commission for Africa.

UNHCR. 2019. *Global Trends: Forced Displacement in 2018.* https://www.unhcr.org/globaltrends2018/.

UNHCR. 2020. *Global Trends: Forced Displacement in 2019*. https://www.unhcr.org/flagship-reports/globaltrends/globaltrends2019/.

UNHCR. 2021. *Global Trends: Forced Displacement in 2020*. https://www.unhcr.org/flagship-reports/globaltrends/.

Valenta, M., and Strabac, Z. 2013. The dynamics of Bosnian refugee migrations in the 1990s: Current migration trends and future prospects. *Refugee Survey Quarterly*, 32(3), 1–22.

Valentino, B. A. 2004. *Final Solutions: Mass Killing and Genocide in the 20th Century*. Cornell University Press.

Valk, J. 2020. Crime and punishment: Deportation in the Levant in the age of Assyrian hegemony. *Bulletin of the American Schools of Oriental Research*, 384(1), 77–103.

Vallet, É., ed. 2021. *State of Border Walls in a Globalized World*. Routledge.

Van Hear, N. 2006. Refugees in diaspora: From durable solutions to transnational relations. *Refuge: Canada's Journal on Refugees*, 23(1), 9–15.

Vang, C. Y. 2020. Creating proper subjects: The politics of Hmong refugee resettlement in the United States. In Pasquetti, S., and Sanyal, R., eds., *Displacement: Global Conversations on Refuge*. Manchester University Press, 29–45.

Van Selm, J., 2014. Refugee resettlement. In Fiddian-Qasmiyeh, E., et al., eds., *The Oxford Handbook of Refugee and Forced Migration Studies*. Oxford University Press, 512–524.

Vargas-Silva, C. 2017. Remittances sent to and from the forcibly displaced. *The Journal of Development Studies*, 53(11), 1835–1848.

Vertovec, S. 2004. Cheap calls: The social glue of migrant transnationalism. *Global Networks*, 4(2), 219–224.

Vickery, M. 1984. *Cambodia: 1975–1982*. South End Press.

von Einsiedel, S., et al. 2017. Civil war trends and the changing nature of armed conflict. UN University Centre for Policy Research. https://collections.unu.edu/eserv/UNU:6156/Civil_war_trends_UPDATED.pdf.

Vukašinović, J. 2011. Illegal migration in Turkey–EU relations: An issue of political bargaining or political cooperation? *European Perspectives*, 3(2), 147–167.

Waldinger, R., and FitzGerald, D. 2004. Transnationalism in question. *American Journal of Sociology*, 109(5), 1177–1195.

Wallerstein, I., 1980. *The Modern World-System II: Mercantilism and the Consolidation of the European World-Economy, 1600–1750*. Academic Press.

Ward, P. 2020. Capitalising on "local knowledge": The labour practices behind successful aid projects – the case of Jordan. *Current Sociology*, 69(5), 705–722.

Watenpaugh, K. D. 2015. *Bread from Stones: The Middle East and the Making of Modern Humanitarianism*. University of California Press.

Watson, S. D. 2009. *The Securitization of Humanitarian Migration: Digging Moats and Sinking Boats*. Routledge.

Watt, L. 2009. *When Empire Comes Home: Repatriation and Reintegration in Postwar Japan*. Harvard University Press.

Weiner, M. 1985. On international migration and international relations. *Population and Development Review*, 11(3), 441–455.

Weiner, M. 1996. Bad neighbors, bad neighborhoods: An inquiry into the causes of refugee flows. *International Security*, 21(1), 5–42.

Weiner, M. 1998. The clash of norms: Dilemmas in refugee policies. *Journal of Refugee Studies*, 11(4), 433–453.

Weitz, Y. 1994. Changing conceptions of the Holocaust: The Kasztner Case. *Studies in Contemporary Jewry*, 10, 211–230.

Whitaker, B. E. 2002. Document. Changing priorities in refugee protection: The Rwandan repatriation from Tanzania. *Refugee Survey Quarterly*, 21(1), 328–344.

Whitaker, B. E. 2003. Refugees and the spread of conflict: Contrasting cases in Central Africa. *Journal of Asian and African Studies*, 38(2–3), 211–231.

White, B. T. 2019. Refuge and history: A critical reading of a polemic. *Migration and Society*, 2(1), 107–119.

Wilson, S. J. 1989. Kossuth and American non-intervention. *Hungarian Studies*, 5(1), 39–48.

Wimmer, A., and Schiller, N. G. 2003. Methodological nationalism, the social sciences, and the study of migration: An essay in historical epistemology. *International Migration Review*, 37(3), 576–610.

Wolman, A. 2019. The role of departure states in combating irregular emigration in international law: An historical perspective. *International Journal of Refugee Law*, 31(1), 30–54.

Wright, T. 2014. The media and representations of refugees and other forced migrants. In Fiddian-Qasmiyeh, E., et al., eds., *The Oxford Handbook of Refugee and Forced Migration Studies*. Oxford University Press, 460–474.

Wyman, D. S. 2019. *The Abandonment of the Jews: America and the Holocaust, 1941–1945*. Plunkett Lake Press.

Yahil, L. 1974. Selected British documents on the illegal immigration to Palestine, 1939–1940. *Yad Vashem Studies*, 10, 241–276.

Yuen, H. K. 2014. Proxy humanitarianism: Hong Kong's Vietnamese refugee crisis, 1975–79. Unpublished Master of Philosophy thesis. University of Hong Kong.

Zaat, K. 2007. The protection of forced migrants in Islamic law. UNHCR. https://www.unhcr.org/476652cb2.pdf.

Zetter, R. 1994. The Greek-Cypriot refugees: Perceptions of return under conditions of protracted exile. *International Migration Review*, 28(2), 307–322.

Zetter, R. 2012. Are refugees an economic burden or benefit? *Forced Migration Review*, (41), 50–52.

Zetter, R. 2021. Theorizing the refugee humanitarian–development nexus: A political-economy analysis. *Journal of Refugee Studies*, 34(2), 1766–1786.

Zhukov, Y. M. 2015. Population resettlement in war: Theory and evidence from Soviet archives. *Journal of Conflict Resolution*, 59(7), 1155–1185.

Ziegler, R. 2015. No asylum for "infiltrators": The legal predicament of Eritrean and Sudanese nationals in Israel. *Journal of Immigration, Asylum and Nationality Law*, 29(2), 172–191.

Ziegler, R. 2017. *Voting Rights of Refugees*. Cambridge University Press.

Zolberg, A. 1997. Global movements, global walls: Responses to migration, 1885–1925. In Wang, G., ed., *Global History and Migrations*. Westview Press, 279–308.

Zolberg, A. R. 2006. *A Nation by Design: Immigration Policy in the Fashioning of America*. Harvard University Press.

Zolberg, A. R., Suhrke, A., and Aguayo, S. 1989. *Escape from Violence: Conflict and the Refugee Crisis in the Developing World*. Oxford University Press.

Zucker, N. L., and Zucker, N. F. 1987. *The Guarded Gate: The Reality of American Refugee Policy*. Harcourt Brace Jovanovich.

Acknowledgments

We will always be grateful for the support of our colleagues, friends, and family who made this book possible. We are especially indebted to those who informed our research by sharing their experiences of displacement and providing humanitarian relief. The Asfour family's story inspired the structure of the text that follows refugees across their countries of origin, transit, and destinations. While we cannot share the Asfours' real names to protect their privacy, we thank them for generously sharing their story.

Many of the ideas in this book were first laid out in a short essay published in 2016 titled "What Drives Refugee Migration?" and a 2018 article in *Annual Review of Sociology* titled "The Sociology of Refugee Migration." Feedback on these earlier works allowed us to refine and develop the ideas in this book, and for that we are thankful to Xóchitl Bada, Simone Baglioni, Susan Bell, Frank Caestecker, Val Colic-Peisker, Nicholas De Genova, Andreas E. Feldmann, Molly Fee, Jonathan Fox, Thomas Gammeltoft-Hansen, Steven Gold, Justin Guest, Renee Luthra, Cecilia Menjívar, Jenna Nobles, Thomas Soehl, and Thomas Spijkerboer.

Our editor at Polity, Jonathan Skerrett, patiently worked with us from the outset to conceptualize the project and see it through. Karina Jákupsdóttir, Assistant Editor in Sociology, shepherded us through the process. Several colleagues generously commented on earlier drafts, including two anonymous Polity reviewers. A special thank you to David Cook-Martín, Laura Madokoro, and Roger Waldinger, whose extensive feedback significantly strengthened the book. We are also grateful to Sara Bellezza, Fátima Khayar Cámara, Jeff Crisp, Elena

Fiddian-Qasmiyeh, Rana Khoury, Jiaqi Liu, James Milner, Lama Mourad, Stephanie Nawyn, Boldizsár Nagy, Linh Thủy Nguyễn, Şevin Sağnıç, Stephanie Schwartz, Karina Shklyan, and Beatrice Waterhouse, all of whom gave of their time and expertise to improve this manuscript.

The Center for Comparative Immigration Studies (CCIS) at UC San Diego was the nest where this egg hatched. We thank Ana Minvielle for her constant encouragement. Much of the research and writing were made possible by sabbatical leave from the UC San Diego Department of Sociology, a postdoctoral fellowship from Brown University's Watson Institute for International and Public Affairs, and support from the University of Washington's Department of Law, Societies, and Justice, as well as the UW Center for Studies in Demography and Ecology.

Versions of this manuscript received valuable feedback from a panel at the 2021 International Association for the Study of Forced Migration conference, a University of Washington "Law, Societies, and Justice Workshare" organized by Steve Herbert, a panel at the 2021 American Sociological Association conference organized by Francisco Lara-García and Van Tran, a workshop at Sciences Po organized by Dawn Chatty and Tamirace Fakhoury, and a UC San Diego graduate seminar on the Sociology of Forced Migration.

In the midst of writing the grim histories in these pages, Marian and Gabriela were a daily reminder to David of all that is good in the world. And, for bringing cheer to the home office during the pandemic's solitary hours of research and writing, he thanks Mars and Apollo. Any typographical errors are from their paws on the keyboard.

Rawan is grateful to Gershon Shafir for his mentorship, friendship, and limitless curiosity. She is thankful to Lindsay DePalma, Jane Lilly López, and Lauren Olsen, who have been her teammates for the last decade. Rawan thanks all her aunties and amos in Jordan – especially Nasma and Narjes – who kept her fed, sheltered, and never feeling too far from home. She is eternally thankful to Sara and Kiki for everything they taught her and to the people who have loved and supported her: Lama and Dana Alhasan, Brandon Faucett, David Marcus, Neda Meier, Lucy Schram, and Amanda Salih. She is blessed to have Ghada, Linah, and Shaam in her life. Most of all, she thanks her parents, Nedal and Mazen, for their love, and Amr, Yousef, Stephanie, and baby Mazen for making life so much sweeter.

Rawan Arar, Seattle, Washington
David Scott FitzGerald, San Diego, California

Index

Page numbers in *italics* refer to figures.